Rituals *and* Riots

Rituals
and Riots

*Sectarian Violence and
Political Culture in Ulster,
1784–1886*

Sean Farrell

THE UNIVERSITY PRESS OF KENTUCKY

Publication of this volume was made possible in part
by a grant from the National Endowment for the Humanities.

Editorial and Sales Offices: The University Press of Kentucky
663 South Limestone Street, Lexington, Kentucky 40508–4008

04 03 02 01 00   5 4 3 2 1

Library of Congress Cataloging-in-Publication Data

Farrell, Sean, 1966-
    Rituals and riots : sectarian violence and political culture in Ulster,
    1784-1886 / Sean Farrell.
        p.   cm.
    Includes bibliographical references (p.   ) and index.
    ISBN 0-8131-2171-X (cloth : alk. paper)
    1. Violence—Ulster (Northern Ireland and Ireland)—History.
2. Riots—Ulster (Northern Ireland and Ireland)—History. 3. Ulster
(Northern Ireland and Ireland)—Church history. 4. Ulster (Northern
Ireland and Ireland)—History. I. Title.
DA990.U46 F345 2000
941.6081—dc21   00-028309

Contents

List of Illustrations

Woodcuts

Maps

Tables

Acknowledgments

In her classic 1971 article, "The Rites of Violence," Natalie Zemon Davis lamented historians' inattention to religious violence. That claim, thankfully, is no longer defensible. Inspired in part by Davis' pioneering examinations of Protestant/Catholic conflict in sixteenth-century France, a generation of scholars have explored the complex links between religious belief, ritual and violence in numerous cultures across the globe. This book owes a tremendous debt to these historians, who have done so much to improve our understanding of this vital area of plebeian culture.

This project has occupied nearly eight years of my life. It would never have been completed but for the help and support of countless individuals. It goes without saying that friends and colleagues bear no responsibility for any shortcomings in this book. These same friends are, however, at least partially responsible for whatever insights exist within these pages. My interest in history was first cultivated at Pomona College, where Robert Woods guided me through my first painful attempts to understand the Irish experience. I continued my studies at the University of Wisconsin-Madison, where I had the privilege to work with a number of excellent scholars. I would like to especially thank Kurt Gingrich, Patrick Tally and Tim McMahon, whose friendship made my tenure in Madison a pleasure. Sunday softball and trips to the Union may not have contributed much to my grasp of modern British and Irish history, but they did help me retain what little sanity I still have. Among many friends in Madison, Robert Mayville and Colleen Forrest deserve special mention for their constant support.

At Madison, I benefited tremendously from the tutelage of Jim Donnelly, whose exacting standards and professionalism provided me with an excellent introduction to the historian's craft. This essay would not have seen the light of day without his knowledge and encouragement. I am also indebted to Suzanne Desan, who introduced me to a number of works on conflict and community that have shaped my interpretation of Ulster sectarianism. Finally, I would to thank Martin Zanger, whose wit and wisdom helped me get through a difficult time at the University of Wisconsin-LaCrosse.

In Ireland, I would like to draw particular attention to the Institute of Irish Studies at Queen's University, Belfast, which acted as a kind of base for my work in Northern Ireland. Ronald Buchanan and Brian Walker were particularly instrumental in creating a supportive and enlightening atmosphere at the Institute. Along similar lines, I would like to thank the archivists and staff at the Armagh County Museum; the Belfast Central Library; the Cavan County Library; the Linen Hall Library, Belfast; the Loyal Orange Order, Belfast; the National Archives of Ireland, Dublin; the Public Record Office, London; the Public Record Office of Northern Ireland, Belfast; and the Union Theological College, Belfast. Providing documents for an impatient historian can be a trying task, a task that was completed with unflinching courtesy and efficiency throughout my tenure in the British Isles. Of course, the archives are not open 24 hours a day, and Jeremy Armstrong, Tony Canavan, Bruce Comfort, Gill McBride and Nicola Sterling provided much needed humor and friendship during my stay in Belfast.

My understanding of the Ulster experience has been sharpened by the work of a number of Irish historians. Although there are far too many individuals to list here, there are a few scholars whose work I have found particularly instructive and stimulating. I would especially like to thank Jonathan Bardon, Marianne Elliott, Tony Hepburn, David Miller, A.T.Q. Stewart, Brian Walker, and the late Frank Wright. Their work has transformed the way we look at Ulster's past. I hope that this study contributes to that conversation.

Since I arrived at Newberry College in Fall 1997, I have been blessed with a number of friends and colleagues who have helped me develop and complete this project. For their friendship and insight, I would like to thank Debbie Black, Garth Kemerling, Russell Kleckley, Bill Long, Joe McDonald, Michael O'Shea, Kay Poston, Jesse Scott, and Keith Wagner. Renee Joiner typed this much of this manuscript with an astonishing degree of efficiency and good humor. My special thanks go to my friend Marquerite Fowler Whitaker, who drew the maps for this book. I would be remiss if I failed to mention my students, who continue to be both the chief frustration and inspiration of my life.

Above all, my greatest debts are owed to Donald and Eleanor Farrell, who have provided the love and support to get me this far. Sticking within the family, I would also like to thank Tim, Kim, and Kathryn Farrell. The light and hope one sees in little Kathryn's eyes is the perfect antidote for the violence and hatred described in this book.

One of the chapters in this book first appeared in article form. An early version of chapter 6 can be found in *Eire-Ireland* 32, nos. 2 and 3 (summer/fall 1997): 52–79.

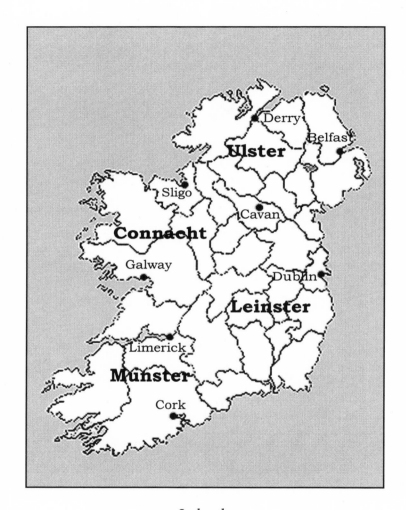

Ireland.

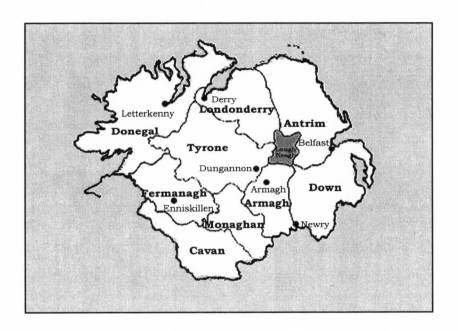

Ulster.

The Study of Sectarian Violence and Modern Ulster History

I cannot conclude this long report without observing on the melancholy fact of a people of one district of the county being so hostily opposed as to arm themselves to such an extent in deadly hatred of one another, as for the first time in my time I witnessed on yesterday. If one party unwarrantably assembled to oppose an ancient custom, the other has been guilty of acts, by wantonly consuming houses over the heads of unoffending women and children which the most savage people might be ashamed of. So long as these party processions are tolerated, so long will this country be subject to similar scenes, and unless some legislative enactment is passed to put a stop to them, there can be no hope of peace in this part of the country, and the two parties will become year by year more hostile and increase in acts of barbarity to one another.

Joseph Tabiteau to Thomas Redington

In the early hours of 12 July 1849, Maj. Arthur Wilkinson positioned his troops on some strategic high ground near Dolly's Brae, a hill located between Rathfriland and Castlewellan in the southern part of County Down. Wilkinson anticipated trouble; local Orangemen had announced their intention to walk in procession through this almost wholly Catholic district. Anyone familiar with communal relations in Ulster knew that such a territorial invasion was likely to result in trouble.

Dolly's Brae itself had been a party flashpoint since the early nineteenth century, when a young Catholic man had been killed there in a sectarian clash. According to local legend, his mother's dying injunction had been to "never let the Orangemen pass."[1] Fortunately, this did not prove to be much of a problem, as both parties developed a kind of informal compact during the intervening years—local Orange lodges simply avoided this controversial flashpoint during the marching season. Unfortunately, this precarious balance collapsed in 1848, when Orangemen commemorated the Twelfth of July by walking in procession through the district for the first time in years. Two factors explain the Rathfriland loyalists' decision to renew their processional tradition in 1848. First, they apparently believed that legislation banning party processions had expired, making their partisan display legal. A second and more important motivation, however, came from the realm of national politics. In the midst of the nationalist agitation that would eventually lead to the 1848 Rising, Orangemen and their allies wanted to use the Twelfth celebration as a demonstration of their firm and unswerving loyalty.

In marching to Lord Roden's estate at Tollymore Park, the Orange processionists had their choice of two routes: an old road leading directly through Dolly's Brae and a new, more circuitous path. In 1848 magistrates and police talked the Orangemen into taking the new road, which they believed would prove less controversial with the local Catholic population. The rerouting of the procession seemed to be successful; there were no major conflicts in July 1848. Unfortunately, the story was not to have such a happy ending.

In the wake of the Twelfth celebration in 1848, local Catholics taunted their Orange foes, circulating a song that condemned the processionists for their cowardice in taking the new road. Faced with such insults, local Orange lodges decided to march directly through the disputed area in 1849. As one magistrate put it, "I think it was a point of honour with the Orangemen to go through the Brae. . . . "[2] The decision to take the old road through Dolly's Brae created a potentially explosive situation. Major Wilkinson was quite right to be anxious.

A group of angry Catholic men and women approached the Brae later that morning, determined to block the passage of the Orange procession. Apparently surprised by the military presence there, they took up a position in a nearby field. Armed with scythes, pikes, and some firearms, this body of anti-Orange activists represented two overlapping social groups: local men and women and a large number of men from nearby Catholic parishes. At the bidding of Major Wilkinson, two Catholic priests attempted to reduce the tension by exerting their tenuous influence among the Ribbon (the name usually given to anti-Orange groups in Ulster) party. After a protracted discussion the priests managed to extract a promise from the Catholic crowd that they would not fire first.

The Orange procession finally approached Dolly's Brae at about eleven

o'clock. Between twelve hundred and fourteen hundred people purportedly took part in the march, which ran from Ballyward church to Lord
Roden's demesne at Tollymore Park. The processionists advanced in typical
fashion; orange sashes and banners abounded and the air shook with the
deafening sounds of the fife and drum. One of the banners reportedly read
"No Repeal," nicely underlining the links between national politics and local communal relations. The marchers clearly expected some sort of trouble;
one magistrate estimated that five hundred men had guns with them.[3] Hoping to keep the two parties apart, magistrates and police positioned themselves at the head of the procession. The tactic seemed to work, as the
marchers filed through the disputed ground with little trouble. There was a
slight disturbance when a group of Catholic women gathered at the road-
side to verbally abuse the Orange processionists, but on the whole the authorities seemed pleased with the relative tranquillity of the morning. As
the procession marched away, Major Wilkinson turned to a Catholic priest,
saying, "Now that they have got through, I hope the Orange leaders will try
and persuade them to return by some other road."[4] Whatever the answer,
the morning had passed as well as could have been hoped.

When the Orange marchers arrived at Tollymore Park, they proceeded
to a large meadow, where a tent and platform had been raised for the day's
festivities. The proprietor of Tollymore Park, Lord Roden, was one of the
true grandees of the ultra-Protestant cause in Ireland. Widely known for
his active role in advancing Protestant religious education throughout the
island, Lord Roden also held the position of Deputy Grand Master of the
Orange Order. As the marchers arrived at Tollymore Park, Roden's servants
provided the processionists with food and beer, which were no doubt welcomed on this unusually hot day. One magistrate, George Fitzmaurice, talked
with Lord Roden himself, asking him to use his influence with the
Orangemen to persuade them to avoid Dolly's Brae on their return march.
Roden answered that while he would certainly make the attempt, he feared
that he had no influence over his plebeian brethren.

Throughout the afternoon several speakers addressed the crowd from
the platform. At least three of the orators doubled as magistrates: Lord Roden,
William Beers, and Francis Beers. Although each had pledged to discourage
their followers from returning via Dolly's Brae, reports indicate that none
of the speakers kept this promise. In fact, William Beers distinctly advised
the Orange party to return home via the more controversial route. The procession would try to force the pass again.

The marchers approached Dolly's Brae at about five o'clock in the afternoon. Catholic women were again in the forefront of the opposition, labeling the Orange processionists as "prisoners of the police." With two-thirds of the procession already through the pass, however, it looked as if the day might end without serious incident. At this point disaster struck. A sound akin to a gunshot or squib emanated from near the head of the procession. Two Ribbonmen responded with gunfire, aiming several shots at the rear of the parade. Chaos broke loose—Orangemen shot wildly at their Catholic enemies, who returned fire as best they could. Finding themselves under attack from the hill, the police, under the command of Sub-Inspector James Ponsonby Hill, charged up the slope to dislodge their Ribbon assailants. The party quickly broke under the assault, and the actual conflict was over in a matter of minutes. Behind the scenes, however, Orangemen remained quite busy. Taking advantage of the confusion of battle, several Orange marchers fired indiscriminately at local Catholic men, women, and children. Loyalists also wrecked seven houses, breaking windows and furniture and setting them ablaze. Seeing the wreckers, the police and military rushed back to stop the carnage but were unable to prevent the destruction of these homes. Major Wilkinson recalled, "The houses were evidently fired by stragglers from the main [Orange] body; saw nine or ten houses, on both side of the road, on fire; Mr. Tabiteau, Mr. Corry, S.I., and the police did all they could to stop the flames."[5] For all their reported efforts, however, the police did not arrest a single Orange suspect.

Thus ended the famous battle of Dolly's Brae. It was a decidedly one-sided conflict. Government estimates placed the number of Catholic dead at thirty. Only one policeman was wounded and no Orangemen were seriously hurt. But the clash at Dolly's Brae resonated much further than this rather obscure rural locality in the southern part of County Down. After a detailed inquiry the British government stripped Lord Roden, William Beers, and Francis Beers of their magisterial duties.[6] In addition, the carnage of Dolly's Brae led the government to pass a new Party Processions Act in 1850, once again banning all party processions in Ireland. The Rathfriland Orangemen had won back their honor, but only at a very high price.

Sectarian violence constitutes one of the defining characteristics of the modern Ulster experience. Since 1780 clashes between Catholic and Protestant crowds have occurred with a depressing frequency in both rural and urban settings throughout the north of Ireland. The Dolly's Brae fight of 1849 was only one instance in a long list of sectarian atrocities committed by both Orange and Green in the long nineteenth century. This should not be particularly surprising to anyone familiar with the contemporary violence that plagues Northern Ireland. Indeed, by viewing Ulster's past through the spectacles of the present conflict, most analysts simply have assumed that Catholics and Protestants have been fighting constantly since Protestant settlers arrived in Ireland in the sixteenth and seventeenth centuries. While this premise obviously contains a great deal of truth, it has led to the creation of an unfortunate gap in Irish historical scholarship; until recently many scholars seem to have believed that such endemic violence was unworthy of detailed academic analysis.

The late John Whyte once wrote that in proportion to size, Northern Ireland was the most heavily researched area in the world, estimating that by 1989 seven thousand items had been published on various aspects of life in this "small corner of a small island."[7] While most of these works are primarily concerned with contemporary conditions in Northern Ireland, recent years have brought a kind of renaissance to Ulster historical studies.[8] This has been particularly true of the late eighteenth and the nineteenth centuries, where a number of important recent works have opened up new vistas and perspectives on this formative period of the modern Ulster experience.[9]

While studies of nineteenth-century sectarian conflict have been comparatively rare, there has been some good work in this critical area.[10] Here, scholars have largely followed in the footsteps of A.T.Q. Stewart, whose groundbreaking *The Narrow Ground: The Roots of Conflict in Ulster* remains one of the most powerful academic analyses of Catholic/Protestant conflict in the north of Ireland. Exploring the seeming continuity of sectarian violence in Ulster, Stewart examines what he views as patterns of conflict in the North over the past four centuries. Eschewing a more liberal or optimistic view of communal relations, he sees the clash as an atavistic one between two communities over the same ground. Stewart's analysis of the relationship between settlement and sectarian violence is particularly powerful; his description of contested territories as "seismic zones" remains a particularly apt metaphor for those areas, such as Shankill and Falls in West Belfast, that have sadly become tragic watchwords for Catholic/Protestant violence.[11]

Building on Stewart's framework, a number of recent works have examined the process and nature of sectarian riots in nineteenth-century Ulster in greater detail, focusing in particular on the ritualized nature of communal conflict. This is an important development, as contrary to popular belief, most communal riots were not spontaneous affairs; party processions and other partisan public demonstrations produced the vast majority of large-scale nineteenth-century sectarian conflicts. As Neil Jarman discusses in *Material Conflicts,* his excellent study of the processional tradition in Northern Ireland, this continuity of form often disguises important changes in meaning.[12] In other words, while the ritualized process that produced sectarian riots in nineteenth-century Ulster (Orange processions and Catholic reactions to them) rarely varied, the specific events and issues that triggered communal confrontation and conflict changed constantly. Taken in conjunction with two sensitive studies of Ulster politics in the forty years before the Home Rule crisis,[13] Jarman's powerful examination of the many important roles played by public ritual in Ulster's tradition of communal violence has transformed our understanding of nineteenth-century sectarianism.

Several themes emerge from any serious examination of the literature on sectarian violence in late eighteenth- and nineteenth-century Ulster. First, despite important and sometimes innovative work, the field remains rather underresearched. Although scholars have begun to explore important aspects of sectarianism in nineteenth-century Ulster, there has been no attempt to provide an in-depth and contextual analysis of this "tradition" of sectarian violence. Despite all of the good work done, a widespread misconception remains within Irish historical studies: sectarian violence in the north of Ireland is almost entirely atavistic and therefore does not merit sophisticated analysis. This assumption can still be found in some of the best works in the field.[14] For most scholars the sectarian violence of nineteenth-century Ulster remains a simple tale of tribal hatred. Why waste precious time and resources on such a depressing and simple story?

Why indeed? Simply because tribalism and atavism rest at the heart of the modern Ulster experience. Riots between Catholics and Protestants (and more importantly, the attitudes that gave rise to such violence) framed the creation of northern society, particularly its formal system of denominational politics. Building on recent work in Ulster historical studies, this book examines the process and nature of sectarian violence in late eighteenth- and nineteenth-century Ulster, focusing in particular on the relationship between sectarian riots and the evolution of the North's divided political culture. In doing so, it hopes to resolve one of the seeming contradictions of recent historiography. If, as Brian Walker persuasively argues in *Ulster Politics,* the years between 1868 and 1886 were the formative period for modern Ulster's divided political culture; if the Loyal Orange Order did not include a majority of Protestant adult males until the last quarter of the nineteenth century, then why did the language of anti-Catholic Protestant unity (which Frank Wright usefully has termed pan-Protestantism) resonate with such depth and vitality when it was raised during these formative years? In this book, I argue that the habitual practice of ritualized sectarian confrontation (and resultant Catholic/Protestant riots) prosecuted by a minority of Ulster Catholics and Protestants was at least partly responsible for the unmatched power of the pan-Protestant message. The choreographed and ritualized character of partisan conflict was especially important. Sectarian festivals and the riots they provoked played integral roles in maintaining, reinforcing, and updating the ideas, myths, and symbols that late nineteenth- and early twentieth-century protagonists used to construct the North's antagonistic but interlocked political culture.[15] In other words, Ulster's nineteenth-century "tradition" of sectarian violence prepared the way for the emergence of a formalized denominational system of politics in the north of Ireland.

Most of the major sectarian riots of the late eighteenth and nineteenth centuries were closely tied to the central issue of power and control in the North. Put simply, Protestants wanted to maintain their ascendant position over Irish Catholics, while Catholics wanted to achieve at least equal citizenship, focusing in particular on reversing the historic dispossession of "their" land and restoring the Catholic Church to its rightful place in society. These conflicting visions of how Irish society should be structured lay at the root of sectarian contention in Ulster. When either group perceived that changes might occur in local, regional, or national power relations, they responded by taking to the streets, asserting their strength in ritual-laden public demonstrations. These provocative displays often produced substantial riots between Catholic and Protestant crowds. The most famous of these occasions is of course the Orange Order's commemoration of King William's historic victories at the Boyne and Aughrim on the Twelfth of July. But while the Twelfth was and remains the most celebrated of these events, it hardly stands alone. Ulster Catholics and Protestants had a host of such holidays; the nineteenth-century calendar literally was filled with partisan festival days. In short, the calendar provided plenty of chances for communal exhibition and provocation.

A careful examination of the process that led to sectarian rioting generates several intriguing questions. What forces triggered such provocative displays and the violence they produced? How did partisan organizations like the Orange Order and the Ribbon societies reconcile the competing claims of sectarian and class allegiance? What was the relationship between national political developments and local communal conflict? If partisan festivals gave rise to sectarian contention, what precise roles did public and private ritual play in this deadly process? How did the social transformation of Ulster from a predominantly rural society to one driven by urban-based industry affect the shape and structure of party violence? And finally, what impact did this tradition of violence have on the evolution of modern

Ulster politics? The following chapters will address these questions. As they do so, it will become clear that to understand the formation of modern Ulster society, one must take into account the importance of sectarian riots and the plebeian beliefs that gave rise to such clashes.

Recent methodological innovations allow us to decipher some of the popular cultural perceptions of these rioters. Over the past thirty years scholars have altered the way we look at popular violence. Inspired by the work of E.P. Thompson and Natalie Zemon Davis,[16] historians increasingly have looked beyond the basic social characteristics of rioters, attempting to read the social meaning reflected in these outbursts of collective action. Such an approach centers on two fundamental questions. First, what legitimizing notions underlay the actions of the rioting crowd? Second, what is the exact relationship between the broader community and the goals, motivations, and behavior of the rioters? While this approach has its shortcomings, the notion that popular culture can act as a mediator of power relationships has allowed scholars to reconstruct how the lower classes played an active role in making their own history and cultural identity.[17]

Two features of this textual approach to popular conflict make it particularly suitable for the study of sectarian violence in late eighteenth- and nineteenth-century Ulster. First, Catholic/Protestant riots almost invariably emerged from set-piece, ritual-laden confrontations, structures that contain a great deal of information about the plebeian belief systems that led to such endemic conflict. Second, by directing analytical attention to lower-class convictions, such an approach gets at the critical variable in Ulster's sectarian conflict—the perceptions of the Catholic and Protestant rioters themselves. Too often analysts concentrate their analytical fire solely on the gentry and clerical classes, which presumably manipulated the comparatively uneducated and primally motivated lower classes of the North. As any perceptive analyst of contemporary Northern Ireland is aware, this model is upside down—one can make a good case that lower-class attitudes and behavior dictated elite response and not vice versa. At the very least, we need to attempt to comprehend the cultural perceptions that motivated and justified participation in Ulster's tradition of sectarian violence.

Sectarian violence and division has long been one of the defining characteristics of the Ulster experience. Of course, Ulster hardly stands alone in its modern experience of communal division created and reinforced by ritualized violence. One of the most positive recent trends in Irish historical writing has been scholars' increasing tendency to place the Irish experience in comparative perspective.[18] From India to the Balkans, a number of societies have attempted to form around contentious and divided political cultures. In India, in particular, ritualized violence has played a number of critical roles in forging, maintaining and even strengthening communal lines of division. If no example offers a perfect parallel to the Ulster experience, the experiences of these divided societies do suggest an instructive (if oftentimes not particularly hopeful) message: Ulster is not alone.

In an important work on late nineteenth-century politics, Brian Walker concludes with an eloquent call for further examination of Ulster's contentious past: "Knowledge of our history, of how and why all this happened when it did, may enlighten us; it may also help us cope with the real burden of the past."[19] Clashes between Catholic and Protestant crowds—which became such a depressingly familiar part of Ulster life during the long nineteenth century—played a critical role in maintaining and exacerbating partisan contention in the north of Ireland. In short, these sectarian riots and the forces that produced them were integral to the formation of modern Ulster society. As such, they surely warrant a more vigorous conversation. This book hopes to further that discussion.

■ 1

Trouble in Armagh, 1784–1798

The first disturbances we had in the north of Ireland, that I recollect, were in the county of Armagh.

James Christie

On 7 July 1796, Edward Cooke, the under secretary in Dublin Castle, wrote a concerned letter to Lord Gosford, the Lord Lieutenant of County Armagh. In this letter Cooke vividly described the recent ouster of Catholic tenants from their homes in north Armagh and the Armagh-Down borderlands. "My Lord Lieutenant learns with the utmost regret that outrages still continue in the county of Armagh and that those persons who style themselves Orange Boys are persecuting the lower orders of the Catholics with great cruelty—burning . . . their houses and threatening the lives of those who will employ them."[1] Like many other contemporary observers, the under secretary proceeded to blame the crisis in Armagh on the inactivity of its weak gentry class.[2] To remedy this situation Cooke argued that the county gentry needed to reassert social control over their lower-class coreligionists. Unfortunately, Cooke's prescription for resolving the crisis fell far short of his rather insightful analysis. In the end, his only suggestion was that the county magistracy should meet in a show of solidarity against the violence.

The disturbances that Cooke described occurred throughout late 1795 and 1796, when vengeful Protestant gangs called Peep O'Day or Orange Boys drove Catholic tenants and their families from the weaving districts of mid-Ulster. Estimates range widely, but somewhere between four thousand and five thousand Catholics fled mid-Ulster in this two-year period. Many of these families traveled to the remote climes of North Connacht, finding new homes in the counties of Mayo and Galway.[3] Ironically, these northern

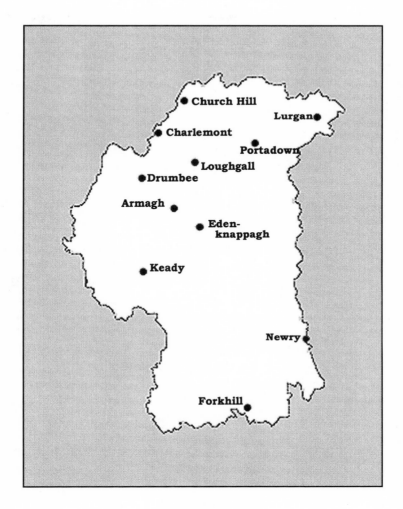

County Armagh.

exiles played a critical role in spreading both the revolutionary ideology and organizational structure of the Defenders and the Society of United Irishmen to the west of Ireland. Not surprisingly, bloodcurdling (and increasingly exaggerated) tales of Orange persecution and massacre in Armagh proved to be an excellent recruiting sergeant for the United Irishmen throughout Ireland.[4]

The Armagh expulsions of 1795 and 1796 constituted the last phase of a protracted communal conflict between the Peep O'Day Boys and the Defenders that raged on and off in County Armagh and its surroundings between 1784 and 1796. Known to historians as the Armagh troubles, these sectarian disturbances played a significant role in pushing Ireland toward revolution in the 1790s. Two of the primary organizations of revolution and counterrevolution in late eighteenth-century Ireland, the Defenders and the Loyal Orange Order, emerged directly from County Armagh. Not surprisingly, a number of historians have examined these disturbances in some detail, offering quite disparate interpretations of the forces behind these critical events.[5]

The scholarly debate on these disturbances largely has centered on the question of motivation; on what precise role economic and political forces have played in triggering the violence in Armagh. Although these analyses often have been quite creative and insightful, no scholar has yet offered a satisfactory interpretation of the Armagh troubles.

In searching for a more inclusive and comprehensive account of these critical events, E.P. Thompson's concept of the moral economy serves as a useful tool for fusing the various political, economic, and cultural forces that shaped this long-running sectarian conflict. The idea of the moral economy first emerged in Thompson's classic 1971 article on food riots in eighteenth-century Britain.[6] Rejecting the traditional view that such clashes were spasmodic reactions to economic grievances, Thompson asserted that the participants' actions were grounded upon "a popular consensus as to what were legitimate and what were illegitimate practices in marketing, milling, baking, etc. This in turn was grounded upon a consistent traditional view of social norms and obligations, of the proper economic functions of several parties within the community, which, taken together, can be said to constitute the moral economy of the poor."[7] According to Thompson, this consensus derived much of its legitimacy from the rioters' selective reconstruction of the traditional paternalist model of food market regulation. In fact, he found that the moral economy of the eighteenth-century English poor largely reproduced the provisions of the *Book of Orders*, a series of emergency measures enacted in times of crisis by the English government between 1580 and 1630. Many food rioters thus believed that they were playing a magisterial role, enforcing their conception of traditional British law against violators of customary practice. While certainly controversial,[8] Thompson's work helped to revolutionize the way we look at collective action, inspiring a generation of scholars to explore the cultural milieu from which popular violence emerged.

Two aspects of the moral economy argument make it a particularly useful framework for the study of Ulster's tradition of sectarian violence. First, by emphasizing the importance of traditional communal expectations in explaining outbreaks of popular violence, it focuses on the issue which lies at the heart of partisan contention in the north of Ireland: the continued relevance and vitality of two interlocked but conflicting visions of how Irish society should be structured. In an important book on Belfast's troubled history, Jonathan Bardon states that "historians have been a little too ready to blame the symptoms rather than search for the underlying causes of this sectarianism, which has its roots deep in Irish history."[9] Thus, most of the works devoted to sectarian contention in late eighteenth and nineteenth-century Ulster focus their attention on organizations and institutions like the Peep O'Day Boys, the Defenders, and the Orange Order.[10] Because it focuses on the beliefs and expectations that gave rise to sectarian clashes, the moral economy framework allows the scholar to move beyond the institutional level, a step that is critical if we are to better understand the evolution of modern political culture in the north of Ireland.

By showing how food rioters used selective reconstructions of the past to legitimize their actions, Thompson's article also stressed the important role played by popular conceptions of history in the prosecution of collective violence. This idea nicely echoes the tradition of conflict in Ulster, where both Catholics and Protestants used mythic narratives of the Irish past to justify their actions. Indeed, popular depictions of history often lay at the center of sectarian riots. At partisan festivals throughout the year, both parties constructed two conflicting accounts of Irish history in elaborate displays of public ritual, provocative rites that gave rise to some of the largest sectarian riots of modern Ulster history.

The Armagh troubles began in the early 1780s because mid-Ulster loyalists perceived that powerful forces were working to overwhelm the sectarian moral economy. The notion of a sectarian moral economy refers to Protestant plebeian expectations regarding their relative position in Irish society. This worldview consisted of a series of presumptions regarding relationships with two broadly defined social groups: Irish Catholics and the Protestant elite (and implicitly, the British state).[11] When both of these relationships were called into serious question in the late 1770s and 1780s, hardline loyalists in mid-Ulster mobilized into action, attempting to enforce their understanding of their traditional rights on the ground.

The sectarian moral economy centered on an exclusivist definition of loyalty and citizenship.[12] Put simply, a sizable majority of Ulster Protestants believed that they had a historic right to superior status over their Catholic antagonists. This belief system had rather straightforward political and economic ramifications. The economic provisions of the sectarian moral economy consisted of a vague sense that Protestants had earned the right to a position of relative economic advantage over Irish Catholics. The Protestant tenant-farmer/weaver in County Armagh did not have to be prosperous (which was lucky for him, as most were not!), but the sight of a Catholic neighbor accumulating wealth was a clear violation of this communal code. More importantly, the loyalists believed that Catholics should be kept down politically—excluded from the Irish polity. Of course, in the late eighteenth century, politics had nothing to do with the franchise for the vast majority of Irish Protestants. For the rank-and-file loyalist, privileges like the right to bear arms and expectations of partisan judicial favoritism were what separated the plebeian citizen from those outside the political pale. As we will see, the right to bear arms was particularly critical. This was not merely about maintaining communal ascendancy over one's foes (although holding a monopoly on weaponry certainly went far in that direction). The right to bear arms also conferred a certain measure of citizenship and above all, a special status to plebeian Protestants.

Like Thompson's food rioters, the ultra-Protestants' exclusivist conception of citizenship was grounded in a selective reconstruction of history. This belief system derived much of its legitimacy from a widespread mythic view of the Irish past that emphasized both the barbarism and revanchism of Irish Catholics—an ideology typically encapsulated in reductionist fashion as a siege mentality.[13] This historical narrative generally focused on the bloody events of the seventeenth century, when Irish Catholics twice rose in rebellion against both Protestant settlers and the British Crown. For loyalists, these events offered ironclad proof that Irish Catholics were not to be trusted with full citizenship rights. Ulster Protestants, by way of contrast, had continually earned their ascendant status throughout these years, maintaining a record of steadfast loyalty and exemplary military service.

But hard-line loyalists did not justify the sectarian moral economy solely in terms of their own perceptions of communal fidelity. Their exclusivist notion of citizenship was also grounded in a popular interpretation of the British constitutional settlement of the late seventeenth century. Plebeian Protestant conceptions of their historic rights were not solely based on illusory myths constructed by members of the Protestant lower classes desirous of maintaining their ascendant status over their Catholic adversaries. They reflected a not entirely inaccurate perception of British law in Ireland. After all, the exclusivist provisions of the Penal Laws provided much of the basis for British governance in eighteenth-century Ireland. In many ways, loyalist expectations regarding communal relationships accurately reproduced the formal terms of penal legislation enacted against Irish Catholics in the early eighteenth century. And these laws were hardly a distant memory. As late as 1780, laws excluding Catholics from formal politics, banning their right to bear arms, and restricting their economic wherewithal existed on the statute books.[14] When the Peep O'Day Boys traversed the weaving districts of north Armagh in search of Catholic arms, they were merely enforcing laws that the naive gentry had allowed to languish. These men clearly saw themselves as defenders of the true Protestant constitution—plebeian magistrates of true British law.

But the sectarian moral economy was not only concerned with regulating communal relationships. It also mapped out a general set of rules and obligations for true Protestants. These generally flowed from assumptions regarding habitual Catholic disloyalty.[15] Working from this premise, loyalist ideology emphasized the need for cross-class Protestant unity (which Frank Wright has termed pan-Protestantism) against the revanchist Catholic threat. Particularly important was the special relationship between lower-class loyalists and the Protestant elite. From a plebeian perspective, the standard for this critical relationship had been established with the penal laws, when both the British government and the Irish ruling classes had rewarded Protestant loyalists by giving them a perpetual right (or so they believed) to an ascendant status over Catholic rebels. By the late eighteenth century, plebeian Protestant activism thus represented a call for the return of traditional partisan paternalism.[16] The notion that plebeian Protestants' historic service had earned them the right to a special relationship with the Protestant gentry lay at the heart of the sectarian moral economy.

Not surprisingly, the worldview that dominated Irish Catholic popular culture differed fundamentally from its loyalist counterpart. This belief system focused on the historic deprivation of the Irish Catholic church and its adherents. At the heart of this mythic narrative lay an understandably deep well of bitter resentment centered on the formal exclusion of Catholics from many critical aspects of Irish society. This sense of dispossession was represented most tangibly in the eighteenth century by the relatively recent loss of landholding rights. The resolute attachment of Irish Catholics to the land of south Ulster would play a central role in the expansion of sectarian antagonism in the late eighteenth century.[17]

Like its Protestant counterpart, this Catholic worldview derived much of its legitimacy from a particular view of the Irish past, a narrative that focused on the status and power lost to Protestant conquest over the previous two centuries. But for all the basic parallels, it would be wrong to view this belief system within the conceptual framework of the sectarian moral economy. The moral economy is essentially a conservative notion, an ideology concerned with preserving the vitality of traditional practices against the onslaught of innovation. For very understandable reasons, Ulster Catholics were not particularly interested in preserving what they had. Instead, their conceptual grid was essentially restorative, a worldview that centered on the need to regain what had been taken from their ancestors. Above all, northern Catholics aimed to resist and roll back the imposition of the sectarian moral economy.

The notion that Ulster Protestants and Catholics had diametrically opposed worldviews is not particularly novel. But it is critical to reiterate these fundamental communal beliefs, for they lay at the heart of Armagh's sectarian warfare in the 1780s and 1790s. The final decades of the eighteenth century were the most traumatic and turbulent years in modern Irish history. To many observers both political and economic trends seemed to open up the possibility of a dramatically new type of Irish society—a vision of the future that challenged both Protestant and Catholic conceptions of how Irish society should be run. The threat to traditional plebeian Protestant expectations regarding their status within Irish society proved to be particularly important, for it was largely the widespread fear of betrayal among lower-class loyalists that drove the Armagh troubles forward.

On the political front, the late 1770s and early 1780s saw a number of attempts to curb some of the worst abuses of the eighteenth-century Irish polity. Pushed forward by a loose coalition of the Irish Protestant elite, generally labeled Patriots, these reform attempts satisfied very few Irish men and women. They both threatened the lower-class Protestant interpretation of the constitutional settlement and whetted the Catholic appetite for more substantial reform measures.[18] By challenging the status quo, these political reforms mobilized two substantial social groups with irreconcilable goals. But it was not merely political developments that drove this crisis forward; structural changes in the Ulster economy also played a critical role in creating an environment ripe for outbreaks of sectarian violence.

The growth of the northern linen economy (centered on mid-Ulster's famous linen triangle) threatened the communal status quo in a myriad of ways.[19] By opening up potential avenues of socioeconomic advancement for Catholic weavers and merchants, the expansion of the linen trade seemingly increased economic competition for Protestants involved in this critical industry. At the same time, it reduced the amount of social control that the Protestant gentry had over their lower-class coreligionists by giving young males increased wages and weakening the traditional vertical social bonds of the old rural economy.[20] Finally, both the growth of the linen economy and efforts to implement "agricultural improvement" dramatically increased social mobility within Ulster, challenging notions of communal settlement on the narrow ground of the north.

The dictates of religious geography made County Armagh particularly susceptible to such challenges. With its population roughly balanced between Catholic and Protestant, Armagh existed as a kind of frontier zone between Ulster's rival communities. Protestant divisions between Anglican and Presbyterian further complicate this picture of communal balance. Each of the three communities had a definite area of strength within the county: Anglicans dominated the northern third; Presbyterians were particularly strong in central Armagh; and Irish-speaking Catholics controlled the southern third of the county. Of course, this map only gives us the general contours of Armagh's sectarian geography. By the late eighteenth century, Catholics, Anglicans, and Presbyterians had settled throughout the county, creating potential zones of confrontation in all three cultural zones. This was particularly true in the county's northern half, which housed a substantial Catholic population to go with its conservative Protestant majority. When political and economic forces challenged the status quo in the late 1770s and early 1780s, northern Armagh provided the primary communal battleground.

With the sectarian moral economy threatened on so many fronts, both Catholics and Protestants mobilized to attack and defend the status quo. In County Armagh the primary issue proved to the prospective arming of Irish Catholics, which first arose with the admission of some Catholics to select Volunteer corps in late 1784. But the arms issue was only one of many; both political and economic trends in the 1780s and 1790s threatened to extinguish many critical aspects of Protestant ascendancy in Ireland. When these political, economic, and cultural forces are fused within the explanatory device of the sectarian moral economy, we gain a more comprehensive understanding of the motivations behind the Armagh troubles. With this framework in place, the Armagh disturbances can roughly be divided into two fairly distinct phases.

In the first stage the forces released by the Patriot attempt to include some Catholics within an expanded Irish polity and the dramatic changes wrought by agricultural improvement and the expansion of the Ulster linen economy threatened hard-line plebeian Protestants' conception of their place in Irish society. The prospect of Irish Catholics legally carrying arms was particularly galling to many lower-class Protestants. In an era when citizenship was often defined by the right to bear arms, many plebeian Protestants viewed their exclusive right to carry weapons as the primary mark of their social superiority over Catholics. Efforts to alter this portion of the Penal Code came as a shock to many loyalists, particularly because it was "their" elite that had proposed the hated reforms. The combined sense of threat and abandonment produced the Peep O'Day Boys, who attempted to reimpose their conception of true law by carrying out violent arms searches on Catholic homes between 1784 and 1788.

The second phase of the disturbances centered on elite efforts to revitalize their ties to lower-class loyalists—that special relationship that lay at the heart of the sectarian moral economy. This process effectively began in 1788, when the Armagh gentry incorporated the Peep O'Day Boys into the newly expanded Irish Volunteers, bringing both arms and legitimacy to their cause. But this relationship was not to be reforged overnight. This would occur only between 1795 and 1797, when the British government and the local gentry, pressed by the turbulent behavior of militant plebeian Protestants and the looming threat of revolution, finally took steps to formalize their special ties to the Protestant lower classes. Loyalist belief found its institutional form in these years with the formation and expansion of the Orange Order and the creation of the Irish yeomanry. By the outbreak of the 1798 rebellion, the sectarian moral economy had been refashioned, much to the liking of the militant Protestant weavers who had done so much to dictate the pace of change.

Challenging the Sectarian Moral Economy

A great deal of mystery surrounds the actual events that triggered communal violence in Armagh. As David Miller states in his insightful article on the Armagh troubles, there are a number of sometimes conflicting explanations for the initial outbreak of communal violence.[21] Miller himself draws heavily on a 1792 pamphlet written by J. Byrne entitled *An impartial account of the late disturbances in the county of Armagh,* easily the most comprehensive contemporary description of the Armagh troubles.[22] In this work a brawl between two Protestants in the Edenappagh townland in July 1784 is supposed to have initiated a cycle of violence which soon engulfed large portions of the county. According to Byrne, this particular clash led to faction fighting, which in the turbulent political context of the 1780s and in the divided and contentious environment of County Armagh soon took on a sectarian character. Although Byrne's explanation for the precise origins of the communal violence remains somewhat suspect, his argument does underline the forces which provided the real impetus for this sectarian war—

the widespread perception among Armagh loyalists that political and economic trends were threatening their historic rights to exclusivist citizenship.

If examined in context, the list of political reforms undertaken in Ireland between 1778 and 1793 is a fairly impressive one. Catholic relief acts were passed in 1778, 1782, 1783, 1792, and 1793. Among their many provisions these bills allowed Irish Catholics to lease and inherit land, to own land outside parliamentary boroughs, to practice law, and finally in 1793 to vote in parliamentary elections. Following a century in which Catholics were virtually excluded from the Irish polity, this rapid series of reforms appeared to be a leading indicator of dramatic changes to come in Irish society.

While this seemingly momentous shift certainly provided a critical backdrop for the Armagh disturbances, it was the formation and evolution of the Irish Volunteers that opened up Ulster's tragic Pandora's box. Originally formed in 1778 to defend Ireland against French invasion, the Volunteers quickly became involved in national politics, providing much of the muscle and momentum behind the Patriot call for free trade and parliamentary reform.[23] In the early 1780s some Volunteer companies went much further, calling for a form of legislative independence at the famous Dungannon Convention of 1782. Although the vast majority of the resolutions approved at Dungannon centered on the need for parliamentary reform and assertions of Ireland's historic rights to legislative independence, two of the resolutions dealt specifically with the Catholic question:

Resolved (with two dissenting voices only, to this and the following resolution)— That we hold the right of private judgment, in matters of religion, to be equally sacred in others as in ourselves.

Resolved, therefore, that, as Men and as Irishmen, as Christians and as Protestants, we rejoice in the relaxation of the penal laws against our Roman Catholic fellow-subjects, and that we conceive the measure to be fraught with the happiest consequences to the union and prosperity of Ireland.[24]

With the Volunteers pressing for such changes in the national polity, Irish politics seemed to be heading in a Catholic direction.

While Volunteer radicalism seemingly faded on a national scale following the "constitutional revolution" of 1782, advanced companies continued to call for fundamental reforms in the way in which Ireland was governed. Some went much further, calling on loyal Catholics to join Volunteer companies throughout Ulster. One such call occurred right in the heartland of Armagh loyalism, at a meeting of the Loughgall Volunteers in June 1784.[25] Of course, rhetoric often failed to translate into reality. Despite the tolerant sentiments expressed in such resolutions, no Catholics were formally admitted to Volunteer companies in Armagh in 1784.[26] In this case, however, reality was less important than perception, for such conciliatory rhetoric only reinforced the prevalent notion that Irish society was becoming less Protestant in character. In Armagh, the suggestion of giving Catholics the right to bear arms was enough to mobilize some outraged loyalists, who began raiding their adversaries' homes for arms in late 1784, a practice that characterized the Armagh troubles until late 1788.[27]

The sectarian disturbances that raged in County Armagh between late 1784 and 1796 were fundamentally rooted in the disruption of the sectarian moral economy. The arms issue raised in early 1780s was clearly the most visible symbol of the ongoing threat to the lower-class ultra-Protestant interpretation of how the Irish polity should be structured. As such, it is obviously the most concrete variable in explaining the outbreak of sectarian violence in Armagh. But there are at least two other factors that need to be incorporated into our analysis. Both of these emerged from the rapid commercialization of the Ulster economy.

If the ability to own weapons was the most visible symbol of the Protestant nature of the Irish polity, relative economic advantage certainly constituted another important part of the Ulster Protestant's sense of superior status. By opening up avenues of material advancement for Catholics, the growth of the Ulster linen trade challenged Protestant conceptions of their own economic hegemony. In the northern part of County Armagh, at least two highly visible Catholic businesses had made substantial advances in the linen trade by the 1780s, the Quigleys of Armagh and Bernard Coyle of Lurgan.[28] Taken in conjunction with the newly won abilities of Catholics to lease, inherit, and own land, the visible prosperity of men like Coyle and Quigley only reinforced the Armagh loyalist's sense of their own declining status vis-à-vis Irish Catholics.

The growth of the linen trade also disrupted the status quo in Armagh by encouraging social mobility. Because of the diminished importance of fertile land, Protestants began to settle on land previously viewed as marginal and therefore Catholic, presenting challenges to long-held settlement patterns. More directly, landlords interested in grasping their share of the profits of the linen trade often wanted "industrious" and "loyal" Protestant tenants to replace their Catholic counterparts. One such man was the colorful nobleman George Robert Fitzgerald.[29] His attempt to generate linen profits by transplanting Ulster Protestants to County Mayo provides us with a nice illustration of the links between commercialization and the rapidly accelerating tempo of sectarian contention in Armagh.

In the summer of 1784, Fitzgerald announced that he wanted to transplant Ulster men and women skilled in the linen trade onto his north Connacht estate in an effort to introduce the linen industry to the region around Castlebar, County Mayo.[30] A large number of families took up this seemingly attractive offer, including a contingent from the Mount Norris area of County Armagh. Unfortunately, these Armagh settlers faced trouble in Mayo almost immediately. To make room for his new tenants Fitzgerald evicted a number of the Catholic occupiers on his Mayo estate. This upset local Catholics, who wrecked the homes of the settlers and banished them from the county. The settlers returned to Armagh angry and disgusted in 1786 and played a central role in quickening the pace of the Peep O'Day Boys anti-Catholic violence in central Armagh.[31] Of course, the vast majority of such incidents occurred not in north Connacht but on the heretofore less valuable peripheral lands of Ulster. The application of the techniques of "improvement" to these marginal and Catholic lands exacerbated existing sectarian tensions between Catholics and Protestants. As we shall see, this factor played a critical role in the "expansion of Defenders, a Catholic secret society dedicated to 'defending' Catholic interests against loyalist aggression," to south Armagh and bordering regions after 1789.

Previous explanations of the Armagh troubles have primarily differed over the question of the relative weight of the political and economic forces behind the sectarian violence. This distinction dissipates when these elements are fused within the concept of the sectarian moral economy. The outbreak of violence in Armagh in the 1780s ultimately was rooted in the perception of a group of Armagh Protestants that they were rapidly losing their ascendant status over Catholics. As they looked around them, there were a number of signs that seemed to indicate a movement toward full Catholic citizenship within the Irish polity. The prospect of losing the last vestiges of their special rights as Protestants proved to be the catalyst behind the formation of the Peep O'Day Boys and the breakdown of traditional forms of social control in north Armagh. The question was, What steps had to be taken to refashion an acceptable relationship between the Protestant elite and their lower-class coreligionists?

Reconstructing the Sectarian Moral Economy

Between 1788 and 1798, members of the Armagh gentry and their plebeian brethren struggled to rebuild connections that would satisfy both parties. Driven forward by both the turbulent behavior of the Protestant lower classes of mid-Ulster and the looming threat of revolution in Ireland, this process was successfully concluded by 1798. Unfortunately, the way in which this Protestant alliance came together only further exacerbated sectarian tensions throughout the north of Ireland. The new overtly communal nature of the strife, in which armed bands of Catholic Defenders clashed with gentry-supported Protestant loyalists, played right into the hands of militant lower-class Protestants, who saw their social ideals institutionalized between 1795 and 1798 with the creation of the Orange Order and the yeomanry.

The outbreak of sectarian violence in 1784 and 1785 presented the Armagh gentry with a delicate problem. Recognizing that the Peep O'Day Boys were the aggressors, the gentry struggled to bring their coreligionists back into line. One of their first efforts came at the spring assizes of 1785, when eight Peep O'Day Boys were brought up for trial. William Richardson, M.P., a gentleman from Rich Hill, spoke on behalf of the accused in the hope that judicial leniency might curb their activities. Unfortunately, Richardson's liberality turned out to be ineffectual. Soon after their release, the Peep O'Day Boys returned to their nocturnal activities.[32] In the following year some sympathetic landlords actually loaned weapons to local Catholics for their protection.[33] While this tactic certainly created a more level playing field for the Defenders, it only gave added impetus to plebeian loyalists searching for Catholic arms.

Gentry efforts were only successful in 1788, when they co-opted the Peep O'Day Boys into expanded companies of the Irish Volunteers. By mid-1789 arms raids on Catholic homes had become a rarity in north Armagh. The decision to bring these militant loyalists into the Volunteers changed the nature of the mid-Ulster conflict, for the gentry essentially had surrendered to the demands of the Peep O'Day Boys. In exchange for their inclusion on the side of law and order, the gentry gave these militant loyalists the two things that they had pushed for between 1784 and 1788: the exclusive right to bear arms and formal recognition of their special relationship to the Protestant elite who controlled the Volunteers. Although the gentry's 1788 decision did effectively halt arms searches in north Armagh, it helped to initiate a new and more deadly phase of the Armagh disturbances.

From late 1788 both the Catholic Defenders and the Protestant Volunteers increasingly marched in public processions designed to mark their territory. These open displays of partisan muscle inevitably led to occasional riots between the two parties. The first such clash occurred just north of Armagh city on 21 November 1788 when a company of the Benburb Volunteers paraded in uniform to Armagh city to attend church services. This company was a new unit of the Benburb Volunteers, part of the effort to bring the more assertive and independent Peep O'Day Boys under the regulatory eye of their Volunteer commanders. The Benburb men marched to Armagh by the Eglish road to the famously ecumenical tunes of "The Protestant Boys" and "The Boyne Water."[34] At one point a gathering of Catholic women surrounded the Volunteers, giving them "a broadside of tongue weapons" and calling them mere Peep O'Day Boys.[35] No violence broke out, however, and the Volunteers marched on to Armagh city. Their return journey would not be so fortunate. Marching home via the same road, the Benburb Volunteers ran headlong into a large Catholic crowd, determined to obtain revenge for the morning's scuffle. A fight ensued between the two parties, and the Volunteers fired into the crowd, killing two men.[36]

Although very few of these set-piece confrontations resulted in violence,[37] they clearly represented a departure from the style of conflict that had predominated in Armagh in the mid-1780s. The aggressive and independent activism of the Peep O'Day Boys was now more or less regulated within the structure of the gentry-controlled Volunteers. In fact, the resident gentry of north Armagh could feel very pleased with the results of their efforts. By late 1789 the arms searches had ceased, and other than the occasional clash between the Volunteers and Defenders, the northern half of the county was relatively quiet.

For all this, communal violence had not left the county. After 1789 the disturbances shifted to the Catholic-dominated areas of south Armagh and the bordering regions of south Down, Louth, and Monaghan. Spurred on by the ongoing transformation of the Ulster rural economy, these border regions provided fertile soil for the growth of Defenderism; with few resident gentry in the area, sectarian contention increased dramatically.

The precipitating factor in the spread of Defenderism and sectarian violence to these border regions seems to have been Protestant encroachment on heretofore Catholic land.[38] By weakening the need for fertile soil, the growth of the linen economy encouraged increased social mobility. Hoping to share in the profits of the expanding economic pie, landlords attempted to settle clusters of Ulster Protestants in the outlying areas of north Connacht, north Leinster, and south Ulster. As was the case in Mayo, the appearance of these new settlers often resulted in the displacement of Catholic tenants. This in turn encouraged the growth of the Defenders, pledged to protect Catholic interests. Sectarian unrest increased dramatically between 1788 and 1791, culminating in the barbaric murder of a Protestant schoolmaster in the infamous Forkhill incident of 1791.

In January 1791, fifty to sixty Defenders forced their way into the home of Alexander Barclay, an Irish-speaking Protestant schoolmaster living near Forkhill. They proceeded to torture and murder Barclay, ripping out his tongue and slicing off his fingers. His wife and brother-in-law were both mutilated in similar fashion. While the actual background is somewhat complex, the murder seems to have been committed in response to a widespread belief that Catholic tenants were to be dispossessed of their land in favor of Protestant settlers. This assault on the "rights" of local Catholics was only reinforced by the appearance of an Irish-speaking Protestant schoolmaster, who would have been expected to convert some of his young scholars to Protestantism. Finally, Barclay's brother-in-law had played a prominent role in a recent assault on the local parish priest.[39] The murder, thus, can be viewed as a ferocious response to a perceived two-pronged assault on Catholic landholding and the Catholic faith. The complexities of the murder were understandably lost on most Ulster Protestants, who simply viewed the Forkhill incident as more proof that Catholics were simply out to massacre the Protestant population of Ireland.

Both the increasing general threat of revolution and particular events like the Forkhill murder helped to push forward the alliance between elements of the Protestant gentry and their lower-class coreligionists. The threat of a sectarian jacquerie seemed to vindicate what militant Armagh loyalists had been saying since 1784. Irish Catholics simply could not be trusted; they needed to be kept down. The tumultuous events of the 1790s certainly lent a great deal of weight to this position. With Defenderism spreading throughout Ireland, the radical Society of United Irishmen agitating in Belfast and Dublin, and the French Revolution raging on the continent and beyond, a majority of the Ulster Protestant elite shifted toward the hardline positions of their plebeian brethren. The time for reform had passed.

The event that initiated the final stage of this process of Protestant reconciliation occurred in north Armagh in September 1795. This was the famous Battle of Diamond, the last set-piece party confrontation of the Armagh troubles. Because the consequences of this clash proved to be so critical to modern Irish history, the Battle of the Diamond and its frenzied aftermath clearly warrant a detailed examination.

Ironically, County Armagh had settled into a period of relative calm in 1793,[40] as the Defenders successfully concentrated on expanding their organization beyond Armagh.[41] This period of tranquility did not last long, however, as sectarian disturbances returned to Armagh in 1794 and 1795. This renewed unrest took on a familiar form: Protestant gangs attacking Catholic homes in north Armagh.[42] In August 1794 General William Dalrymple vented his frustration in a letter to the government: "Many of them are preparing for flight the moment their little harvests are brought in; some are gone to America, others to Connaught. Their houses are placarded, and their fears excessive. . . . The Catholics conceive the fault to be mine, that I am partial and attached to their enemies, supposing me to possess powers not in me, and when I advise them to apply to the magistrates, their answer is constantly that their own case is hopeless."[43] Repeated attacks on Catholic homes in north Armagh produced a predictable rise in communal tension in this old battleground. Things finally came to a head in September 1795.

The Battle of the Diamond began as just another ritualized show of strength between Protestant and Catholic parties. The Diamond, a crossroads near the village of Loughgall, emerged as a party flashpoint in June 1795 when a fight between a Catholic and a Protestant almost erupted into a major sectarian riot. On this occasion a magistrate arrived in time to settle the dispute.[44] In September the authorities would not be so lucky.

On 17 September 1795 a party of Defenders gathered on a hill near Loughgall. This was no mere local band. The Defenders had traveled from as far away as the border regions of Louth and Monaghan and carried a number of guns. Local Protestants responded quickly to the threat, gathering in strength on a nearby hill. Over the next two days the two parties engaged in a form of ritualized combat, firing harmless shots at each other from hill to hill. Presumably tiring of the game, the two parties agreed to a truce on Saturday, 19 September, at the behest of a local magistrate and the local parish priest. As had happened countless times before, the affair seemed as if it would end without the taking of a single life, becoming yet another rather innocuous display of party strength. By the afternoon of 20 September both sides began to return to their homes.

Unfortunately, a new band of Defenders arrived just as the contest seemed to be ending. Not bound by the terms of the truce, the newly arrived Defenders attacked on the following day. On the morning of 21 September, they fired down the hill toward the cluster of houses in the Diamond. Greatly outnumbered, the Protestants who remained quickly took up firing positions in Dan Winter's house. Well-armed and comparatively secure, the Protestant party quickly routed the attacking Defenders. An estimated thirty Catholics perished in the clash; no Protestants died. The famous Battle of the Diamond was over, a seemingly unremarkable, if tragic, event in the communal violence of the Armagh troubles.[45]

If the Battle of Diamond did not seem to be particularly consequential at the time,[46] it eventually found itself lodged within the mantra of famous dates that make up the hard-line Ulster Protestant folk view of Irish history: "1641, 1689, 1690, and all that." With a script that could have been written by a mediocre playwright, the events at the Diamond embodied the "siege mentality" that remains so vital to understanding Ulster Protestant culture. But we should not linger in such abstractions, for the Battle of the Diamond's primary importance did not reside in the clash itself or even in its later importance to ultra-Protestant mythology.[47] This seemingly unremarkable conflict gave rise to the two closing acts of the Armagh troubles: the formation of the Orange Order and the Armagh expulsions of 1795 and 1796.

Following the Battle of the Diamond a group of the victors gathered at James Sloan's house in the village of Loughgall to form a "defensive association" of Ulster Protestants.[48] They quickly fashioned a rough series of rules and regulations, all centered on the necessity of preserving and protecting the Protestant character of the Irish polity. The Loyal Orange Order emerged from these small beginnings, an institution that would shape the history of modern Ulster.

Aided by the looming threat of revolution, Orangeism quickly spread among plebeian Protestants in mid-Ulster throughout late 1795 and 1796. By late 1796 there were fourteen lodges in the town of Lisburn alone.[49] The primary impetus behind this new organization was decidedly plebeian. Even Col. William Blacker, a man who never lost an opportunity to emphasize the respectability of the Order, chronicled the lack of support given to this new body by Armagh's resident gentry.[50] With the Protestant elite hesitant to endorse this new organization wholeheartedly, Orangeism's immediate impact was minuscule on a national level. This would not change until 1797, when a sizable number of Dublin's Protestant elite formed a special gentleman's lodge. But if members of the elite wavered in these early years, their plebeian brethren remained quite busy. With the local balance of power tipped in their favor following the Battle of the Diamond, Protestant gangs reminiscent of the Peep O'Day Boys renewed their attacks on Catholic homes in Armagh on an unprecedented scale.[51]

The most common form of intimidation employed was that standard Irish institution, the threatening notice. Placards proclaiming "To Hell or Connaught" regularly were nailed to the doors of Catholic homes in mid-Ulster in these years. The wrecking gangs went further on many occasions, actually destroying the property within the house, including the looms and spinning wheels needed to make a living.[52] None of this was new. But while the style of violence was familiar, the scale and geographic expanse of this sectarian pogrom did represent something novel. This campaign of intimidation lasted into late 1796 and spread beyond the borders of Armagh, disturbing the counties of Down, Tyrone, and Londonderry.[53]

Fearing for their lives and not trusting the local judicial system, many mid-Ulster Catholics escaped to north Connacht. As previously noted, between four thousand and five thousand Catholics fled mid-Ulster in 1795 and 1796.[54] Most refugees settled in Mayo and Galway. James Cuffe, a Mayo landowner, traveled to the town of Ballina, where "about sixty men, as nearly as I could guess attended, and I must own that the account they gave of themselves was most melancholy and affected me much."[55] In another letter Cuffe indicated that almost all of the exiles were weavers by trade. In talking to the Ulstermen, Cuffe discovered that most had fled in fear of the Peep O'Day Boys' nocturnal visits. Many of these Catholic fugitives blamed their plight on the inattentiveness of the Protestant gentlemen of Armagh.[56]

Contemporary opinion generally concurred with this opinion. Figures ranging from the Lord Lieutenant to United Irish propagandists focused their wrath on the Armagh magistracy.[57] Some were particularly harsh: "In consequence of the shameful supineness of the magistrates, the Orange Boys are still permitted to continue their depredations in the north with impunity. If this system of spoilation is much longer acquiesced in by the magistrates, the sufferers must be driven to despair, and considering themselves as put out of the protection of the law, they will necessarily associate for their own defense and will become recruits to the Jacobin Club established at Belfast."[58] This analysis proved to be correct, as the Armagh expulsions eventually played a critical role in forging closer ties between the Defenders and the United Irishmen.

An examination of the geography of the wreckings supports the idea that the "inattentiveness" of the Armagh gentry lay at the center of the ejections. Several Mayo landlords compiled detailed lists about the northern emigrants, catalogs that contain critical information about the exiles' occupational and geographic backgrounds.[59] James Cuffe's list is particularly helpful. In a letter to Dublin Castle, Cuffe provided an inventory of the northern heads of households who had recently settled in the vicinity of the Mayo towns of Foxford, Crossmolina, and Ballina. The vast majority of these families came from Armagh and Down. More revealing, a substantial percentage of the emigrants came from parishes dominated by members of the Armagh gentry who would play central roles in the growth of the Orange Order.[60]

Magistrates and estate owners like William Brownlow, William Richardson, Joseph Atkinson, and James Verner gave their plebeian coreligionists a free hand in intimidating Catholic families. This should not be surprising. Faced with the threat of a largely Catholic rebellion, landlords who were staunch Protestants to begin with were very unlikely to punish those responsible for ridding their estates of potential adversaries. By tacitly protecting plebeian perpetrators from the law, these gentlemen also furthered their hard-line credentials with their lower-class brethren, help-ing to ensure that they would receive their future support.[61]

The British government in Ireland found itself in a somewhat unset-tling situation. Faced with the treat of armed rebellion, Dublin Castle could not afford to alienate any section of the loyalist population. At the same time, the government had to do something to quell the disturbances in the North. Writing from Dungannon, Thomas Knox expressed this predica-ment in a letter to Dublin Castle in August 1796: "As to the Orangemen, we have rather a difficult card to play. They must not be ultimately discounte-nanced; on the contrary, we must in a certain degree uphold them, for with all their licentiousness, on them we must rely for the preservation of our lives or properties, should critical times occur. . . . I hope I shall be able to manage it so with our Tyrone people that they shall not be lost to the cause of their king and country, and at the same time be kept within due bounds."[62] The problem, then, was how to strengthen loyalist forces in Ireland while regulating their excesses.

Faced with a similar problem in 1788, the Armagh gentry had co-opted the Peep O'Day Boys within extended companies of the Irish Volunteers. This move had solved the immediate problem of arms raids in north Armagh but understandably alienated the county's Catholic population, thereby contributing mightily to the spread of Defenderism. In 1796 the govern-ment resolved its dilemma in like fashion, giving commissions to local no-tables to raise yeomanry corps from among the loyal population. The tactic looked good on paper, dramatically increasing the manpower at the government's disposal and giving it a greater degree of social control over newly formed yeomanry corps.[63] Unfortunately, things did not work so smoothly on the ground.

In raising the yeomanry, the government left many critical decisions about the nature and composition of the corps in the hands of local no-tables. This was particularly true for conservative noblemen, who were given much more latitude than their more reform-minded brethren. Such critical questions as whether to include or exclude Catholics were left up to local interests. In Ulster this meant that the yeomanry took on a strongly Orange hue in many localities.

The Orange character of much of the Ulster yeomanry was not merely a reflection of the sentiments of the unyielding conservative elite. The loy-alist character of the yeomanry often was defined by the rank and file, who simply refused to serve with known Protestant reformers or Catholics.[64] By maintaining the "true blue" purity of local corps, plebeian loyalists were able to impose their own exclusivist notion of loyalty on to a state-sponsored institution. The yeomanry thus represented exactly what ultra-Protestants had been agitating for since 1784: an almost entirely Protestant military organization that reflected the exclusivist view of citizenship held by many militant lower-class loyalists in Ulster. In many ways the yeomanry was the perfect institutional expression of plebeian loyalist ideology. It was a powerful public instrument that tangibly reflected their superior status over Irish Catholics.[65] With the formation of the yeomanry in 1796–1797, the sectarian moral economy had been successfully reconstructed.

The entrance of militant loyalists and Orangemen into the yeomanry brings our story full circle. By early 1797 ultra-Protestants had finally achieved what they had fought for since 1784: state and elite recognition of their superior position vis-à-vis the Catholic population. The commander of the British army in the north of Ireland, Lieut.-Gen. Gerard Lake, symbolically acknowledged this point in the town of Lurgan on 12 July 1797, when he formally reviewed Orange processionists marching in full partisan regalia.[66] The decade-long struggle was now over; the sectarian moral economy had been successfully refashioned. It would not face such a serious challenge again until the late 1820s, when Daniel O'Connell's triumphant crusade for Catholic emancipation forever changed the course of Irish history.

Previous examinations of the Armagh troubles have focused on showing how specific political and economic forces shaped and facilitated this long-running sectarian conflict. While these efforts have dramatically increased our understanding of aspects of the Armagh disturbances, they have failed to provide a comprehensive explanation for these critical events. To understand the outbreak of sectarian warfare in Armagh, one has to examine the ways in which the dramatic political and economic changes of the late eighteenth century shaped communal expectations in Ulster.

Following a century of relative stasis, the last decades of the eighteenth century witnessed a series of events that seemed to indicate revolutionary changes in the character of Irish society. With the threat of a Jacobin insurrection seemingly diminished, members of the Protestant gentry began to remove some of the economic and political restrictions that had kept Irish Catholics down throughout the eighteenth century. Between 1778 and 1793 the Irish Parliament passed Catholic relief acts that gave Catholics the right to own and inherit land, enter previously proscribed professions, and vote in parliamentary elections. While Irish historians have tended to emphasize the hesitant and incomplete nature of these reforms, they nonetheless represented a dramatic departure from the exclusivist policies that had characterized the Penal Age in Ireland. Put simply, the general tide of events seemed to be flowing in a Catholic direction.

This shift was not confined to matters of parliamentary politics, for the events that triggered the outbreak of sectarian violence in Armagh did not occur within the ornate halls of College Green in Dublin. Instead, the peculiar evolution of the Irish Volunteers proved to be the primary destabilizing force in Armagh. The prospect of Catholics legally bearing arms within companies of the Volunteers provoked militant plebeian Protestants into action in the weaving districts of mid-Ulster. For these men the idea of Catholics possessing the right to bear arms was the ultimate violation of the sectarian moral economy—a powerful belief system rooted in the idea of the Protestant right to exclusive citizenship within the Irish polity. It was not just a question of self-defense. The arms issue was simply the most tangible and potent symbol of the ongoing shift in the balance of power in Ireland. It was viewed as a leading indicator of plebeian Protestants' declining status vis-à-vis Irish Catholics.

The impact of this trend was particularly forceful in Armagh because of the destabilizing impact of the linen trade. Centered on the famous linen triangle of mid-Ulster, the region's new protoindustrial economy broke down many of the pillars of the old rural economy, promoting both increased levels of social mobility and economic opportunities for many Ulster men and women. In doing so, however, this process challenged fundamental conceptions of religious geography and economic hegemony in the north of Ireland. Like the political changes initiated by the Patriots and their Volunteer allies, the linen economy presented a series of profound challenges to the status quo in Ireland. County Armagh's tenuous demographic balance between Catholic and Protestant made this situation even more dangerous.

Faced with these dramatic changes, plebeian Protestant loyalists fought to hold back the tide by imposing their conception of ascendancy on areas of mid-Ulster in the 1780s. Nurtured on a rich belief system that stressed the unchanging and rebellious nature of Irish Catholics, militant Protestant weavers formed the Peep O'Day Boys, whose arms raids on Catholic homes epitomized the first phase of the Armagh troubles, a period which lasted until 1788. These vengeance groups wanted nothing less than the restoration of the sectarian moral economy.

Between 1788 and 1798 both the Armagh gentry and the British government attempted to refashion an acceptable relationship with their zealous lower-class coreligionists. In both cases the militant loyalists of mid-Ulster achieved their goals. Faced with the turbulent anti-Catholic behavior of the Peep O'Day Boys in the mid-1780s, the Armagh gentry brought members of these partisan wrecking gangs into the newly expanded companies of the Irish Volunteers. While this step did bring an end to arms searches in north Armagh, it essentially amounted to the surrender of the gentry to the aims of the Peep O'Day Boys, who received both weapons and elite recognition of their superior status in the deal. This relationship eventually was consolidated and institutionalized within the ranks of the Loyal Orange Order in the late 1790s and beyond.

The British government found itself in much the same position in 1796 and 1797. With the prospect of rebellion growing day by day, Dublin Castle found itself desperately short of reliable military personnel. To meet this need and to help regulate the excessive loyalist zeal of Protestant wrecking gangs, the government allowed trusted notables to raise yeomanry corps from the local loyal population. This proposal was met with unstinting enthusiasm among Ulster loyalists, who flocked to the standard of these new government-sanctioned military units. Much like the Orange Order, the yeomanry provided both legitimacy and institutional structure for the loyalist cause. With the formation of this state-sponsored body militant Protestants had, with the substantial aid of the threat of revolution, imposed their idea of what constituted loyalty (and citizenship) on the very institutions of the British state in Ireland.

The character of the Wexford rebellion in 1798 only reinforced and legitimized this perspective. Widely-circulated reports of the sectarian barbarities perpetrated at Scullabogue and Wexford Bridge provided fresh material for a belief system already centered on the bloody sectarianism of the seventeenth century.[67] This reductionist interpretation of the rebellion quickly spread throughout Ireland, helping to reinforce and expand the loyalist interpretation of how Irish society should be structured. It was reports of the sectarian brutality of the rebellion that truly closed this chapter of Irish history. The Society of United Irishmen's vision of an Ireland free from communal strife would have to wait. After 1798, Ireland gradually returned to its "natural" state, with society firmly divided by a sectarian chasm between Catholic and Protestant. By 1800 the exclusivist character of plebeian Protestant ideology had returned to the center of British governance in Ireland. The militant Protestants of mid-Ulster could now rest easy—their vision of Irish society had prevailed and would dominate Irish politics for the next two decades.

■ 2

The Orange Order and Catholic Resistance, 1795–1820

The Orange Society is, above all things, Protestant, exclusively Protestant, but not sectarian.

R.M. Sibbett, *Orangism in Ireland and Throughout the Empire*

On the morning of 12 July 1813 several Orange lodges assembled in front of the Linen Hall in Belfast to commemorate the anniversary of the Battle of the Boyne. The size of the gathering was not particularly impressive—if anything, there were fewer Orangemen present than on previous occasions. From the Linen Hall the Orangemen marched out of Belfast with drums beating and colors flying to a field near the town of Lisburn, where they joined their brethren for an afternoon of partisan celebration.

The Belfast lodges returned from the Lisburn meeting at about seven o'clock in the evening. Determined to continue their festivities, a large group marched through the city toward the house of a sympathetic publican named Isaac Thompson. As the small procession marched through the city center, a hostile crowd of men, women, and youths traded insults with the marching Orangemen. These verbal exchanges quickly altered an already tense situation, and the two groups were soon throwing stones and brickbats at each other instead of words. The outnumbered Orangemen charged down Hercules Street toward the relative safety of Thompson's pub. Fleeing the angry crowd, the Orangemen slipped into their place of shelter. Refusing to give up their supposed prey, the crowd attacked the pub, hurling stones that shattered several windows. After a few minutes the besieged Orangemen responded with terrible effect. Emerging from the pub, several men fired shots into the crowd, killing two young men and severely wounding four others. Only the sudden appearance of the military prevented further tragedy, putting a halt to this rather one-sided battle. After dispersing the unruly crowd, several magistrates proceeded to Thompson's house, where they arrested two men who had taken a leading part in the clash.

The Belfast riot of 1813 was now over. Excepting the two fatalities, the conflict itself proved to be a rather small affair—it was neither widespread nor lengthy and did not disrupt Belfast society in any measurable way. It was a noteworthy event, however, for the riot of 1813 was the first organized sectarian riot between Orange and Green in nineteenth-century Belfast. It would not be the last.[1]

Over the past thirty years scholars have dramatically altered the way we look at collective violence. Following the lead of George Rudé, E.P. Thompson, and Natalie Zemon Davis, historians have destroyed the old stereotype of the wholly irrational and anarchic mob, replacing it with a more nuanced and contextual view of popular conflict.[2] One of the central themes of the massive riot literature is the idea that the unruly activities of the crowd often were driven by quite rational goals and shaped by the precepts of popular culture.[3] Such diverse events as the religious riots of sixteenth-century France and the bread riots of eighteenth-century England are now viewed as goal-oriented and highly organized affairs. Viewed from this perspective, riots and popular demonstrations can provide a window into the plebeian attitudes and assumptions that direct and legitimize collective action.

The power of this approach is not limited to the historical study of the streets of London or Lyon. These same ideas are applicable to the examination of sectarian violence in Ulster, for like the Belfast riot of 1813, most party clashes in nineteenth-century Ulster emerged from set-piece confrontations, occurring at partisan festivals, fairs, and political assemblages. The Twelfth of July was only one of a myriad of sectarian commemorations that provided the arena for some of the bloodiest clashes in nineteenth-century Ireland.

But it was not only the set-piece nature of Ulster riots that structured the character of communal contention. To prosecute this conflict, both plebeian loyalists and their Catholic adversaries created sectarian organizations, the Loyal Orange Order and a series of Catholic associations usually labeled Ribbon societies. The existence of associations devoted to the public observance of partisan festivals greatly enhanced the structured nature of party violence. Almost every sectarian riot of prefamine Ulster was directly tied to the provocative actions of the Orange Order or its Catholic enemies. Indeed, during times of political controversy, Ulster's sectarian societies could virtually choreograph outbreaks of communal violence. For Orangemen and their Catholic foes, such conflicts served as much more than simple trials of party strength—clashes between Orange and Green also helped to maintain the relevance and vitality of their two conflicting visions of how Irish society should be structured.

Both the fundamental ideology and activities of the Orange Order rested on the same narrow conception of loyalty detailed in the previous chapter. Put simply, many Ulster Protestants believed that they had a historic right and need to a special and ascendant position vis-à-vis Irish Catholics in relation to both the Protestant elite and the British state in Ireland. When the events of the last decades of the eighteenth century challenged this view, both plebeian and elite Protestants worked hard to refashion an acceptable relationship based on these exclusivist ideals. This process was given tangible form with the creation of the Orange Order in September 1795.

Forged against a backdrop of revolutionary turmoil, the Orange Order served as the institutional embodiment of the sectarian moral economy. Orangeism's strength centered on a simple implicit contract between its plebeian members and a substantial section of the Protestant elite. This Orange covenant was designed to defend loyalists' exclusivist interpretation of Irish citizenship. Of course, the existence of broad ideological agreement within the Order should not be viewed as evidence as any kind of monolithic consensus. Not all Orangemen held the same view as to what constituted the critical elements of the sectarian moral economy. Plebeian Orangemen, for example, placed much more emphasis on the Order's processional tradition than did their elite brethren, who generally viewed the marching season with ambivalence at best. This particular difference of opinion was especially critical, for the violent results of the processional tradition brought the Orange Order into seemingly annual conflict with both Ulster Catholics and the British government throughout the nineteenth century.

Not surprisingly, many Ulster Catholics fought against the imposition of this worldview. In prefamine Ulster this attitude took the tangible form of Catholic crowds violently blocking the progress of Orange processions on the Twelfth of July and other partisan festival days. Opposing Orange public demonstrations provided the main impetus for the evolution of what has been termed the Ribbon tradition in the borderlands of south Ulster. Unfortunately, as we shall see, the term Ribbonism has become too loaded to retain much analytical utility. For that reason, we will limit the use of the term, abandoning it when describing the myriad of other associations and groups that gathered to challenge Orange dominance. Although these societies played a critical role in preserving the symbols and language of a nascent version of Irish nationalism, they were primarily oppositional in nature—and as such must be viewed as a synthesis of both conspiratorial and communal elements, primarily focused on fighting the public exhibition of Orange hegemony.

A broader examination of early nineteenth-century northern Catholic street politics recognizes not only the formal underground networks of Ulster Catholics described by Tom Garvin in his groundbreaking article on Ribbonism,[4] but also groups like the Freemasons, who opposed Orange demonstrations in the first decade of the nineteenth century, and the Catholic men, women, and children who commemorated St. Patrick's Day by marching in procession through town and countryside. By refusing to submit to the aggressive imposition of the sectarian moral economy and by openly asserting a worldview more representative of the northern Catholic experience, these groups acted as a rough lower-class parallel to the growing self-confidence and politicization of middle-class Irish Catholics.

The following chapter examines the critical role played by partisan institutions in the prosecution of sectarian violence in the early nineteenth century. In particular, it focuses on the relationships between these evolving partisan associations, popular politics, and sectarian contention. The institutionalization of communal conflict had a dramatic impact on prefamine Ulster society, continually updating and reinforcing the sectarian chasm that had long characterized northern life. These tribal voices and the riots they provoked would later play an integral role in the formation of Ulster's divided system of formal politics. But we get ahead of ourselves. To comprehend the evolution of political culture in nineteenth-century Ulster, we must first examine the plebeian beliefs that gave rise to the North's sectarian associations and its habitual communal conflict. Because the Loyal Orange Order's provocative public behavior produced the vast majority of these clashes, Orangeism will be examined first.

The Formation of the Orange Order

The Loyal Orange Order emerged in the aftermath of the Battle of the Diamond in September 1795, when several of the principal Protestant combatants met at James Sloan's house in the Armagh village of Loughgall. The men who assembled at Sloan's inn that day were decidedly not members of the Protestant elite—middling farmers and weavers from across mid-Ulster dominated this first meeting. Led by James Wilson, a farmer from the estate village of Dyan in County Tyrone, and James Sloan, a Loughgall innkeeper, these men created the original framework for the Orange Order, a defensive union of Protestants dedicated to advancing the Protestant cause.[5]

The idea of creating a Protestant defensive association was certainly not new to mid-Ulster. Plebeian Protestant organizations like the new Orange Order had flourished on a local level throughout the linen triangle since the early 1780s.[6] In many ways the Orange society was merely the most successful in a long line of Protestant defensive associations. The key to understanding this process lies in defining the term defensive, for these men were not only defending their lives from the physical assaults of their Catholic adversaries, they were also defending their historic right to an ascendant position over an increasingly assertive Catholic population.

Defining defensive association in this manner helps to explain the formation of plebeian Protestant organizations in mid-Ulster throughout the 1780s and 1790s. Angered by the gentry effort to eliminate the last vestiges of the Penal Laws and genuinely frightened (not without reason) by the increased confidence of their Catholic enemies, many lower-class Protestants banded together to defend their exclusivist vision of Irish citizenship. As previously noted, both the Peep O'Day Boys and several of the expanded companies of the Irish Volunteers certainly fit this model. When the Volunteers were abolished in 1793, ultra-Protestant activists quickly moved to fill this vacuum.

The most important of these new associations came together in the early 1790s in the estate village of Dyan, located between the towns of Benburb and Caledon in the southeastern corner of County Tyrone. Called the Orange Boys Society, this organization was the brainchild of James Wilson, one of the men responsible for the formation of the Orange Order in September 1795. Wilson viewed the Orange Boys as a more disciplined and organized version of the Peep O'Day Boys—a necessary response to increased Catholic agitation in the area. As a small, local organization, the Orange Boys Society itself was a minor player on the Ulster stage.[7] But the society's legacy would prove much more enduring than the organization itself, as Wilson's Orange Boys Society provided one of the primary models for the Orange society formed at James Sloan's inn in September 1795.[8]

Two factors set the Orange Order apart from its less influential predecessors. First, this new society was able to act as an umbrella organization for the burgeoning number of loyalist associations springing up all across Ulster. All of these new societies had one important difference from their ancestors—the approval of a growing section of the Protestant elite. Concerned with the spread of the United Irishmen and the Defenders, members of the gentry began to actively encourage the formation of defensive associations. Not surprisingly, a number of these new Protestant bands were closely tied to men who would prove influential in the evolution of early Orangeism: Col. William Blacker, Rev. Phillip Johnston of Lisburn, and Rev. Holt Waring of Lurgan.[9]

This points to the second key factor in the Orange Order's success—its ability to attract the support of influential members of the Protestant elite. Like so much else, this was primarily a matter of timing.[10] The Orange Order stepped onto the Irish stage just as the island careened toward violent revolution. While gentry support for the Order was not particularly strong at the outset,[11] members of the elite quickly came to see this new society as a powerful bulwark against rebellion.[12] Faced with the impending threat of revolution, many landlords actively encouraged the formation of defensive associations and lobbied vehemently for the creation of the yeomanry.[13] Both would provide fertile soil for Orangeism's growth.

Two factors made the formation of the Irish yeomanry in October 1796 particularly crucial. First, by giving government sanction to local Protestant defensive associations, the yeomanry gave members of the gentry the opportunity to lead and control these potentially disruptive bands of plebeian loyalists. This in turn helped to solidify the foundation for the uneasy lower-class/upper-class alliance that would characterize the Orange movement throughout the nineteenth century.[14] It was the involvement of a substantial sector of the gentry, spurred on by the increasing threat of revolution in Ireland, that really set the Orange Order apart from its predecessors.

The creation of a gentleman's Orange lodge in Dublin in June 1797 put a formal seal on this relationship. While the new lodge attracted little initial attention, it soon had a decisive champion in the capital city in Patrick Duignean, the powerful advocate-general. By early 1798 several of the most influential members of the Protestant party had joined the Order—an impressive list that included John Claudius Beresford and Sir Jonah Barrington.[15] Orangeism had clearly come a long way from its plebeian roots in County Armagh. With the formation of the Dublin gentleman's lodge, the Orange Order had taken a giant step toward becoming a national movement.[16]

This process was finalized by the Wexford rebellion, a conflict that most contemporary observers viewed as a simple sectarian bloodletting. While modern historians have shattered this simplified image of the Wexford struggle,[17] contemporary opinion could not achieve such distance. The vast majority of Ulster Protestants viewed the rebellion as a simple sectarian jacquerie, an interpretation that lent credibility to what the hard-line plebeian Protestants of mid-Ulster had been saying all along—that the revanchist goals of Irish Catholics had not changed since the seventeenth century. With its exclusivist conception of loyalty reinforced by the sectarian interpretation of the recent rebellion, the Orange Order moved toward the center stage in Ireland. By the turn of the century it was poised to be a major player in the political life of the country.

The formation of the Orange Order thus represented the successful culmination of a long process that emerged from the radical political and economic changes that threatened to transform Ulster society in the final decades of the eighteenth century. Frustrated by the naïveté of an elite that believed it could now safely reform the anti-Catholic provisions of the Penal Laws, die-hard Protestants mobilized to keep their Catholic enemies from upsetting the communal balance in mid-Ulster. Only when Ireland tumbled toward revolution in the mid-1790s did a substantial section of the Protestant elite come to share this view. Faced with the growing threat of rebellion, influential members of the Protestant establishment recognized the utility of these loyalist associations. After mid-1796 these men forged crucial links with the newest and most successful of these defensive unions, the Orange Order, giving the organization the legitimacy and elite leadership that its plebeian creators had wanted from the outset. In short, the formation of the Orange Order must be viewed as a critical part of the Protestant effort to reconstruct the sectarian moral economy, a belief system seemingly validated by the harrowing tales that emerged from Wexford in 1798.

Several misconceptions about early Orangeism dissipate when its early history is viewed as a critical part of the refashioning of the sectarian moral economy. First and foremost, the Orange Order was not an aristocratic creation designed to dupe the Protestant lower-classes. Although the gentry did flock to the Orange standard as the threat of revolution approached, Protestant weavers and farmers threatened by an increasingly assertive Catholic population brought the Order to life. As the Orange historian Col. Robert H. Wallace states, the Orange system was "conceived and brought forth by humble men."[18] It is quite true that the elite quickly gained control of the commanding heights of the Order. But they did so on essentially plebeian terms, vowing to defend a hard-line, exclusivist vision of the ideal Irish polity.

Nowhere are Orangeism's popular roots more evident than in the original rules and regulations devised by Sloan, Wilson, and their compatriots in September 1795. Unfortunately, no copies of the original "Armagh rules" have survived. Luckily, we can reconstruct an adequate substitute. In doing research for his official history of Orangeism in the late nineteenth century, Colonel Wallace discovered a lodge book issued to Orange lodge number

670 in 1798.[19] Because early warrants were copied directly from the original rules and regulations housed at Sloan's residence in Loughgall, Wallace believed that the rules and regulations contained in this lodge book provided an exact replica of the bylaws set down in September 1795. While they may not be an exact copy of the Armagh rules, the "bye-laws and regulations of the Orange Society meeting in Ballymagerney" do provide an interesting look into the popular cultural perceptions that inspired the creation of the Orange Order.

Bye-Laws and Regulations of Orange Lodge 670

1. Members to meet on a regular basis.

2. Drunkeness and disorder not allowed, 'least the harmony of the Meeting should be disturbed.'

3. One Irish half guinea shall by paid by the person depositing a certificate.

4. Visitors excluded until business is finished.

5. 'That no Roman Catholic can be admitted to our Society by any mains, and our reason for so objecting against them is in memory of the bloody Massacre which they Committed on Our Forefathers.'

6. All applicants for admission must prove their good character.

7. Each member of the Lodge is bound to 'venture life and fortune' to assist the king and his lawful successors 'against All his or their Enimises as loing as he or the Maintanes the prodestand Religion.'

8. Members who do not conform to the Rules and Regulations will be expelled.

9. 'That We are to mete the 12 Day of July in Every year and go to Whatseover plase of Worship Shall bee aggred upon and our reason for so meetnig and Assembling on that Day is in Memory of King William the prince of ororrnge Who bravly Suported And freed us from Popish Slavery Which ought to be kept By all true prodestants thrughout his Mayestys Dominion.'

10. People should not seek admission to the Lodge if they doubt their ability to conform to its Laws and Constitution.[20]

A careful examination of these early rules and regulations raises several points of interest. First, the very style and language of the document point to Orangeism's plebeian roots. This is not an elegant production—its numerous spelling errors and convoluted grammar reflect the lack of formal education that one would expect from farmers and weavers. Later versions of the bylaws would prove to be much more polished efforts, reflecting the increasingly respectable leadership of the Order.[21] In Orangeism's first years, however, the organization's rules and regulations clearly mirrored its more humble social origins. But these local ordinances do much more than simply reflect the plebeian roots of Orangeism. They also give us a somewhat unique opportunity to examine the popular attitudes and beliefs that inspired and shaped the early Orange Order. In short, they help us get to the heart of what I have termed the sectarian moral economy.

Orangeism was above all else a Protestant organization, no Catholics allowed. Orangemen typically provided two reasons for excluding Catholics from the Order. The first of these concerned religious belief. Along with the overwhelming majority of Irish Protestants, the initial Orangemen firmly believed that the religious and political teachings of Roman Catholicism were simply incompatible with fundamental Protestant conceptions of civil liberty.[22] Of course, such beliefs were pervasive throughout the British Isles. In her groundbreaking study of British patriotism, Linda Colley has shown just how important anti-Catholicism was in the formation of a British national identity.[23] Roman Catholicism, with its emphasis on centralized religious authority and the importance of hierarchy and discipline, was typically equated with intolerance and tyranny. For obvious reasons, this belief was especially potent in Ulster. Testifying before the Select Committee on Orange Lodges in 1835, the Rev. Mortimer O'Sullivan, the rector of Killyman parish and a staunch Orangeman, claimed that the persecution of heretics remained at the heart of Roman Catholic doctrine.[24] Such religious beliefs only reinforced the loyalist perception of the social and political threats posed by Irish Catholics.

These attitudes were not the sole preserve of conservative ultra-Protestants; they permeated the highest ranks of liberal and "enlightened" Irish Protestantism. Even Theobald Wolfe Tone, revolutionary leader of the United Irishmen and author of the famous pamphlet *An Argument on Behalf of the Catholics* believed that Roman Catholicism was something of a dying superstition.[25] This belief was one of the few things that all Irish Protestants shared. But while it was important, religious belief was not the primary reason for excluding Catholics from this loyal association. It was the supposed lessons of history rather than the tenets of religious dogma that provided Orangeism's founders with the dominant elements of their ideological framework.

This view of the Irish past focused on the violent events that dominated the seventeenth-century narrative—the rebellions of the 1640s and

1688–1691. The folk memory that inspired the farmers and weavers who founded the Loyal Orange Order centered on two particularly dramatic events: the Catholic massacre of Ulster Protestant civilians in late 1641 and the siege of Derry in 1688–1689.[26] These two incidents provided the moral underpinning for a powerful interpretation of the Irish past, usually characterized as a "siege mentality." This view of Irish history portrays Irish Protestants as a besieged people called upon to repel an unending series of assaults. The siege of Derry is usually given pride of place and prominence here as the enduring symbol of Ulster Protestant myth of deliverance.[27] As countless commentators have duly noted, the siege motif has always resonated with a particular power in the north of Ireland.

Of course, we have to be very careful when discussing the "Protestant view of Irish history." Recent scholarship rightly has stressed the diversity of the Protestant experience. As Brian Walker cautions in an important article, there has never been a monolithic and unchanging unionist sense of history. Until the last decades of the nineteenth century, large sections of the Ulster Protestant population did not view "1641, 1689, 1690, and all that" as a constant reminder of the Irish Catholicism's unchanging threat. The famous mantra of symbolic dates, so often marched out by commentators to illustrate the siege mentality of Ulster Protestants, meant different things at different times to the various communities of northern Protestantism.[28]

But while it is true that the siege motif cannot be used to characterize a static Protestant sense of Irish history, it did resonate with unmatched power in times of crisis. This narrative had obvious appeal in the 1790s, especially among the Anglicans and Presbyterians who had been involved in the Armagh troubles. The explicit reference to the 1641 massacres in the Ballymagerney bylaws reflects the potency of this belief system for the conservative loyalists of mid-Ulster.[29] James Wilson and James Sloan and their followers firmly believed that the lessons of Irish history clearly showed that Irish Catholics could never be trusted with the full rights of citizenship. The cataclysmic events of the 1790s only served to update and reinforce this belief.

It was this view of history that shaped the formation of the Orange Order and its defensive predecessors. Faced with the unchanging threat posed by Irish Catholics, Protestants needed to forget their petty differences and band together behind their natural leaders to face the common enemy. Of course, this call for partisan paternalism was conditional in nature; as long as their "natural leaders" led them in the right direction (i.e. keeping the Catholics down), they would dutifully follow. In short, the Orange view of

Irish history did more than justify the exclusion of Catholics from the Order. It also pointed to the necessity of uniting all Protestants behind the Orange Order's strenuous efforts to keep Catholics in their place.

The annual marching season served as one of the Orange Order's primary tools in its self-declared mission to defend and maintain its Manichaean vision of the Irish polity. Ritual reconstructions of this worldview were particularly noticeable at the annual Twelfth of July celebration, when Orangemen assembled to commemorate King William's historic triumph at the Battle of the Boyne in 1690.[30] The explicit reference to the Twelfth celebration in the bylaws printed above points again to the Orange Order's middling origins, for the marching season was of special importance to plebeian Orangemen. While members of the elite certainly participated in public commemorations of the Twelfth from time to time—especially in times of crisis—processions were of particular significance to plebeian members, who saw the marches as their opportunity to convey their superior position to their Catholic foes.

For the rank and file, Orange processions symbolized their active participation in continued Protestant dominance over Ulster society. As the official historians of Orangeism have stated, "Where you could walk, you were dominant, and the other things followed."[31] When the rules and regulations were revised in 1799, the Order's leaders removed all references to the Twelfth in an effort to stress the responsibility of the organization. This made little difference on the ground, however, as the processional "tradition" became increasingly important in the first decades of the nineteenth century.

Finally, the principles espoused in Orange bylaws acted as more than rules and regulations for the organization. In the minds of Orangemen and their supporters these principles provided a set of standards for all Ulster Protestants. The ninth rule of the Ballymagerney regulations proclaims that the Twelfth of July celebration is a commemoration of "King William, the Prince of Orange, who bravely supported and freed us from Popish slavery—which ought to be kept by all true Protestants throughout his Majesty's dominion."[32] Ulster Protestants who deviated from these principles (i.e. those who believed that the conciliation of Catholic grievances would solve the problems of Irish society) were viewed as either ignorant fools or traitors. In short, Orangemen believed that they represented true Ulster Protestantism. This was quite a bold claim for an organization that only involved a minority (however substantial) of Ulster Protestant males until late in the nineteenth century.

But if the Orange Order did not immediately attract a majority of Ulster Protestants, it did take hold among substantial sectors of the rural population. Of course, a number of loyalist associations had existed in the rural northern environs. What made the Orange Order different was that its members managed to forge and maintain an alliance between its plebeian rank and file and influential members of the Protestant elite. The Order's successful fusion of lower-class and elite interests was based on an implicit covenant between the two social groups.[33] Put simply, members of the Orange elite pledged to maintain and protect the sectarian moral economy in exchange for the political and military support of the rank and file. This peculiar cross-class alliance proved to be the key to the Order's remarkable durability and strength.

The motivations behind elite acceptance of this compact seem simple enough. Faced with the threat of revolution in the 1790s, the Orange Order provided both the Protestant elite and the British government with a large body of zealous loyalists. As the British commander-in-chief in Tyrone, Brig.-Gen. John Knox, succinctly stated, the Orangemen were "the only description of men in the north of Ireland that can be depended upon."[34] In a time of military crisis the value of such a fervently loyal body could not be overstated.

But the plebeian connections achieved through the auspices of the Orange Order retained their usefulness long after the tumult of 1798 had subsided. The Orange rank and file continued to act as a bulwark against social and political upheaval in prefamine Ulster. But Orangeism served as much more than a counterrevolutionary force. The organization also provided conservative members of the rural elite with a relatively constant and largely dependable source of political support. In an era when economic power increasingly was shifting to an industrial and urban base, the political ties engendered by the Orange Order allowed the rural elite to retain a level of political support disproportionate to their economic position in Ulster society. While Orange leaders often were embarrassed by the robust sectarianism displayed by their lower-class brethren on the Twelfth of July,[35] this was a small price to pay for the many benefits gained from their Orange connections.

The motivations behind plebeian acceptance of this deal are no more complex. The Orange covenant answered the loyalist call for partisan paternalism that lay at the heart of the sectarian moral economy. It placed members of the Protestant elite at the head of a loyalist association pledged to keep the Irish polity exclusively Protestant. Of course, this really was not a problem at the outset of the nineteenth century. In the aftermath of the 1798 rebellion the Protestant interest reigned supreme. Led by Lord Clare, Patrick Duigenan, and John Foster, hard-line ascendancy politicians successfully resisted the lukewarm British desire to twin Catholic emancipation with the Act of Union.[36] With the Orange party firmly entrenched in Dublin, rank-and-file Orangemen could be sure of a sympathetic government.

This was important, for the ascendancy of the Orange party in Dublin brought a number of very tangible benefits to the rank and file. Perhaps the most significant of these favors centered on the marching season. As previously noted, the right to walk on the Twelfth of July was particularly important to rank-and-file Orangemen, who viewed the processional tradition as a critical symbol of their communal ascendancy. With their leaders and allies in influential positions, plebeian Orangemen received elite and government support (or at least tolerance) for their often disruptive processions. Although government figures rarely participated openly in such partisan ceremonies, they did allow Orange processionists to march with relative impunity. There would be no serious attempt to curb party processions until the advent of the Wellesley administration in the early 1820s.

But the advantages that lower-class Orangemen received from this compact were not merely symbolic. Members also gained the substantial benefits of a widespread system of partisan paternalism. Preferential treatment for members of the Order was particularly evident in Ulster courtrooms, where plebeian Orangemen often enjoyed special protection within the notoriously partisan judicial system of the north. Elite members could shield their Orange brethren from the full punishment of the law in a number of ways. As magistrates, men like Col. William Verner or Col. William Blacker often protected their fellow Orangemen by conducting incomplete or partial investigations of disturbances involving their loyalist followers. One such occasion occurred in the wake of the Maghery wreckings of 1830, when Col. William Verner attempted to cover up for his militant coreligionists by refusing to aggressively pursue any of the participants. Unfortunately for the wreckers, a rival magistrate soon arrived on the scene and demanded a legitimate investigation of the disturbances.[37] This was not the norm; when a magistrate wanted to protect loyalists from the full reach of the law, he was well positioned to do so.

If Orangemen actually faced judgment, Orange leaders could use their positions and influence to affect the course of a criminal trial. With their ability to select juries and give partisan charges from the bench, such officials could offer a great deal of protection for their lower-class brethren. At the very least, they could mitigate the severity of punishment. Orange members of the gentry and clergy often did this by acting as character witnesses for their plebeian coreligionists. Giving "good characters" was a critical service, for the favorable testimony of a gentleman or a pastor almost always reduced a defendant's sentence. Finally, Orange defendants regularly received financial assistance in their judicial dealings. The Grand Lodge of the Loyal Orange Order set up a fund for the defense of "Orange brethren who conduct themselves well, and who may be unjustly prosecuted."[38] These abuses of the law were not seen as such by rank-and-file Orangemen, who viewed these actions as their historic right—an integral part of the sectarian moral economy. Although the Orange Order could not offer its members total legal immunity, Orangemen operated in full knowledge that the law generally was on their side.

The power of this Orange covenant is best illustrated by the outrage expressed by Orangemen on those few occasions when the standards set by the contract were not upheld. When members of the Protestant elite failed to measure up to the criteria for true Protestant behavior outlined by Orange principles, the Orange rank and file typically reacted with bitter indignation. Because Dublin Castle was loath to attack its Orange supporters while Britain remained at war with France, clashes between plebeian Orangemen and government officials centered on a local rather than a national stage prior to 1815. Not surprisingly, the primary area of contention was the judicial arena. Liberal Protestant magistrates and clergymen often proved reluctant to give Orangemen the preferential judicial treatment that they believed was their historical right. When Protestant elites failed to provide such protection, angry Orangemen often displayed sharp opposition to their social betters.

In the summer of 1802 a party of Orangemen and yeomen fired without authority on an "unoffending group of Catholics." After an inquiry into the events the sheriff of County Down, H.W. Kennedy, took two of the men into custody and got warrants for the arrest of several others who had taken part in the attack. Kennedy recorded the loyalists' bitter anger in a letter to the undersecretary, Alexander Marsden: "a great discontent prevails among the yeomen that their comrades should be committed for the offence and they have intimated that they will not allow it."[39] Four years later, when a Tyrone magistrate named Richard Wilson charged eleven Orangemen with attacking the home of a Tyrone Catholic named Constantine O'Neill, he was labeled a "pervert Protestant."[40]

The most famous attack on Orangeism in the first decades of the nineteenth century occurred in a courtroom far removed from Ulster's narrow ground. Speaking before the grand jury of County Wexford, Judge William Fletcher intoned:

I have found that those societies called Orange societies have produced most mischievous effects, and particularly in the north of Ireland. They poison the very fountains of justice; and even some magistrates, under their influence, have, in too many instances, violated their duty and their oaths. I do not hesitate to say that all associations—whether of Orangemen or Ribbonmen, whether distinguished by the colour of Orange or of Green—all combinations bound to each other by the obligation of an oath, in a league for a common purpose, endangering the peace of the country, I pronounce them to be contrary to law.[41]

Fletcher's statement equating members of the Orange Order with their Ribbon enemies was particularly galling to Orangemen. After all, Orangeism existed to protect Ireland from such nefarious conspiracies. When Fletcher gave a similar speech before the grand jury of County Armagh in 1818, the Order quickly published a spirited rebuttal.[42]

These public breaches in Protestant unity were relatively rare in the early decades of the nineteenth century. One of the reasons why Orangemen recalled Justice Fletcher's charge with such lasting bitterness was because it nearly stood alone in the public record. For the most part, members of the Protestant elite supported or at least tolerated the often disruptive behavior of lower-class Orangemen. The sectarian moral economy was safe from above. Instead, danger came from a much more predictable source—Ulster Catholics.

Ulster Catholic Resistance, 1800–1820

The examination of secret societies in eighteenth- and nineteenth-century Ireland has proven to be one of the richest fields of inquiry in recent Irish historical studies. From the Whiteboys of the 1760s to the antigrazier campaigns of 1890–1910, Irish agrarian movements have been extremely well served by historians.[43] While the editors of a prominent collection of essays on Irish agrarian violence are right to stress the unreaped harvest that remains,[44] the study of Irish secret societies has effectively transformed the face of Irish social and economic history, helping to give nonelites a solid presence within the Irish historical narrative.

Despite the attention devoted to secret societies in recent years, wide areas of investigation remain relatively untouched. One of the most prominent of these concerns the evolution of underground Catholic political organizations between 1798 and 1848. With a few notable exceptions,[45] the Ribbon tradition of prefamine Ireland has not received the same attention as its agrarian counterparts. In many ways our knowledge about Ribbonism has not advanced much beyond Maj.-Gen. Robert Dalzell's 1816 assessment: "That these societies do actually exist in several parts of the district I believe there is no doubt, but I have not as yet been able to get any clue to enable me to state confidently when such meetings are held."[46] It is as if the Defender tradition died with the revolutionary failure of 1798, only to be reignited by the ardor of the rebels of 1848. If we are to understand popular politicization in prefamine Ireland, the subject of Ribbonism clearly merits more attention.

Historians traditionally have taken a rather cynical view of the Ribbonmen. Much of this attitude stems from the rather shaky character of the sources available for the study of Ribbonism. For obvious reasons, the statements of paid informers and the seemingly paranoid observations of Protestant landlords afraid for their property do not provide a particularly sound foundation for objective analysis. As General Dalzell's comment implies, contemporaries also had a notoriously difficult time putting their finger on the exact nature of Ribbonism. In 1811 Lord Downshire received the following letter about the Ribbonmen from William Todd Jones, of Dromore, County Down: "I learn, my Lord, that there are nocturnal meetings of the peasantry in this county, and that we Protestants are all to be killed and salted up for export by the express polite invitation of his Holiness to the Irish Catholics, under the good-natured suggestion of Bonaparte Himself . . . , but all Tanderagee was up, and thus it is that fools or Knaves circulate their fears or invent alarming rumours to answer individual designs."[47] Testifying before the Select Committee on Orange lodges in 1835, Sir Frederick Stovin, the inspector general of police in Ulster, observed: "I have very great doubts about Ribbon societies. I never could find out anybody that could show me a Ribbon society or find me the members of one."[48] By contrast, one prominent Orange clergyman claimed that with the exception of about twenty people, every Catholic in the mid-Ulster parish of Killyman belonged to the Ribbon societies.[49] Clearly, Ribbonism lay in the eye of the beholder. In this situation it is easy to see why modern historians have been somewhat reticent to examine this elusive subject. Historical research has only recently begun to shed light on this shadowy world.

Joseph Lee was the first modern historian to examine the Ribbonmen in some detail. Unfortunately, Lee's groundbreaking essay in *Secret Societies in Ireland* has several problems. These mostly stem from his use of the term Ribbonism, for like many nineteenth-century writers, Lee employs the word interchangeably with Whiteboyism. For Lee, then, Ribbonism encompassed such disparate movements as the Ribbon movement of 1819–1820, the

Rockite movements of 1821–1824, and the antitithe agitation of the 1830s. Lee thus locates the center of Ribbon activity in Roscommon, Kilkenny, Tipperary, Limerick, and Queen's County.[50] These are not the Ribbonmen participating in the north's party riots. Because of his misuse of terminology, Lee's essay is of limited value to scholars interested in Ulster's tradition of sectarian violence.

The most insightful work on Ribbonism has been done by Tom Garvin. In an important article Garvin rejects Lee's economistic interpretation of the Ribbon tradition, replacing it with an account that stresses the political nature of the Ribbon societies.[51] Garvin sees the Ribbon tradition as an important bridge between the Defenders and later nationalist organizations. Despite the fragmentary nature of his source material, he claims that "Ribbonism was nationalist, Catholic communalist if not sectarian, and vaguely in a populist mode, with much millennial admixture."[52] To support this contention Garvin points to two factors: the remarkably consistent character of informers' accounts on the nature of the Ribbon societies and the similar geographic patterns of the Defenders and the Ribbonmen. This last point is especially critical. Although two formal Ribbon networks existed— one based in Dublin and the other in south Ulster—the territorial similarities between Defenderism and Ribbonism lead Garvin to assert that the Ribbon societies originally were rooted in the sectarian battlefields of the north. This seemingly simple point serves as an important corrective to Lee's contention that Ribbonism was centered on the agricultural heartland of west Leinster and north Munster.

But the links between the Defenders and Ribbonmen went much deeper than mere geography. Garvin claims that the Ribbonmen also acted as agents of popular politicization. Like the Defenders, the Ribbonmen developed extensive networks over considerable distances, forging intimate ties with conspiratorial movements across Ireland, the most notable being the Ribbon movement active in Clare, Galway, and Roscommon in the years 1819–1820. These networks helped the Ribbonmen to maintain and extend Defenderism's nebulous web of nationalist ideas and symbols. In short, Garvin sees the Ribbonmen as direct descendants of the Defenders. He thus attributes to the Ribbon societies a much greater measure of political purpose and organization than past historians have accorded them.[53]

Tom Garvin's insights into Ribbonism represent a dramatic advance in our understanding of underground political organization in prefamine Ireland. Two aspects of his work are especially helpful: his analysis of the territorial similarities between Defenderism and Ribbonism and his emphasis on the Ribbon societies' role as curator of the language and rituals of Irish nationalism. By placing the Ribbonmen in their correct historical and geographic context, Garvin's analysis contributes greatly to the study of communal relations in early nineteenth-century Ulster.

Unfortunately, there are several problems with Garvin's account. The limited scope of Garvin's source material does not support some of the more extensive assertions he makes about the nature of the Ribbonmen. There can be no doubt that the Ribbonmen existed in some form. The territorial parallels between Ribbonism and Defenderism and the remarkable harmony of informers' accounts are simply too strong to be written off as coincidental. Futhermore, the consistent nature of the Ribbon societies' bylaws and rituals convincingly support Garvin's assertion that the Ribbon tradition played a critical role in the preservation of popular Catholic nationalist symbols and ideas.

Problems arise, however, when we try to examine how the Ribbon societies actually functioned outside their lodge meetings. There is little concrete evidence linking the underground activities of the Ribbon lodges to the sectarian riots that sporadically disrupted the Ulster countryside in the first decades of the nineteenth century. Although Ribbon symbols and rituals point to a worldview diametrically opposed to the public assertions of the Orange Order, any statement as to the Ribbon societies' precise role in blocking Orange processions must be seen as somewhat speculative. Without such proof, analysts run the danger of merely reflecting the ultra-Protestant belief that the entire Irish Catholic population belonged to conspiratorial secret societies designed to drive Protestants from Ireland. Garvin's narrow focus on the formal networks of the Ribbon societies must be adjusted if we are to better understand the relationship between Ribbonism and sectarian violence in Ulster.

To more effectively evaluate the nature of northern Catholic participation in early nineteenth-century sectarian conflict, we need to adopt a slightly different perspective. Rather than focusing exclusively on the formal underground networks of the Ribbon societies, Catholic participation in these clashes must be viewed as the communal response of some Ulster Catholics to the Orange Order's open assertion of partisan dominance.[54] This more communal focus brings two distinct advantages to our analysis. First, by largely abandoning the term "Ribbonism," we avoid some of the problems that stem from over a century of habitual misuse. More importantly, this new approach better accommodates the diversity of Catholic organizations and individuals that publicly challenged Orange hegemony in prefamine

Ulster. In the early nineteenth century, groups ranging from Catholic Free-mason lodges to loosely organized musters of Catholic men, women, and youths all gathered to oppose Orange processions. If we are to understand the vigorous Catholic response to loyalist marchers' public aggression, these groups clearly need to be taken into consideration.

This communal focus does not entail abandoning Garvin's insights into the formal organization of the Ribbon societies. These groups clearly played an integral role in preserving the relevance and vitality of the symbolic language and rituals of Irish nationalism. Furthermore, there is significant evidence that Ribbon lodges played a catalytic role in many early nineteenth-century sectarian clashes. Ulster Catholic participation in these partisan conflicts was clearly a rather complex mix of communal and conspiratorial opposition to Orange public assertion.

Two critical themes emerge when northern Catholic responses to loy-alist display are examined from this perspective. First, the changing nature of Ulster Catholic participation can be connected to the ongoing process of popular politicization among the Irish Catholic population. As the second decade of the nineteenth century progressed, Catholic challenges to Or-ange public display became both more frequent and more formidable. Put simply, an increasing number of Ulster Catholics became less willing to suffer the open insults of Orange processionists. These confrontations led to more sectarian riots, as both parties attempted to gain control of public spaces in the north of Ireland. This phenomenon clearly mirrored the grow-ing self-confidence of middle-class Irish Catholics in the first decades of the nineteenth century. As such, it should be viewed as a critical part of the politicization process that reshaped prefamine Irish society.

This more inclusive focus also acknowledges the participation of both women and children in many of the sectarian clashes in nineteenth-cen-tury Ulster. In light of the virtual exclusion of women from modern Irish historiography,[55] the critical roles played by women in these conflicts are especially interesting. Catholic women participated in nearly every attempt to block Orange marches in prefamine Ulster. In fact, party riots repre-sented one of the few public spaces where female participation was not only tolerated but welcomed.

Above all, however, this communal focus attempts to rescue this criti-cal subject from a certain cynicism engendered by its problematic source material. By viewing the "Ribbon" tradition as public opposition to the imposition of the sectarian moral economy, we can evaluate what actually occurred on the ground. Only then, perhaps, can cynicism be effectively avoided.

Challenging the Orange Consensus, 1800–1821

To any veteran observer of the Ulster scene, the Aughnacloy races of December 1818 seemed like an invitation for trouble from the very outset. Recent meetings in mid-Ulster had been the occasion of some serious clashes between the Orange and Green. Party rioting had just disturbed the Armagh races, where a Catholic man had been badly beaten by three loyalists from County Tyrone. The Aughnacloy races seemed to offer the perfect opportunity for a renewal of party hostilities. Expecting trouble, Capt. Edward Moore, the head of the local yeomanry, placed a number of his men at the racecourse.

The crowd arriving in Aughnacloy that day for the races seemed to confirm Moore's anxiety. As the races approached, an unruly body of Protestants from the Dyan district marched through the main street to the racecourse. At the same time a disorderly crowd of Catholics from the Trugh area of County Monaghan arrived for the races. A large number of the Trugh men carried sticks. While no clashes occurred before the races started, both parties clearly had prepared for the worst.

As the races concluded, it seemed as if Captain Moore's fears might prove unfounded. The Dyan men began their northward journey home, and a large crowd of Catholic men, women, and children started walking toward the River Blackwater and County Monaghan. It looked as if the day might pass without serious confrontation. But this happy scenario was simply not to be. As the Tyrone men reached the base of Mill Street, the tense atmosphere finally gave way when one man shouted, "Who was for Dyan?" A group of the Trugh men immediately set upon the offender, and the anticipated party fight had begun.

Most of the fighting occurred near the bridge over the Blackwater, where both parties quickly became engaged in a stone-throwing battle. One group of Catholic women played a critical role in this first phase of the clash, gathering stones from the hillside and carrying them in their aprons to the battlefield. Hoping to quell the riot, members of the yeomanry sprinted toward the bridge area. With their commanding officer absent (inexplicably, Captain Moore remained at home), the yeomen brandished their weapons in an attempt to intimidate the rioting parties. The threat of gunfire was enough to bring a temporary halt to the clash, and cooler heads attempted to prevail upon the two parties to leave. Both groups stated that they would go home only if their enemies did the same. After several minutes of this stalemate the Dyan men began to head northward, and it seemed as if the clash was over.

As the Dyan men turned to march home, however, a triumphant shout came from the Trugh men. They had forced the Orangemen to leave the field—the day was theirs. To drive this point home they hurled a shower of stones upon their Protestant enemies. This proved to be too much for the Dyan loyalists and several members of the yeomanry, who immediately turned in fury and charged up the hill, firing wildly at their foes. Finding themselves outgunned, the Monaghan party broke and fled in the face of this renewed attack. One man and one woman were killed in the initial hail of fire. Another woman lay seriously wounded as the rout came to a close. After the clash had ended, members of the yeomanry celebrated with some of the armed members of the Dyan party by marching to the partisan sounds of the fife and drum. Aughnacloy was theirs.[56]

The Aughnacloy riot of 1818 demonstrates several of the real difficulties faced when examining the relationship between Ribbonism and sectarian violence. The clash was obviously premeditated in one sense—both parties arrived with weapons in hand. Furthermore, a later investigation into the origins of the riot revealed that the Trugh party had scoured the Monaghan countryside for supporters.[57] As one police report stated, at the very least both parties had come to the races determined not to suffer the slightest public insult.[58] At the same time, the active participation of both women and children argues for a more communal approach, as would the absence of any evidence tying any Ribbon lodges to the actual clash. Like most prefamine sectarian riots, the Aughnacloy riot of 1818 combined elements of both communal and conspiratorial violence.

The party clash at Aughnacloy also effectively highlights the style of most prefamine clashes between loyalists and their Catholic opponents. As previously noted, sectarian riots generally emerged out of set-piece confrontations. Both parties used occasions like races, fairs, and traditional partisan festivals to test party strength and assert their antagonistic visions of how Irish society should be structured. While most public demonstrations did not produce violent conflict, these exhibitions of partisan strength triggered most of the largest sectarian riots of nineteenth-century Ireland, as both parties attempted to establish hegemony over contested public spaces. The Ulster calendar literally was filled with opportunities for such sectarian displays—from fairs to the Twelfth of July, both parties had plenty of chances to play their provocative and often deadly game. With the Orange party's dramatic victory in the aftermath of the 1798 rebellion, it should not be too surprising that Orangemen generally took the offensive in the first decades of the nineteenth century, provoking Catholic reactions that sometimes led to serious party riots.

Although the Orange victory at the Battle of the Diamond and especially the traumatic events of 1798 certainly shattered any semblance of communal balance in Ulster, Orange public displays did not go unopposed in the first decade of the nineteenth century. Catholic challenges to the Orange Order initially were both small and infrequent. Given the totality of the Orange victory in 1798, this was not too surprising. What is interesting about turn-of-the-century Catholic resistance is not its magnitude but its source. The first set-piece confrontations of the nineteenth century were clashes between members of the Orange Order and local Freemason lodges.

Freemasonry has never occupied a particularly cherished place in modern Ireland. Closely identified with both Orangeism and Communism in the twentieth century (quite a feat in itself), Irish Freemasonry has been the subject of much speculation and little good analysis.[59] This seems somewhat surprising given the number of Irish secret societies that used masonry as a model for their organizational structure. A brief examination of the history of Freemasonry in early nineteenth-century Ulster reveals an organization that differed radically from its modern reputation. To begin with, Freemasonry was both popular and strongly Catholic. An 1804 survey of Irish Freemasonry lists 104 lodges in County Antrim, 92 in Tyrone, and 151 in Armagh, Down, and Londonderry. According to the official historians of Irish Freemasonry, these lodges were largely Catholic in membership. Furthermore, Freemasons often became involved in the frequent quarrels of the 1780s and 1790s, fighting with groups of Orangemen, Defenders, and United Irishmen.[60]

Given the nature of communal relations in Ulster, it was perhaps inevitable that Catholic Freemasons would come into conflict with Orangemen. Still, when the Freemasons' modern reputation as an anti-Catholic organization is considered, it does seem ironic that it was the Freemasons who initially maintained the Defenders' anti-Orange legacy in the first years of the century. Local Freemason lodges engaged Orangemen in several public fights in 1802 and 1803. The first and most famous of these clashes occurred in the market town of Kilrea, County Londonderry, in June 1802.

On 7 June 1802 a substantial crowd gathered in Kilrea to attend the local fair. The day passed quietly, and by late afternoon the vast majority of the participants had returned to their homes. Things changed dramatically at about six o'clock, when an unruly party of Freemasons appeared in the center of town. A number of the masons shouldered large sticks, moving through Kilrea challenging the fifteen to twenty Orangemen who remained at the fair. Led by the master of their Vow Lodge, the Freemasons attacked the outnumbered Orangemen, beating them handily and forcing them to take refuge in a house. The crowd continued to assault the house, shattering several windows with large stones. Surrounded by their foes, the Orangemen fired into the crowd, killing two and wounding several others. The over-powered Catholic attackers fled the battlefield, leaving the Orangemen alone to celebrate their victory.[61]

Writing in the wake of an official investigation into the Kilrea riot, one prominent observer blamed the crisis on a familiar problem: the lack of effective mechanisms of social control in the border region between Londonderry and Antrim. In assessing the factors that led to the party clash, Alexander Knox, Lord Castlereagh's secretary, pointed to the absence of resident gentlemen in the area. In his view, the sectarian passions of the Catholic and Protestant lower classes could only be regulated by the judicious power of the resident gentry—a clear echo of the social-control thesis put forth by J. Byrne and his Armagh contemporaries in the late eighteenth century. In this letter Knox described the way in which the clash between the Freemasons and the Orangemen reflected the familiar sectarian divide of northern society: "I wish, lest I should not have been sufficiently clear, to direct your attention to the curious sameness of wording in so many of the affidavits—in which masons and Roman Catholics stand . . . versus yeomen and Orangemen—as if the latter were one united body and the former another united body in a state of permanent, systematic enmity."[62] Knox correctly implies a direct link between the Defenders of the late eighteenth century and Freemason lodges like the one that triggered the Kilrea violence. In the years following the Act of Union the Defender tradition of anti-Orange activism largely was carried on by Catholic lodges of Freemasons. These bodies constituted an important bridge between the Defenders and the Ribbon societies and their supporters in the Ulster Catholic community. Irish Freemasonry thus played a significant part in the evolution of Ulster Catholic sectarian associations.

While the Freemasons did not long remain the primary vehicle for Catholic hostility to Orangeism, Kilrea was not the final clash between the two parties. Two weeks later, the two parties clashed near Downpatrick. Two men were killed this time.[63] In 1803 a Tyrone correspondent reported a series of faction fights between lodges of Orangemen and Freemasons, "that is, really the Loyalists and the United Irish." The two parties had battled at Dromore and Fintona and were reportedly preparing to renew their hostilities at a new location. Sounding a familiar theme, George Porterfield complained that there were no local men of consequence to keep the Freemasons and Orangemen under control. If something was not done, he declared, Tyrone would soon become another Armagh.[64]

Porterfield need not have worried, for the changing nature of Irish Freemasonry ensured that it would not remain the catalyst for anti-Orange activism. Pressured by both the sectarian realities of nineteenth-century Ulster and the hostility of an increasingly organized Catholic Church, Freemason lodges soon came to better resemble their modern reputation—somewhat respectable and almost entirely Protestant.[65] While one military commander claimed that Catholic secret societies in Donegal were using Freemasonry as a front for their conspiratorial designs as late as September 1813,[66] the torch of anti-Orange activism soon was passed to new organizations.

The years between 1804 and 1810 proved to be relatively quiet in the north of Ireland. While a serious party clash occurred in Armagh city on the Twelfth of July in 1806 when members of the Limerick militia attempted to block the progress of Orange procession,[67] this era saw few truly substantial party confrontations. Lacking a tangible foe, the Orange Order began to show signs of decay by 1809–1810. Participation in the July processions had even fallen off. While Orangeism and its allies remained firmly entrenched within the northern judicial system and at Dublin Castle, the movement clearly had lost much of its spirit and momentum.

If Orangeism seemed to have lost its direction, the events of 1811–1812 served to rejuvenate the organization. The reasons for an Orange resurgence lay with one single factor—the reemergence of the Catholic question at the heart of British and Irish politics. The renewal of activity on this front centered on the activities of the Catholic Board, a body long dominated by conservative Catholic aristocrats, traditionally dedicated to petitioning parliament to remove remaining Catholic disabilities. Upset at the turmoil created by the veto controversy of the previous year and reinforced by the Catholic hierarchy's increasing political involvement, the Catholic Board pursued a more aggressive strategy in 1811. This new attitude was best symbolized by the Board's decision to send its annual petition for Catholic relief directly to the prince regent instead of the usual route through the lord lieutenant and chief secretary. Needless to say, Dublin Castle was not amused.[68]

Predictably, increased levels of Catholic political activity rekindled the Orange Order, sparking a renewal of "Orange and Protestant" spirit throughout the north of Ireland.[69] This should not be surprising, since any serious assertion of Catholic political muscle touched on the raison d'être of Orangeism—the defense of their exclusivist interpretation of the Irish polity. But not all the threats to Orange hegemony occurred within the world of high politics. The appearance of a Catholic secret society in Ulster in late 1811 and 1812 augmented the political threat posed by the activities of the Catholic committee. After 1811 the Orangemen again had a somewhat tangible enemy to fight—the Ribbonmen.

The first references to the Ribbonmen describe their appearance in the counties of Antrim and Down in late 1811.[70] In his *Autobiography* William Carleton has left an account that highlights Ribbon strength in his home county of Monaghan: "I now discovered that the whole Catholic population, with the exception of aged heads of families, was affiliated with Ribbonism."[71] While Carleton's dramatic license certainly should be taken into account, there is no doubt that the resuscitation of Catholic political hopes and the consequent reaction of the Orange Order triggered a revival of the remnants of the old Defender system across portions of Ulster.[72]

Contemporaries were well aware of the symbiotic relationship between Orangeism and Ulster Ribbonism. Testifying before the 1825 Committee on the State of Ireland, John Dunn commented, "Whenever the system of Orangemen set up, the other begins, and once they begin, no one can say where they end."[73] Ten years later, the Earl of Gosford echoed these sentiments: "I think that the violence of the two parties leads to that of the other side."[74] In the minds of most early nineteenth-century observers, Ulster Ribbonism primarily existed to combat the public provocations of the Orange Order.

Ribbon oaths reflected the anti-Orange origins of these societies. Contemporary accounts of these oaths are remarkably consistent. One contained in Carleton's *Autobiography* is typical, calling for preferential dealing with Catholics and protection from "Orangemen or heretics."[75] Some oaths went further, making vague reference to the national cause.[76] Carleton himself certainly believed that the Ribbon societies were born of Orange triumphalism: "The truth, however, is, if there can be an apology for Ribbonism, that it was nothing more nor less than a reactive principle against Orangeism, of whose outrages it was the result."[77] Like Defenderism, Ulster Ribbonism was largely the product of the Orange attempt to reimpose its exclusivist vision of the sectarian moral economy onto Ulster society.

While it remains notoriously difficult to obtain an exact picture of just who belonged to the Ribbon societies, there are some suggestive clues hidden within the myriad of police reports and informers' accounts about prefamine Ribbonism. Unfortunately, these documents reveal little about the social background of the vast majority of the Ribbonmen. Without such data one can only provide the rather banal speculation that the rank and file of the societies were universally Catholic and undoubtedly drawn from the lowest ranks of Irish society.

Fortunately, the police were able to gather a great deal more information about Ribbon "leaders." Most of these had occupations firmly embedded in the upper strata of the lower classes. Nearly half of the Ulster leaders implicated in an 1839 trial were publicans, clearly reflecting the publican's social importance within the Irish prefamine community. The occupational backgrounds of the remainder were divided fairly equally between artisans, laborers, and farmers.[78] Of twenty-three suspects in County Louth, seven were farmers, three were publicans, and twelve were artisans or laborers.[79]

Both Tom Garvin and Michael Beames have used this data to emphasize the urban and petit-bourgeois character of the Ribbon leadership.[80] While this emphasis is undoubtedly correct, part of this can be attributed to the geography of Ribbonism. The Ribbon societies had three primary areas of strength in prefamine Ireland—all three were regional centers of trade and domestic industry: the proto-industrial countryside of south and east Ulster, Dublin, and the eastern seaboard counties. Ribbon leaders clearly reflected the social milieu from which they came. When a police report listed twenty-one suspected Ribbon leaders in the Buncrana district of County Donegal, fourteen were farmers.[81]

Despite its simple anti-Orange origins in Ulster's communal battlegrounds Ribbonism evolved into a rather extensive and complex organization; one that performed a number of critical social functions for its membership. For many Ribbonmen the association played an important socializing role in their lives. A number of police informers fondly recalled the sense of brotherhood and fraternity found within Ribbon networks. As one man testified, "I was fond of the Ribbon Society—some of my pleasantest [days] were spent in it."[82] In an era when overpopulation and market forces were mercilessly transforming Irish society, covert meetings in the smoky back rooms of public houses offered a comforting sense of mystery and belonging to Ribbon members.[83]

But Ribbon networks clearly were not typical nineteenth-century friendly societies. Intimidation and violence were never far from the surface—not all of it directed at the Orange enemy. Many Ribbonmen seem to have been pressed into service. At the 1822 trial of Michael Keenan, the police agent Michael Coffey related how he was first inducted into the Ribbon societies: "I saw a note in the window informing me that I was considered a Protestant and an Orangeman in the country—that I might thank my friends that one opportunity was afforded me, and that I ought to avail myself of it."[84] William Carleton told a similar, if less menacing, tale in his *Autobiography*. Brought to an initiation ceremony in Monaghan in 1813, Carleton's hesitation in joining up was only overcome by two glasses of particularly strong whiskey.

The appearance of Ribbon societies and the revival of Orangeism in 1811–1812 ushered in an era of renewed sectarian contention in the north of Ireland. Threatened by the revival of Catholic political activity in 1810–1811, plebeian Orangemen attempted to reassert partisan hegemony at provincial fairs and festivals. Of course, the Order's annual celebration of the Twelfth of July was the most important of these occasions. With sectarian tension rising in the north, the marching season provoked several serious party clashes between 1811 and 1815. In each case Catholic opposition to Orange processionists seems to have been primarily communal in nature—a fact underlined by the active participation of women and children in these conflicts. The area surrounding the market town of Letterkenny, County Donegal, proved to be a particularly contentious district.

The stage had been set in July 1810, when several Orange lodges paraded from Milford and Rathmelton to Letterkenny. According to a local magistrate, the Orange processionists "did not exert a peaceful demeanour" (a wonderful understatement), taunting the Catholic population as they walked through this predominantly Catholic region. A Catholic body finally attacked the offending Orangemen as they approached Letterkenny. When the parties were brought to trial at the next petty session, they declared themselves to be reconciled and were released on their own recognizance.[85] The truce did not last long.

In the early summer of 1811 sectarian hostilities were renewed in Donegal when Orangemen attacked a group of Catholics at the Rathmelton fair.[86] Sectarian tensions rose dramatically in the wake of this riot, as both parties prepared for the upcoming Twelfth. One magistrate reported that notices had been found calling for the Catholics of surrounding counties to come to Letterkenny to help block the upcoming procession. Furthermore, it was reported that those Orangemen who were also members of the yeomanry intended to march in uniform on the Twelfth—a further provocation.[87] Clearly, government officials had good reason to worry.

In fact, sectarian tensions in east Donegal reached such a pitch in the summer of 1811 that a local Protestant clergyman, the Rev. Arthur Kenny, published a pamphlet against the Orange processional tradition. In his essay Kenny argued that Orangemen should simply give up their custom of parading because it offended Catholics, who believed that the processions "are the annual commemoration of the murder of their ancestors by the ancestors of the opposite side."[88] Kenny's appeal has a predictable effect—none—and local Orange lodges celebrated the Twelfth with their customary zeal. Fortunately, local magistrates and other government officials were able to keep the two parties apart. For all the threats of conflict, both real and imagined, Letterkenny enjoyed a relatively tranquil Twelfth of July in 1811.[89]

Such was not the case in 1813 in Belfast, where a large Catholic crowd rioted with Orange processionists in the city center. While rapid military reaction contained the clash, two people were killed in the affray.[90] Again, the Catholic response to the provocation offered by Orange marchers seems to have been communal. At a later trial witnesses testified that it was "the people" who had surrounded and attacked the offending processionists. Others underlined the prominent role played by Catholic women in the clash. William Booth, for example, stated that he saw several women breaking up pavement stones and carrying them to the fray in their aprons. Women also participated in the fight itself, throwing stones at Isaac Thompson's public house.[91] The task of blocking Orange processions was the job of the entire Catholic community.

There was an intimate relationship between the rise of Catholic national political activity in the years 1810–1811 and the riots at Letterkenny and Belfast. As previously noted, the aggressive tactics of the Catholic Committee in these years sparked a renewal of loyalist spirit throughout Ulster. As would occur throughout the century, Orangemen attempted to employ the July marching season to show Catholics who remained on top.

It is the Catholic response to these efforts that is interesting, for the renewed determination to block Orange processions in the years following 1810 clearly mirrored the resurgence of Catholic political confidence on the national stage. This was not a coincidence. As the Catholic question resurfaced at the center of Irish politics in 1810–1811, Ulster Catholics became increasingly unwilling to simply submit to the insults offered by the Order's annual marching season. While blocking Orange processions may not signify the highest mode of popular politicization, it certainly reflected the increasing level of confidence among Ulster Catholics. In some ways Catholic opposition to the marching season should be viewed as a rough lower-class parallel to the growing self-assuredness of the rising Irish Catholic professional and middle classes. As Daniel O'Connell and other Catholic leaders challenged the last vestiges of the Penal Laws on the national level, plebeian northern Catholics increasingly contested the Orange Order's efforts to symbolically formalize its dominance of Ulster's public spaces. These struggles would resurface in the 1820s, when O'Connell's crusade for Catholic emancipation threatened the very heart of Orange belief.

But Orange processions did not produce all of the sectarian riots of the early nineteenth century. Catholic crowds often clashed with known Orangemen or members of the yeomanry at northern fairs in the years 1812–1814. This was especially true in parts of County Down, where the activities of local Thrashers, or Ribbonmen, dramatically heightened sectarian tension. Things finally came to a head at the Ballynahinch fair of February 1812.

Party feeling was running high in south-central Down in early 1812. Tension centered on the activities of the Thrashers, a Catholic secret society whose lodges reportedly extended throughout east Ulster. The Thrashers seem to have been a regional variant of the early Ribbonmen.[92] One local correspondent vividly described a Thrasher funeral that had recently occurred between Newry and Rathfriland. His letter described an affair reminiscent of Whiteboy rituals in the south and west of Ireland—seventy men marching in loose military array with white handkerchiefs worn around their necks.[93] Whatever the accuracy of such reports, they certainly aroused Protestant sentiment in the winter of 1812.

The Twelfth of February 1812 was a fair day in the small town of Ballynahinch. Participants from all across south-central Down attended the fair. While partisan passions occasionally reared their heads throughout the day, no serious quarrels broke out. This was fortunate, for Ballynahinch had neither magistrates nor yeomanry to maintain the public peace. Party tension finally gave way to violence in the early evening, when groups of Orangemen and Thrashers assaulted one another with sticks and stones. The fight expanded quickly; the *Belfast Newsletter* later reported that at least three hundred combatants participated in the battle.[94] Several Orangemen retreated to the cover of sympathetic houses, which were promptly stoned by the Catholic crowd. Firing from the safety of his own home, an Orangeman named Patrick Thompson shot and killed a man named McAllister from the neighboring village of Loughinisland.[95] Finding themselves outgunned by their Orange opponents, the Thrashers fled the battleground at Ballynahinch.

With party feelings up, sectarian clashes disrupted local fairs all across Ulster between 1812 and 1815. Substantial riots occurred in or near the towns of Killeter, Maghera, Garvagh, and Kilkeel. The latter was particularly extensive; Orangemen wrecked fifty Catholic homes in Kilkeel after driving their adversaries from the town.[96]

These clashes all had a depressing familiarity about them. Indeed, it was in the early nineteenth century that Orangemen and their Catholic opponents began to shape the Ulster institution known as the party riot— an event that the men and women of Belfast would later develop into something of an art form. To initiate sectarian contention at these fairs, bodies of Catholic men typically moved about the center of the fair issuing public challenges to any Orangemen or yeomen who would respond. Orangemen usually answered the challenge and soon were involved in partisan battles with members of the Catholic crowd. Weaponry in this first stage of the riot was usually limited to sticks and stones. Although participants certainly received serious wounds from these organic missiles, few deaths occurred in the first phase of party conflict.

The second act in this murderous and ritualized form of combat proved to be far more dangerous. Typically finding themselves outnumbered, Orange combatants retreated to the relative safety of a sympathetic house. Besieged there by their Catholic assailants, the better-armed Orangemen (often members of the yeomanry) resorted to gunfire. This usually ended the riot by killing or wounding several members of the Catholic crowd and driving the remainder from the contested ground. Victorious loyalists typically celebrated their achievements with partisan festivals, symbolically renewing their partisan claim to each precious inch of Ulster soil.

Like the party riots produced by Catholic attempts to block Orange processions, partisan clashes at fairs combined the activities of conspiratorial and communal organization. There certainly seems to have been some planning involved in many of these sectarian riots. Witness the groups of Catholic men taunting their Orange opponents or carrying weapons to the fairs. In fact, I would argue that Catholic sectarian associations played a catalytic role in many nineteenth-century party riots by challenging Orangemen and yeomen with open assertions of derision and hatred.[97] But if members of organized secret societies started many of these riots, conflict soon expanded to include members of the community. Communal participation is underlined by the active roles played by both women and children, who often fought and died in these clashes. Fighting Orange hegemony in the public arenas provided by fairs and festivals was not the special preserve of any secret society; these clashes involved elements of the whole Catholic community.

Most sectarian clashes in prefamine Ulster came from Catholic attacks on Orange processions and other provocative exhibitions of Orange ascendancy. But the Catholic contribution to northern sectarian violence was not entirely oppositional in nature. Using the Orange processional tradition as a model, Ulster Catholics increasingly celebrated partisan holidays like Saint Patrick's Day with sizable public gatherings and marches of their own.

Catholic processions were certainly not new to the north of Ireland. After all, they had played an important role in escalating sectarian tension in County Armagh in the late 1780s. But the renewal of the Catholic marching "tradition" in the 1810s touches on something more significant than the mere return of ritualized displays of communal hostility. Like Catholic challenges to Orange marches, Saint Patrick's Day marches reflected the growing confidence of the Ulster Catholic community, for these processions were designed to perform the same functions as their Orange counterparts: to mark Catholic territory and to openly display partisan strength. Some of these displays could be quite impressive. On 17 March 1816 an estimated one thousand men marched through Hilltown, County Down.[98] As Orangeism's official historians stated, "Where you could walk, you were dominant, and the other things followed."[99] Whether they were Orange or Green, party processions centered on one thing—the ritualized display of partisan power.

But if Ribbon processions were designed to replicate the tribal exhibitions of the Orange marching season, they proved to be less provocative in the 1810s. This was primarily a function of sectarian geography. Ulster Catholics, unlike their Orange adversaries, typically did not route their processions through contested settlement areas. In the early nineteenth century, at least, Catholic festivals generally remained in predominantly Catholic townlands and parishes. While such displays certainly caused a great deal of anxiety for magistrates and other public officials,[100] they did not produce major outbreaks of sectarian rioting between 1815 and 1821. Ulster Catholics would not use such marches to challenge notions of Orange hegemony and territorial control until the mid-1820s, when Daniel O'Connell's crusade for Catholic emancipation shook the foundations of Irish society.

But this was not the only factor responsible for the decline in the overall level of sectarian violence between 1815 and 1821. One of the major contestants in the North's partisan warfare, the Orange Order, experienced a dramatic falloff in these years. The forces behind Orangeism's decline are not difficult to understand. With the Napoleonic Wars won and the Catholic Board suppressed, the Orange Order found itself without a tangible enemy. The organization eventually became mired in a series of internal disputes centered on the willingness of a number of provincial lodges to abide by the strict rules and regulations set down by the Grand Lodge.[101] Even enthusiasm for the July anniversaries waned—a sure sign of trouble for the Order.

Of course, sectarian clashes did not disappear from the Ulster stage. Partisan riots occurred in Aughnacloy and Kilrea in 1818 and Crebilly, County Antrim, in 1819.[102] With no serious challenge to the sectarian moral economy on the horizon, however, plebeian loyalists refrained from some of their more provocative exhibitions, thus dramatically reducing the number of opportunities for sectarian conflict. The reduction in the level of partisan violence did not indicate any major sea change in northern attitudes on either side. Party sentiments would burst forth soon enough, triggered by the reemergence of the Catholic question at the center of British and Irish politics in the 1820s.

In the midst of a report on the state of the north of Ireland in May 1814, Gen. John Burnet described Ulster as being generally quiet, "whatever may be the sentiments of the people"[103]—a statement that nicely captures the essence of communal relations in Ulster in the first two decades of the nineteenth century. While levels of sectarian animosity certainly remained high, serious incidents were relatively rare, especially when compared with those southern counties disturbed by extensive agrarian movements. When the Rev. Mortimer O'Sullivan testified that more outrages had been committed in County Tipperary in two years than had been committed in all of Ulster between 1800 and 1835, he was probably not far from the truth.[104]

This is an important point, but the overall level of party conflict in prefamine Ulster was not nearly as important as its style. For the first two decades of the nineteenth century witnessed the institutionalization of sectarian violence in the north of Ireland. Contrary to their reputation as primal and spontaneous affairs, nineteenth-century riots between Orange and Green were almost universally set-piece confrontations. These clashes typically emerged out of carefully constructed public environments. As we have seen, the region's numerous fairs and partisan festivals gave both sides ample opportunities to test their strength, as each party attempted to impose its power on various northern public spaces. The structured nature of party violence was enhanced by the formation and evolution of partisan organizations ardently devoted to the maintenance of these two conflicting visions. These sectarian societies first found their feet in these early nineteenth century decades.

Outbreaks of sectarian violence were closely tied to events on the national political scene. When the Catholic Board in Dublin initiated a more aggressive campaign against the last vestiges of the Penal Laws in 1811, it awakened an "Orange and Protestant" spirit throughout the north, as Orangemen and their allies mobilized to combat Catholic advances. This in turn sparked an increasingly assertive northern Catholic response to the naked exhibition of Orange hegemony. When the Catholic question receded somewhat into the shadows after 1815, public clashes between the Orange Order and their Catholic opponents followed suit. Clearly, sectarian riots were linked closely with national political developments.

But the connections between national politics and party clashes in the north were more complex than that. Catholic attempts to counter Orangeism's public hegemony grew more frequent and more formidable as the century progressed; a trend that clearly parallels the rising confidence of the Irish Catholic community. While Ulster Catholics' increasing willingness to assault the public assertions of the Loyal Orange Order may not represent the highest form of popular politicization, it does symbolize the growing Catholic challenge to the Orange Order's exclusivist vision of the Irish polity. This threat would only increase in the 1820s, when Daniel O'Connell led his historic crusade for Catholic emancipation.

3

National Politics and Sectarian Violence, 1821–1829

> *If it were necessary to defend the constitution against the attack of popery,*
> *he would, agreeably to orders already given, meet 200,000 armed*
> *Orangemen in Belfast and cut down the enemies of the county. At present,*
> *however, he would entreat of the Orangemen of Ireland to remain tranquil*
> *and not to offer violence to anybody.*
>
> Rev. Harcourt Lees

Writing in the mid-1830s, Col. William Blacker remembered 1821 as a par-ticularly disastrous year for Ireland, the first hour of what was "absurdly called conciliation." Looking back, Blacker pointed to King George IV's visit to Dublin on 27 August 1821 as the first sign that British government in Ireland was shifting away from its Protestant foundations. In Dublin that day, a vast concourse of prominent Irish men and women greeted the obvi-ously drunk monarch. Particularly noticeable in the crowd were the great Catholic leader Daniel O'Connell, who paid elaborate homage to the visit-ing king, and the Catholic hierarchy, who greeted the British monarch in full panoply. For Blacker the presence of such enemies to Protestantism represented "the first pandering to popish party feeling" of the decade.[1] It would not be the last.

From 1800 to 1820 few Orangemen could complain about the general nature of British governance in Ireland. While Daniel O'Connell and the Catholic Board had successfully pushed the Catholic question to the fore between 1811 and 1814, there had been no serious challenge to Orange hegemony in Ireland. This changed dramatically in the early 1820s, when a series of events threatened to overturn the exclusively Protestant character of the Irish polity. Loyalists responded to these threats to the status quo as they had in the late eighteenth century, mobilizing against their enemies throughout Ulster. This had the predictable effect of increasing the level of sectarian violence throughout the decade. There were more violent clashes between the Orange and Green in the 1820s than at any time since the bloody sectarian warfare of the 1790s.

Taking stock of the state of the country in the early 1820s, Colonel Blacker and other Orange leaders could point to a number of disheartening trends. The first of these was the virtual explosion of violent agrarian agitation in the southern and western counties of Clare, Cork, Kerry, Galway, Limerick, and Tipperary. For understandable reasons, most Ulster Protestants equated rural violence with nationalist conspiracy. For many loyalists the unprecedented expanse and violence of the Rockite movement of 1821–1824 updated and confirmed the traditional notion that Irish Catholics merely were waiting for the right opportunity to drive every Protestant from the island. This was only reinforced by the widespread dissemination of Pastorini's prophecies, an extremely popular Catholic millenarian tract that predicted Protestantism's imminent destruction in 1825.[2]

But that was not all. Orangemen and their allies also worried about Dublin Castle's apparent shift away from an exclusively Protestant system of government. Accustomed to having the law operate in their favor, ultra-Protestants felt betrayed by the Wellesley administration's hesitant efforts to reform the administration of justice in the early 1820s. Two major initiatives particularly incensed the Orange rank and file: the creation of a professional police force and the government's efforts to curb partisan celebrations in Ireland. Although these changes often proved more symbolic than substantive, they still created resentment among the Orange rank and file.

While all of these forces played important roles in heightening partisan animosity in the 1820s, one factor towered above the others in creating such a hostile climate. Not surprisingly, this controversy centered on national politics and the Catholic question, namely, Daniel O'Connell's momentous crusade for Catholic emancipation. It was the Catholic Association's revolutionary campaign to eliminate the last vestiges of the Penal Laws that stoked the fires of Protestant resentment throughout the north of Ireland.[3] This should not be surprising. Throughout its existence Orangeism's vigor had been closely tied to the rise and fall of the Catholic question. When passage of Catholic emancipation seemed imminent in the late 1820s, Orangemen and their allies furiously worked to block the impending legislation. Ultra-Protestant hostility to the measure knew few bounds, as emancipation was designed to shatter the exclusivist conception of British and Irish citizen-

Lt. Col. William Blacker. (*Dublin University Magazine* 17
[January-June 1841], facing p. 628.)

ship that rested at the heart of Orange belief. With such important matters on the line, plebeian loyalists mobilized to stop the Catholic tide at all costs, a move that pushed party rancor in the north to even higher levels.

But the substance of the Catholic demands was not the only factor responsible for the Protestant backlash. Matters of style were also critical. O'Connell's strategy of using mass popular pressure to force the British parliament to pass Catholic emancipation certainly was not designed to soothe traditional Protestant fears about Irish Catholic designs. With its massive public demonstrations and political meetings, the Catholic Association appeared to be little more than an aboveground version of the Ribbon societies. Few Ulster Protestants would have quibbled with Sir George Hill's unflattering assessment of the association: "The Ribbon system, or as the new term is, the Catholic Association, is in considerable activity here and the adjoining counties."[4] Even liberal Protestant supporters found the popular nature of the campaign unsettling. In an age when democratic politics were unheard of, O'Connell's mobilization of the Irish Catholic masses was truly revolutionary—doubly so in a nation as deeply divided as Ireland.

With such potent forces arrayed against the maintenance of the status quo, militant Protestant activists found themselves in a situation similar to the one that occurred in the late eighteenth century. Loyalists responded as they had in the 1790s, using the Orange Order and the newly created Brunswick clubs to mobilize the weight of political pan-Protestantism against emancipation. The strategy seemed to work in Ulster, where thousands flocked to the revived Orange standard. This had a predictable result in the north, where sectarian conflict occurred with much more frequency as the decade progressed. Just as it had in the past, the rise of Catholic politics and the corresponding ultra-Protestant reaction increased partisan animosity in Ulster, creating an environment ripe for sectarian violence.

Outbreaks of party rioting in the 1820s can be roughly divided into two phases. In the first, which lasted from the autumn of 1821 to mid-1826, the forceful reemergence of Catholic political aspirations triggered an uncompromising Protestant reaction, raising sectarian passions throughout Ulster. Nor was this one-sided. As the decade progressed, northern Catholics increasingly engaged their Orange foes in contests for local and regional supremacy. With party feelings up on both sides, sectarian riots erupted with some frequency at the region's partisan festivals and fairs.

Communal rivalry only intensified in the second half of the decade. As it became clear that Catholic emancipation might soon become the law of the land, hard-line Protestants accelerated their efforts to block the impending legislation, bringing party hostilities to fever pitch. This second phase started with the general election of 1826, when the Catholic Association gave its overt support to candidates in Armagh, Cavan, and Monaghan. Rather inevitably, such an effort deepened the sectarian battle lines throughout the north. Still, levels of party violence subsided somewhat after the excitement of the election, and there were hopes that things would return to normal. Three dramatic events in 1828 shattered these hopes: Daniel O'Connell's famous victory at the Clare by-election, the resultant formation of Brunswick clubs throughout the north of Ireland, and Jack Lawless's "invasion of Ulster." In the final months of 1828 and throughout 1829, party violence reached its highest level since the barbarities of the late 1790s. It would subside only in the early 1830s, as Orangemen and their supporters came to realize that they still controlled the commanding heights of northern society.

Daniel O'Connell's successful crusade for Catholic emancipation is one of the watershed events in Irish history, an event that Fergus O'Ferrall rightly has described as the birth of Irish democracy.[5] O'Connell himself seemed to believe that emancipation might give him the chance to alter the sectarian fabric of Irish society. "It is one of the greatest triumphs recorded in history—a bloodless revolution more extensive in its operation than any other political change that could take place. I say political to contrast it with social changes which might break to pieces the framework of society. This is a good beginning and now, if I can get Catholics and Protestants to join, something solid and substantial may be done for all." Sadly, O'Connell would fail in that endeavor. Indeed, by challenging the Protestant nature of the Irish polity, the struggle for Catholic emancipation hardened Ulster's historic sectarian divide, helping to solidify the foundation for the evolution of the north's tribal political system. Given the strength of the two irreconcilable visions that dominated northern political culture, the formation of such a nakedly tribal system of popular politics seems nearly inevitable.[7] But if the question of inevitability remains a matter of debate for historians, one thing remains undeniable: the political controversies of the 1820s dramatically furthered the sectarianization of Ulster society. These same battle lines would remain in place until the 1880s, when another political crisis deepened and consolidated communal division in the north.

Challenging the Orange Consensus, 1821–1826

At the outset of the 1820s the Orange Order seemed to have reached the low point of its thirty-year existence. Writing in December 1822, Daniel O'Connell certainly indicated that he did not think much of his traditional foes: "As to the Orangemen, it is actually ludicrous to see the way in which they are backing out of this affair. They are a paltry set and I hope will soon cease to have any political influence or existence."[8] The disintegration of Orange morale originated about the time of the Napoleonic defeat in 1815, when, finding itself without the unifying effects of a tangible enemy (O'Connell's Catholic Board had been suppressed in 1814), the Order had fallen into a series of internal disputes over rules and regulations. These only increased in 1820, when the Grand Lodge attempted to reassert its control over some of its wayward brethren by publishing new rules and regulations.[9] Although the furor created by the Grand Lodge's effort died down quickly, it was hardly an auspicious beginning for the 1820s. Clearly, the Orange movement was lacking both spirit and discipline as the decade began. This changed dramatically in the early 1820s, when a confluence of antagonistic forces brought a vigorous if uneven renewal to militant political Protestantism throughout Ireland. In broad terms, loyalist resurgence after 1821 was largely the product of a growing feeling that the Catholic threat loomed larger than it had since the tumultuous 1790s. For the first time since the Act of Union, the Orange consensus was under siege. In perfect keeping with Ulster loyalist myth, the first challenge to Orange hegemony came from a supposed ally in the struggle to uphold the ascendancy—Dublin Castle.

In December 1821 Richard Colley Wellesley, the flamboyant brother of the Duke of Wellington and the new Lord Lieutenant of Ireland, arrived in Dublin to take office. The new viceroy made his formal state entry into the capital with a characteristically grandiloquent flourish; shamrocks adorned the heads of his horses. Wellesley's appointment generally had been viewed as a blow to the Orange party in Ireland—the new Lord Lieutenant came to Dublin with a decidedly pro-Catholic reputation. As the head of a liberal regime it was expected that he would attempt to conciliate Irish Catholics by striking at some of the more provocative aspects of Orange hegemony in Ireland. Daniel O'Connell certainly viewed the appointment as a sign of better things to come: "Lord Wellesley is, I conceive, the harbinger of emancipation and is determined to put down the Orange facton."[10] While the Wellesley administration was to be something of a disappointment for Irish Catholics, it quickly earned the disapprobation of the Orange Order and its ultra-Protestant allies.

Upon arriving in Dublin, the Lord Lieutenant immediately moved to appease Irish Catholic opinion, dismissing the notoriously Orange attorney-general, William Saurin, and replacing him with a noted liberal, William Conyngham Plunkett. While Saurin's removal was offset by the retention of anti-Catholic under-secretary, William Gregory, and the appointment of the solidly Protestant Henry Goulbourn as chief secretary, it was a symbolic blow to an Orange party unaccustomed to such overt challenges to its ascendancy. Taken alone, however, the Saurin dismissal was not enough to produce a demonstrative reaction from Ulster Orangemen. While most hardline Ulster Protestants certainly looked askance at the government's conciliatory stance toward Irish Catholics, they remained relatively quiescent in the hopes that Wellesley would go no further in the following year. They were to be greatly disappointed.

Dublin Castle took two steps in 1822 that further undermined Orange confidence in the new administration. The first of these touched on the partisan celebrations so important to plebeian loyalists. In 1821 the Lord Mayor of Dublin, Abraham King, had banned the Orange Order's traditional dressing of King William's statue in the hopes that this might help to prevent an outbreak of party violence during King William IV's visit to the Irish capital. When a new Lord Mayor, John Smyth Fleming, used this precedent to permanently ban the ceremony in 1822, he received the full support of the Wellesley administration. Infuriated Dublin Orangemen attempted to defy the mayor's edict by dressing the statue—a move that led to a public clash with a group of O'Connell's supporters.[11]

But the government's assaults on Orange privileges did not stop at such symbolic measures. In fact, one government measure struck at the heart of Orange strength—the partisan administration of justice in Ulster.[12] Entitled the Irish Constabulary Act, this bill created a new rural police force in Ireland. In marked contrast to the Orange-dominated yeomanry, both Catholics and Protestants were to enlist in this new police force. This was a serious blow to the Orangemen, whose exclusivist interpretation of loyalty rested on the notion that only loyal Protestants could be trusted to preserve the peace in Ireland.

But loyalist objections to the Irish Constabulary did not end with the religious composition of this new body. Put simply, the new force was designed to take policing functions away from their beloved yeomanry. This represented a serious blow to rank-and-file Orangemen, many of whom received a measure of power and status from their positions in the yeomanry. The disproportionate importance of the yeomanry in Ulster can easily be seen by examining its geographic distribution, as shown in Table 1:

Table 1. Irish Yeomanry by County, 1821

Antrim	2,851	Kilkenny	219
Armagh	1,789	Limerick	232
Cavan	2,269	Londonderry	1,895
Cork	665	Monaghan	1,764
Donegal	634	Tipperary	509
Down	2,636	Tyrone	2,840
Dublin	187	Waterford	63
Fermanagh	2,432	Wexford	248
Kerry	558	Wicklow	1,087

Source: Belfast Newsletter, 18 May 1821.

Clearly, the Irish yeomanry was a largely Ulster institution. Only two counties outside of the north had over one thousand active members in 1821—Wexford and Wicklow. Significantly, the Orange Order had a solid foothold in both of these counties. Of course, Orangemen certainly were free to join the new police force (and many did so). But the Irish Constabulary, with its centralized control, greater discipline, and more ecumenical composition, did not hold the same appeal for Ulster loyalists as the yeomanry. For many Ulster Protestants, the creation of this new police force was just another sign of the ongoing assault on Protestant Ireland.[13]

Things finally came to a head in the winter of 1822. Controversy again centered on the issue of Orange public display in central Dublin. When Wellesley and the Lord Mayor blocked an attempt to decorate King William's statue for the Orange holiday of 4 November, a group of Dublin Orangemen decided to take action against the offending Lord Lieutenant. The result was the farcical "Bottle and Rattle" riot of 1822. On 14 December, Wellesley attended a performance of Oliver Goldsmith's *She Stoops to Conquer* at the New Royal Theatre in Dublin. A particularly boisterous crowd attended that evening, interrupting the play several times to call for the singing of "God Save the King." The cast complied, but the disruptions continued, as several Dublin Orangemen shouted loyalist slogans and heaped abuse on the Lord Lieutenant and other political opponents. One group of militants took advantage of the confusion to express their opposition to the Lord Lieutenant, hurling a series of objects at Lord Wellesley in his viceregal box—a wide selection of wayward missiles that included the blade of a watchman's rattle, an empty bottle, and an orange labeled "no popery." Although the Lord Lieutenant certainly was not threatened in any serious way by the attack, Dublin society was shocked by the Orange assault on the Viceroy. While the attorney general's attempt to convict several Orangemen for conspiracy failed in front of a Dublin grand jury, the tawdry spectacle of loyalists openly assaulting the Lord Lieutenant was a public-relations disaster for the Orange Order.[14]

Although the events at the Royal Theatre that night can be viewed as nothing more than bad comic opera, the "Bottle and Rattle" riot of 1822 reveals the depths of Orange animosity created by Wellesley's rather hesitant attempts to curb some of the more provocative aspects of Protestant rule. The message was clear: if the government failed to live up to the standards of governance contained in the Orange covenant, hard-line Protestants would have to take things into their own hands. It was the advent of the Wellesley administration, with its avowed policy of conciliating Irish Catholics, that initiated an era of renewed loyalist activism in the early 1820s.

The Wellesley administration's efforts to remove some of the more partisan aspects of British governance in Ireland created widespread anger among hard-line Ulster Protestants accustomed to having the government unequivocally on their side. This sense of abandonment was particularly acute in the outlying districts of Ulster, where Protestants suddenly found themselves about to swamped by the Catholic tide. In the predominantly Catholic district of Keady, County Armagh, Robert Maxwell complained that local loyalists lived under siege and would soon suffer at the hands of their Catholic adversaries. Maxwell was particularly critical of the government, whose attacks on the Orangemen ("honourable but much pointed at") had done so much to undermine loyalist morale.[15] With the government's public support for Orangeism seemingly on the wane, many northern Protestants felt vulnerable, a situation that redounded to the favor of traditional loyalism throughout Ulster.

But Dublin Castle's shift toward neutrality was not the only force threatening the status quo in the early 1820s. Another source of anxiety emanated from the southern and western counties of Cork, Clare, Galway, Kerry, Limerick, and Tipperary, where agrarian disturbances of unprecedented scope and violence swept across the countryside. Always hypersensitive to any type of agitation among the Irish Catholic peasantry, hard-line Ulster Protestants certainly were well aware of the massive Rockite movement that disturbed Munster society from 1821 to 1824. The Grand Lodge's February 1822 report reveals just how the Rockite movement animated Irish loyalists: "The Grand Lodge have to state with great satisfaction that those disagreements which unfortunately took place in the Order, on the change of

1820 are subsiding apace. . . . The serious appearance which the unhappy disturbance in the south has assumed, and the insurrectionary spirit which has been found to prevail elsewhere, though not yet so openly manifested, has had the effect of causing members to take shelter beneath the wings of the association, which has ever been found the securest refuge of the loyal in the hour of peril."[16] For many loyalists the Rockite movement's sheer expanse provided seemingly incontestable support for the Orange contention that Irish Catholics remained fundamentally disloyal and dangerous. Not surprisingly, it proved to be an excellent recruiting tool for the Order. In its 1822 report the Grand Lodge claimed to have issued twelve warrants for new lodges and added hundreds of individual members in recent months.[17] By portraying agrarian movements like the Rockites as Catholic conspiracies designed to overthrow the state, the Order created a situation where it could step forward as the defender of true Protestantism. This gave Orangemen the chance to tap into the rich myth system of Ulster loyalism—that siege mentality which legitimized their partisan behavior.

While the Orange Order certainly viewed agrarian movements as dangerous, the primary force behind the loyalist revival of the early 1820s was the reemergence of the Catholic question at the center of British and Irish politics. Of course, this was not just a question of having a liberal regime at Dublin Castle. By 1823–1824, Irish Catholic leaders had turned the new Catholic Association into an umbrella organization of extraordinary power, using the innovative mechanism of the Catholic rent and the decisive participation of the Catholic clergy to mobilize the Irish Catholic masses behind a constitutional campaign for emancipation. Conservative Protestants could not fail to see the increased respectability accorded to Catholic leaders by prominent figures in the British and Irish governments.[18] With the conciliatory Wellesley administration at Dublin Castle, unprecedented levels of agrarian violence spreading throughout the south of Ireland, and Daniel O'Connell initiating a massive political campaign for Catholic emancipation, the Orange consensus that had ruled Irish society for the first two decades of the nineteenth century was called into question. The days of exclusively Protestant rule in Ireland suddenly seemed numbered.

With the status quo threatened on so many fronts in the early 1820s, militant Ulster Protestants again rallied to the Orange standard. Communal divisions hardened throughout Ulster as both communities mobilized to attack and defend the status quo. The sectarian atmosphere of the north, contentious throughout the prefamine era, dramatically deepened in this time of renewed political controversy. As one Strabane man put it: "A great portion of the population have become bound to each other by Orange and

Ribbon obligations, and a great portion [are] intimidated."[19] Hard-line plebeian Protestants reacted to the resurgence of Catholic politics in the early
1820s as they had in the final decades of the eighteenth century and in the
early 1810s: using ritualized public demonstrations to express the weight of
loyalist opposition to emancipation. Not surprisingly, this resulted in an
increase in the level of partisan violence.

The annual marching season offered the best opportunity for such elaborate public displays of Orange power. For years Twelfth of July celebrations
had provoked controversy throughout the north. In times of contention,
however, such processions were by no means confined to July. In May and
June 1824 the liberal Protestant lawyer George Ensor[20] repeatedly reported
on the nightly provocations offered by loyalist drumming parties around
Charlemont, County Armagh:

Your answer of the 4th of June to my communication of the 29th ultimo states—
'that I have not stated whether the public peace has been disturbed by the persons
beating the drums and playing fifes, nor whether they have assembled in any manner contrary to law or for an illegal purpose.' I have stated facts and I repeat that
drummers and fifers, sometimes four together, . . . [have] a large drum parade,
frequently every week, and annoy the country from about eight to nearly midnight
by their noise and their intent; this I state in my own knowledge, and on my knowledge I am persuaded [that] evil will ensue if this be permitted.[21]

Although the provocation offered by Charlemont loyalists failed to produce the sectarian clashes predicted by Ensor, such partisan displays inevitably increased the incidence of party violence throughout Ulster, where
Catholics increasingly responded to such Orange exhibitions. This was particularly true of the Twelfth of July celebrations, which triggered sizable
party riots in Armagh, Belfast, Dungannon, Keady, and Newry between 1821
and 1825.[22]

But Orangemen were not alone in using processions and other forms
of ritualized public demonstrations to display their partisan strength. Ulster Catholics began to celebrate Saint Patrick's Day in a like fashion, using
processions to intimidate their adversaries. Such marches provoked furious
outrage in a loyalist community already upset at the government's unwillingness to suppress the Catholic Association. The reaction of one Monaghan
loyalist was typical: "I wish to direct your attention to, with every loyal man
in the empire, . . . a procession of Ribbonites in 1820, when Thomas Lamb
of Monaghan, one of the holy Roman Catholic priests who was arrested by
Colonel Blacker in McCone's house in Armagh, headed above three hun-

dred Ribbonmen through Killaneil to the town of Knockboy with the insignia of the Knights of St. Paddy around his hat on which was written . . . the motto, 'Death or Liberty.'"[23] Already upset with the Wellesley administration's stance against Orange celebrations in Dublin, Ulster loyalists were infuriated by the government's inability to curb such rebel marches. The "rank hypocrisy" of allowing rebel processions while putting down loyal commemorations only further alienated hard-line Protestants from the government.

But partisan festivals were not the only public occasions that produced party clashes in the first half of the decade. Provincial markets and fairs increasingly became known as "fighting fairs" in these years, providing an arena for often fatal tests of strength between Orangemen and their Catholic opponents. These clashes often had a domino effect within the afflicted region, as the defeated party attempted to gain revenge at the next fair. While the level of violence never approached that characteristic of agrarian movements in the south and west of Ireland, newspaper accounts of such party fights became depressingly familiar in the heightened sectarian atmosphere of the early 1820s.

The most substantial party riot of this period occurred at Maghera, County Londonderry, on 12 June 1823. Tensions had been running high throughout the eastern part of that county since 26 May, when Catholic and Protestant parties had clashed at a fair in the nearby town of Dungiven.[24] On 12 June crowds congregated in Maghera for the town's annual summer fair. Already pressured by the sheer numbers attending the event, security arrangements were further complicated by the absence of the local magistrate, the Rev. J.S. Knox.[25] Still, with an entire regiment of the military on hand to preserve the peace, there seemed to be little enough to worry about.

Like so many of these affrays, the Maghera riot seems to have originated in an argument that had little to do with communal rivalry.[26] The trouble reportedly started when an intoxicated man got into an argument with a local publican over his bar bill. Police responded quickly, arrested the man and marched him off to jail. Seeing the prisoner taken into custody, members of the crowd attending the fair came to his aid, rescuing him from the offending constables. A body of Catholics apparently used the confusion to attack their Orange enemies, forcing a number of Orangemen and other Protestant fairgoers to seek refuge in a house frequented by a local Orange lodge. The crowd continued its attack on the Orange sanctuary, hurling stones at the house and breaking its windows.

Hearing the commotion, Ensign James Elliot, the officer in charge of the military in the magistrate's absence, marched his regiment down Maghera's main street in an attempt to quell the rioters. Elliot's maneuver had little effect, apparently defeated by the crowd's knowledge of government regulations. Knowing that Elliot could not order his men to fire without the magistrate's permission, the rioters continued their destructive work, and Elliot soon withdrew his men to the safety of the barracks. Meanwhile the party clash took a murderous turn, as several Orangemen directed gunfire at their assailants from positions inside the house. Several bullets took deadly effect, killing four and wounding several in the Catholic crowd. Suddenly overwhelmed, the crowd fled, leaving local Orangemen free to celebrate their victory long into the night. And celebrate they did, marching in procession to the sounds of fife and drum, breaking windows and doors, and firing into Catholic houses throughout Maghera. The Orangemen had won the day and commemorated the achievement of their newly acquired ascendancy with the rites of partisan destruction.[29]

In the aftermath of the riot, several commentators grappled with exactly what had gone wrong at Maghera. In his report the commander of the British army in Ulster focused his attention on the absence of effective mechanisms of social control in Maghera that day. In particular, he regretted the absence of the local magistrate, whose presence, he believed, would have prevented the bloodshed.[28] There was certainly a great deal of truth in the report. One of the striking things about the Maghera riot was the manifest ineffectiveness of the military response. Reverend Knox's presence would have lent the security forces some badly needed credibility.

In contrast, the Irish press predictably devoted most of its attention to the question of who bore the blame for the Maghera riot. Rather inevitably, editorial opinion generally echoed the shape of the national political debate over Catholic emancipation. Newspapers on both sides of the divide used the occasion to attack standard party shibboleths. The *Derry Journal* castigated the leaders of the Catholic Association, whose incendiary harangues allegedly had inspired this Catholic attack on innocent Protestants. The more liberal *Freeman's Journal* took a different tack, blaming the high level of party animosity in the north on the provocative effect of Orange party processions.[29] Whatever the real motivations behind the Maghera riot, there was no arguing the fact that partisan passions had reached a dangerous level in the north of Ireland.

While the resurgence of Catholic politics in the early 1820s revived hardline plebeian Protestantism throughout Ulster, this did not necessarily translate into an era of renewal for the Orange Order. This seeming contradiction stemmed from the troubled relationship between the Order and the Wellesley administration. Orangeism had always derived much of its strength from its intimate relationship with the British government in Ireland—a connection that legitimized the Orange imposition of the sectarian moral economy on Ulster society. This relationship deteriorated in the early 1820s. Events like the "Bottle and Rattle" riot and the Maghera riot did not help to ease the already tense relationship between the Order and the Wellesley administration. Nor was governmental criticism confined to the halls of Dublin Castle. In the wake of the Maghera riot, parliamentary critics of the Order like Joseph Hume stepped up their attacks on Orangeism.[30] By the late summer of 1823 the Order was decidedly on the defensive.

Faced with such a hostile environment, Orange leaders took several steps to placate the Order's governmental critics. In each case the Grand Lodge's actions reflected the suddenly reactive nature of the Orange movement. The first of these moves occurred in June 1823. Sensing Orange weakness, two of the prominent leaders of the Catholic Association, John Lawless and Daniel O'Connell himself, petitioned the Lord Lieutenant to halt the impending Twelfth of July celebrations throughout Ireland. The Grand District Lodge of Dublin responded to this prospect with a policy of appeasement, publishing an address to the members of the Orange Order. Although they strongly defended the right to march on the Twelfth, Orange leaders advised members to use their influence to prevent any public celebration on that day.[31] While the edict largely was obeyed in the urban centers of Belfast, Derry, and Dublin, Orange processions again produced violent clashes in several parts of County Armagh.[32] Orange leaders might be willing to compromise the processional tradition to maintain the favor of a heretical British government, but their plebeian brethren in mid-Ulster were not quite so flexible.[33]

In July 1823 Orangeism was forced to take another step backward when the British parliament passed the Unlawful Oaths Act. To avoid censure, the Grand Lodge again revised the rules and regulations of the organization, abolishing its secret oath in order to maintain the legal status of the Order.[34] While the revisions did not seriously disrupt the movement, the fact that Orangeism was forced to reconstitute itself again reveals the newly defensive posture of the Orange party. This growing trend was only confirmed in the following year, when the Grand Lodge took the drastic step of banning the upcoming July celebrations. In a resolution of the Grand Lodge, the deputy grand master, James Verner, explained the reasoning behind this dramatic move: "To act in the most strict conformity with an order which tends so strongly to show how much the members of the Orange Association are willing to sacrifice to the feelings, and even prejudices, of their fellow subjects and how desirous they are that no excuses should be left for ascribing any of the disorder that affect Ireland to their conduct or ex-ample."[35] As in 1823, this directive from the Grand Lodge met with consid-erable success—the Twelfth passed off with relative tranquillity in most districts. It was not totally successful, however. Despite the Grand Lodge's resolution, Orange processions produced several party affrays in 1824, in-cluding a fatal riot in Newry and a serious clash near Ballygawley, County Tyrone.[36]

The suddenly inhospitable political climate of the 1820s presented Or-ange leaders with a critical dilemma, as irreconcilable pressures from above and below threatened Orange unity. Orangeism had always derived much of its strength and legitimacy from its pseudoformal relationship with the British government in Ireland. Unfortunately, the concessions deemed nec-essary to maintain these good relations offended the men who formed the backbone of the Orange movement. Hard-line plebeian loyalists wanted nothing to do with concession and conciliation. Faced with the reemer-gence of a serious Catholic threat, rank-and-file Orangemen responded in the same way they had for the past half-century, using ritualized displays of strength and violence to reaffirm their ascendant position. These tactics were precisely the ones that the Orange elite wanted to avoid. Orange lead-ers and their allies were busy trying to argue that Orangeism was a neces-sary component in preserving the peace in Ireland. Nothing was more devastating to this argument than the violent antics of the Twelfth of July.

These conflicting forces from above and below created a great deal of tension within the movement. When the Grand Lodge made concessions to conciliate the British government, it risked permanently alienating militant loyalists. Orange leaders were acutely aware of the danger posed by taking such a course of action. Testifying before the Select Committee on Orange Lodges in 1835, elite members repeatedly stressed the Order's moderating influence on the rampant sectarianism of plebeian Protestantism. Stewart Blacker was particularly succinct: "I think I have said before that the statute [to ban the Order] would affect only the higher orders and the more intel-ligent members of the society, who at present moderate the movements of the great mass of the body, composed of the lower and humbler classes, and the statute, in carrying that into effect, so far from allaying any party spirit or animosity, would feed it, by taking that safeguard, to cause a much stron-ger collision between the opposite parties."[37] By choosing a course that fun-damentally clashed with that favored by the rank and file, Orange leaders risked a return to the 1780s, when plebeian loyalists had formed indepen-dent "defensive associations" like the Peep O'Day Boys in order to impose their own exclusivist beliefs on mid-Ulster society. With militant loyalism on the rise, the renewed formation of such disruptive bands was a distinct possibility.

But not all of the differences of opinion within the movement revolved around class issues. There is considerable evidence of a regional split within the Orange Order as well. Put simply, the government-centered attitudes of the Dublin Grand Lodge clashed with the more traditional, unyielding loyalism of Ulster Orangemen. When Dublin grandees publicly canceled the Twelfth of July celebrations, many northerners bitterly resented the sudden apostasy of the Grand Lodge. Opposition to such conciliatory gestures was not confined to the rank and file. One prominent Ulster Orange leader, Col. William Verner, went so far as to suggest the formation of a provincial Grand Lodge in Armagh. Verner wanted to undermine the monolithic authority of the Dublin Grand Lodge, giving Ulster Orangemen a greater measure of autonomy. Only the determined opposition of another prominent Ulsterman in the movement, Col. William Blacker, kept this proposition from dividing the Orange Order along regional lines.[38]

If Orange leaders were torn between conciliating the British government and maintaining ties with their plebeian brethren, there is no mistaking the path they chose to take. Between 1823 and 1825 the Dublin Grand Lodge consistently sacrificed the loyalist principles and processions dear to northern Orangemen in order to maintain the Order's ties to the government. Unfortunately, this course of action was as ineffectual with the British government as it was unpopular with lower-class Orangemen.

This became clear in the spring of 1825, when in the midst of an extended and heated parliamentary debate, Robert Peel indicated that the Orange Order would fall under the terms of the new Suppression Act. Although the legislation primarily was designed to suppress the Catholic Association, government officials used the opportunity to ban all such political societies in Ireland in the name of communal balance. Predictably, the new legislation faced no serious opposition in parliament, becoming law on 9 March 1825. Faced with such censure, Orange leaders decided to maintain the same conciliatory course that they had charted over the previous three years. At a meeting of the Grand Lodge in Dublin on 18 March 1825, they took the extraordinary step of voluntarily dissolving the organization.[39] To justify its actions, the Grand Lodge of Ireland declared: "At no period was the institution in a more flourishing condition or more highly respectable in the numbers added to its ranks. Notwithstanding which, the parliament of the United Kingdom have considered it necessary that all political societies should be dissolved. Of course, our society is included. It therefore becomes our duty to inform you that any lodge meeting commits a breach of the law."[40] Thus with one sudden declaration the Grand Lodge brought the contentious existence of the Orange Order to a close—or so it seemed to most contemporaries. Even Charles Brownlow, a prominent Orange leader in County Armagh and one of the earliest parliamentary defenders of the Order, conceded that "he did not apprehend that the Orange societies would continue in Ireland after the bill had passed."[41] That such an important institution in prefamine Irish society could virtually disappear with such rapidity was truly remarkable.

Reaction to the Grand Lodge's circular was exceptionally muted. Running true to the concessionary course charted throughout the mid-1820s, Orange leaders used only thoroughly respectable political avenues to protest the forced dissolution of their society. Several petitions were drawn up objecting to the inclusion of the Order under the terms of the Suppression Act. One such effort was drafted by the grand secretary of the order, James Verner. Predictably, Verner focused on the Order's role in preserving the peace in Ireland since its inception, arguing that it was unjust to outlaw men whose only fault was "an overexuberance of loyalty."[42] Needless to say, such a petition made very little impact.

Orange leaders were only marginally more effective in parliament, where they soon gained a high-profile forum to conduct a defense of the organization. This was provided by a select committee of the House of Lords—a body appointed in 1825 to inquire into the state of Ireland. Two Orange leaders, Col. William Verner and the Rev. Holt Waring, attempted to exonerate the organization before the select committee. While much of the evidence taken before the committee was quite damaging to Orangeism's reputation, these men effectively countered some of the more malign assertions made about the nature of the Orange Order.[43]

If testifying before the select committee gave Orange leaders some small measure of satisfaction, there was no disguising Orange weakness in 1825. With the Order formally disbanded, no loyalist associations existed to counter the rising Catholic tide. One prominent Orange clergyman, Sir Harcourt Lees, immediately attempted to fill this void, forming the Loyal and Benevolent Orange Institution of Ireland.[44] Lees envisioned this new Orange association as more of a religious society than the Loyal Orange Order. The new organization's evangelical orientation can be seen in its initial address: "This association is formed by persons desirous of supporting the principles and practices of the Christian religion, to support and relieve distressed members of the institution, and to offer assistance to such other religious and charitable purposes."[45] The new association's religious mission was reinforced by its close ties to the leaders of the Second Reformation. Lord Farnham, a chief leader of that evangelical Protestant effort to convert Irish Catholics, was a crucial supporter.

The Christian orientation of this new institution undoubtedly was responsible for the movement's ability to maintain a legal presence in Ireland. But Lees's synthesis of traditional Orangeism and evangelical Protestantism failed to capture the imagination of plebeian loyalists. It is not difficult to understand the reasons behind the new association's failure to attract rank-and-file Orangemen. Hereward Senior has put it succinctly: plebeian Orangemen "had little enthusiasm for an organization so obviously designed to keep them on a tight leash."[46] Although this new Orange institution did play an important role in providing organizational continuity until the Order formally reconstituted itself in 1828, it simply never caught on among the plebeian Protestant population of rural Ulster, who seemingly preferred the partisan power politics of the old Order to the religious homilies of Lees and other evangelical preachers.

Nowhere was the Loyal and Benevolent Orange Institution's lack of appeal to hard-line loyalists more evident than in County Armagh, where both Col. William Verner and Col. William Blacker refused to patronize the new Orange association. Without the active support of these leaders of traditional loyalism, the new organization stood little chance of success in the Orange heartland of mid-Ulster. Whatever the intentions of Harcourt Lees, this new institution would not carry the torch of loyalist activism in the late 1820s.

It has been said that the voluntary dissolution of the Orange Order in March 1825 ended an era of Orange history.[47] This statement is somewhat misleading, for the formal adjournment of the Grand Lodge was merely the final act in a process of institutional decay that originated with the advent of the Wellesley administration in 1821. Ironically, this phase of organizational decline coincided with a period of renewed party confrontation in Ulster, as both Protestants and Catholics mobilized to defend and attack the status quo. Faced with a hostile administration at Dublin Castle and a Catholic political movement of unprecedented strength, plebeian loyalists reacted as they always had, using ritualized exhibitions of strength and violence to reimpose their dominance over Ulster's narrow ground. These attempts were largely unsuccessful in the early 1820s, as both the British government in Ireland and the Orange elite refused to sanction such a violent response to the rise of mass Catholic politics. Much of the reason for this failure lies with Daniel O'Connell and the Catholic Association, who maintained a remarkably disciplined and nonviolent political campaign.

But one question remained: how long would they be able to sustain such an approach?

Once More into the Breach: Ulster, 1826–1829

If the Orange Order was in desperate straits in 1825, on the surface its Catholic opponents appeared to be in little better shape. Divided by the veto controversy and suppressed by the Unlawful Societies Act of 1825,[48] the Catholic Association found itself at its weakest point since its 1823 foundation. The veto controversy proved to be especially distracting, as radicals such as the Belfast journalist John Lawless attacked Daniel O'Connell for his apostasy in supporting the "wings" provision in Sir Francis Burdett's failed relief bill of 1825.[49] Although O'Connell was able to announce the formation of a New Catholic Association in the summer of 1825, thus evading the Suppression Act, his Catholic political machine would not regain its full strength until the spring of the following year.[50]

The general election of 1826 transformed this situation. Of course, the coming election was not uniformly positive for supporters of the Catholic cause, who knew that ultra-Protestants would use the occasion to raise the always potent antipopery cry throughout the British Isles. But the sense of opportunity provided by the election easily outweighed any foreboding, for the coming elections gave the Catholic Association a chance to test its strength throughout Ireland. And this it did, contesting elections in seven counties: Armagh, Cavan, Dublin, Louth, Monaghan, Waterford, and Westmeath. Many of these elections proved to be bitterly contentious affairs, as both ultra-Protestants and Catholics (through the medium of liberal Protestant candidates) took the opportunity to press their two irreconcilable visions of how Irish society should be structured. With so much on the line, these battles would not be contained within the realm of electoral politics.

The election itself was a dramatic success for the Catholic cause, as candidates backed by the Catholic Association won seats in Armagh, Dublin, Louth, Monaghan, Waterford, and Westmeath. By revealing the revolutionary potential of the mobilized Catholic electorate, the 1826 elections sounded the death knell of the Irish Protestant polity. Even the *Dublin Evening Mail,* that consistent supporter of fervent political Protestantism, bitterly acknowledged the dramatic impact of this watershed election.[51] Although historians rightly have focused their attention on the historic contests in Waterford and Louth,[52] Ulster hosted several contested elections. Given the nature of the issues involved, it was rather inevitable that these electoral struggles became flashpoints for sectarian conflict. Like fairs and other public festivals, contested elections provided an arena for partisan violence. With sectarian tension already high because of the growing assertiveness of Irish Catholics (and the knee-jerk response of militant loyalism), it was only natural that party riots marked the general elections of 1826. The most dramatic of these clashes occurred in the "sectarian cockpit" of Ireland—County Armagh.

The contest in Armagh is of particular interest because of the background of the candidates involved. Although four men formally announced their candidacies for County Armagh's two parliamentary seats—the two sitting members, Col. Henry Caulfield and Charles Brownlow, plus Col. William Verner and John Burgess—the real contest pitted Brownlow against Verner for the second seat.

In normal times a man like Charles Brownlow would never have been challenged by an Orange magnate like Verner. Brownlow, who had held a parliamentary seat for County Armagh since 1813, was a member of a prominent Armagh family and above all a fellow Orangeman. But these were not normal times, and by 1826 Charles Brownlow certainly was not a typical Orangeman. After championing the Orange Order in the House of Commons for years,[53] Brownlow suddenly switched course in 1825, publicly declaring his support for Catholic emancipation.[54] This quickly earned him the bitter enmity of Armagh Orangemen, who viewed Brownlow as an apostate and heretic. In opposing such a "Lundy,"[55] Colonel Verner based his candidacy on his solid "true blue" credentials. This would not be a friendly election.

The contest formally began on Friday, 23 June, when supporters proposed and seconded their candidates at a spirited meeting at the sessions house in Armagh. Tensions were already high in the city, where members of the constabulary had prevented an election riot from breaking out the previous day—one day before the election began! The town's buildings reflected differing political allegiances all throughout the election; public houses proudly displayed their partisan orientation, placing placards up that alternatively read, "Colonel Caulfield's friends here, Colonel Verner's friends here, Mr. Brownlow's friends here."[56]

Given the bitter feelings involved, the elections got off to a relatively good start. The first day of polling passed without violence, as supporters found more creative ways to attack their opponents. When Colonel Verner took to emphasizing the greater respectability of his followers, one wag in the Brownlow camp quickly circulated a poster which caricatured the na-

Table 2. Election Results, County Armagh, 1826

Col. Henry Caulfield	2,897
Charles Brownlow	2,563
Col. William Verner	1,894
John Burgess	730

Source: *Belfast Newsletter*, 30 June 1826; Brian Walker, ed., *Parliamentary Election Results in Ireland, 1801–1922* (Dublin: Royal Irish Academy, 1978), 36.

ture of Verner's support—a placard that depicted a ragged peasant shouting "Vermin Forever!" (Verner's campaign slogan was Verner Forever!) Verner's supporters lost no time in issuing a vicious rejoinder—an election handbill that highlighted Brownlow's treachery in abandoning the Orange cause: "The last speech and true declaration of Judas B—n-ow, member of parliament, who was hung and burned in effigy for Judaism, P—y, and endeavouring to subvert the present constitution, according to the sentence mutually agreed upon by numerous assemblage of his old friends and constituents."[57] Such was the punishment meted out to a Protestant who betrayed his fellow Orangemen.

The situation deteriorated the following day, as Charles Brownlow moved considerably ahead of Verner in the poll. One particularly serious riot broke out between the "true blues" and the "green party" in the city center. The trouble started when a group of Brownlow supporters marched toward Colonel Verner's committee rooms in English Street. Verner's followers quickly moved out to defend their territory, initiating a party clash in which several of the combatants were wounded by various stone projectiles and well-placed stick blows. The loyalists eventually pushed back their opponents, taking possession of Brownlow's own tally rooms. The riot was only broken up by the appearance of a party of the 72nd Regiment stationed in Armagh city to preserve the peace during the election period.[58]

Unfortunately for Verner, his supporters turned out to be better fighters than voters. As the polling progressed, Brownlow extended his lead over the "gallant colonel." This seemed to exacerbate the situation on the ground in Armagh; several small-scale clashes between Orangemen and their Catholic opponents occurred throughout the city on Monday, 26 June.[59] Tensions subsided gradually as it became clear that Verner had failed in his attempt to unseat Charles Brownlow. When the results were finally announced on 29 June, Brownlow's margin of victory was surprisingly substantial. (See Table 2.)

The election results reveal an important truth; even in the Orange heartland of Armagh, the strength of hard-line loyalism did not lie in the middling tenant farmers who dominated the pre-1832 county electorate. Orange support came from lower down the social ladder. Colonel Verner finally defeated Brownlow in 1832, taking a parliamentary seat he would hold well into the middle of the century. This mattered little in 1826, however, when Verner's supporters were kept outside the polling booth, where their influence was limited to engaging their Catholic enemies in a series of sectarian riots.[60]

Similar scenes of partisan violence dominated the other Ulster elections in 1826. Four people were killed in election riots in Monaghan and Cavan. A major riot broke out in Monaghan when the Catholic supporters of Henry Robert Westenra assailed the carriage of the anti-emancipation candidate, Charles Powell Leslie. This quickly led to conflict between Westenra supporters and the police, who shot three of the former dead in the melee. A similar situation occurred in Cavan, where a clash between rival parties led to the death of a Catholic supporter of Charles Coote.[61] In Ulster, the Association's electoral triumphs proved quite costly indeed.

If the northern elections had been particularly violent in 1826, the Catholic Association achieved a tremendous victory throughout Ireland. Pro-emancipation candidates won seats in six out of the seven contested elections, including two of three in Ulster. Only in Cavan did a candidate who was backed by the association lose, and even there the results were remarkably close given the financial difficulties of both pro-emancipation candidates.[62] Outside of Cavan, candidates supported by the Catholic Association swept the board, demonstrating the power and potential of a disciplined Catholic electorate. This election had a truly revolutionary impact on British and Irish society: after 1826 Catholic emancipation was only a question of timing.

The seeming inevitability of Catholic emancipation only furthered the sectarianization of Ulster society. With the Catholic threat on the doorstep, hard-line loyalists mobilized to protest the impending changes. Not surprisingly, they employed familiar ritual-laden public demonstrations to convey their inveterate opposition to emancipation. Of course, not all Orange messages were directed toward politicians. This tactic also had the useful effect of exhibiting loyalist strength to their Catholic adversaries. And this was important: sensing an historic victory over their Orange opponents, northern Catholics increasingly responded in kind, triggering a dramatic upswing in communal violence across Ulster. According to the reports of the *Belfast Newsletter,* approximately twice as many sectarian riots occurred between 1826 and 1829 as in the period between 1821 and 1825.[63] As emancipation approached, the narrow ground narrowed considerably.

It did not take long for the increased level of sectarian tension to take violent form following the 1826 election. One week after the polls had closed, a serious sectarian riot occurred at the Crebilly fair near Ballymena, County Antrim. Party fighting at Crebilly was so fierce that police "durst not interfere." The "Ribbonmen" eventually emerged victorious, driving their Orange foes from the fair. In typical Ulster fashion they celebrated their newly won ascendancy by marching in triumph into the neighboring town of Ballymena.[64] Such riots were not confined to one area of the province. A week later, Monaghan loyalists clashed with a local Catholic band at the Clones fair. Catholic fairgoers apparently triggered the conflict, shouting "Down with the Protestants!" as they moved through the town center. Local Orangemen struck back, driving their Catholic opponents from the fair.[65]

The contentious spirit of the 1826–1829 period in Ulster is captured well in a long and detailed letter written by the Rev. Patrick A. Murray, a professor at Maynooth. In this letter Murray recalled his childhood days in Clones:

My native town, which is situated in the upper part of County Monaghan, became about the middle of 1827, and continued for a time after, perhaps the most renowned scene in all Ireland of perpetual conflicts between Orangemen and Catholics. . . . These attacks, in every instance commenced by the Orangemen, were repeated from week to week afterwards on market days, but especially on the fairs which were held on the last Thursday of each month. . . . An Orange flag was always hoisted on the Twelfth of July from the steeple of the Protestant church. On the occasion above alluded to, of the first of the "fighting fairs" as they came to be known, after the streets had first been cleared by the Orangemen and the yeomen, the former paraded them in all directions and in large bodies, waving their bludgeons over their heads and calling for the face of a papist or a penny boy [supporter of the Catholic Association].[66]

The professor's Catholic partisanship aside, it is clear that both parties were ready to do battle. All that was needed was a spark to set if off.

The event that triggered this new phase of party confrontation was Daniel O'Connell's famous victory in the County Clare by-election of June 1828.[67] O'Connell's triumph was certainly not the first assertion of Catholic voting power in Ireland. The Catholic Association had demonstrated its political might in the general election of 1826, driving members opposed to emancipation from their parliamentary seats across Ireland. But it was O'Connell's victory in Clare that truly transformed the situation. By standing for a seat that he could not take as a Roman Catholic, O'Connell directly challenged the exclusivist conception of British and Irish citizenship that had structured the Irish polity since the late seventeenth century. The gauntlet was down.

Conservative Irish Protestants responded quickly to this affront. Alarmed by the remarkable success of the Catholic Association and by increasing signs that the British government was going to concede emancipation, several prominent ultra-Protestant aristocrats organized a vigorous "no-popery" campaign throughout Britain and Ireland. This took institutional form on 15 August 1828 with the establishment of the Brunswick Constitutional Club, an organization founded "on the principles of preserving the integrity of the Protestant constitution."[68] Led by such Orange stalwarts as the Earl of Enniskillen and Lord Farnham, these loyalist associations aimed to mobilize and express hard-line Protestant opposition to Catholic emancipation.

Egged on by the threat posed by emancipation, the Brunswick clubs attracted plebeian loyalist support throughout the province. Not surprisingly, former members of the disbanded Orange Order made up the vast majority of the rank and file. An examination of the Brunswick club formed in Portadown on 25 September 1828 illustrates the typical activities and composition of this new organization. Headed by Joseph Atkinson and Col. William Blacker, the Portadown Brunswick club quickly attracted militant Protestants from the traditionally Orange parishes of northeast Armagh. By November the club claimed 177 members.[69] Like other local Brunswick clubs, the Portadown club concentrated on mobilizing the weight of Protestant public opinion against emancipation by organizing petitions against the impending legislation.[70] To help consolidate these local efforts the organization later published a newspaper, the *Star of Brunswick*. This journal was designed to act as a conduit for "the spirit of Protestantism which is now abroad."[71] The combat had now been fully joined.

Worried by the formation and rapid expansion of the Brunswick clubs, Daniel O'Connell and other leaders of the Catholic Association quickly moved to counter their "new" opponents. On 5 August the finance committee of the Catholic Association commissioned John Lawless, a long-time Belfast journalist, to lead a nonviolent and disciplined Catholic mission through the province of Ulster. Lawless's mission had two primary goals: to undermine the development of the Brunswick clubs and to stimulate the collection of the "Catholic rent" in the north. But O'Connell clearly envisioned other benefits for the Association. Keenly aware of complaints against the notoriously partisan administration of justice in Ulster, O'Connell hoped that Lawless's march would hearten Ulster Catholics long oppressed by local Orange triumphalism and help to shift their allegiances from the anti-

Orange Ribbon societies to his own political organization.[72] "The mission of Mr. Lawless is one of the greatest importance. Lawless may be arrested, but the compensation would outweigh the insolence offered. He will organise the collection of Catholic rent in as many parishes as possible, abolish secret societies, and soothe and allay irritation caused by the orgies of the Orangemen."[73] Despite O'Connell's hopes, the Lawless mission did very little to soothe sectarian relations in the north of Ireland.

If the Catholic Association wanted to challenge Ulster loyalism on its own turf, they could not have chosen a better man than John Lawless. As the editor of a weekly radical newspaper, *The Irishman,* Lawless had long played an active role in Belfast politics. He brought both radicalism and a colorful sense of showmanship to the meetings of the Catholic Association, where he frequently berated Daniel O'Connell for his hesitancy and conservatism. While certainly an effective gadfly, Lawless was not a particularly effective political leader. This was partly a matter of personality, a point made nicely in Charles Gavan Duffy's wonderful description of Lawless: "the soul of honour, always interesting and exhilarating, and sometimes exhibiting, unexpectedly, sound judgment."[74] But whatever Lawless's defects as a leader within the Catholic Association, his talents were well suited to awakening the slumbering north. Unfortunately, Lawless would soon discover that the spirits roused by his mission would have been better left asleep.

Traveling north from Dublin, Lawless and his entourage were welcomed enthusiastically in Kells and Drogheda. The people of Drogheda gave the mission a particularly spirited greeting, drawing Lawless's carriage through the center of town in triumph. There he met with clergymen and local Catholic leaders, hoping to draw on their prestige and influence. He also held several public meetings in the area, effectively using his considerable oratorical skills to stimulate donations and enthusiasm for the Catholic cause. Heartened by this initial success, Lawless remained in the border regions of Louth and Meath for several weeks, receiving widespread acclaim from the largely Catholic population.

Things became more complicated as Lawless headed east for County Monaghan and Ulster. The first signs of trouble appeared in the town of Collon, County Louth. Collon parish had a considerable Protestant population; it had been the parliamentary seat of John Foster, the famous leader of late eighteenth-century hard-line Protestantism. When the Lawless mission arrived in Collon in mid-September, plebeian loyalists gathered to block his entry into town. While no serious outbreaks of violence occurred that day, the confrontation between Lawless's supporters and local Protestants was an ill harbinger of things to come.[75]

From Collon, Lawless proceeded to the town of Carrickmacross in southeastern Monaghan. At a public meeting there Lawless issued a direct challenge to his opponents throughout the county: "they had fought the fight at Collon and succeeded and . . . on Tuesday he would require twenty thousand men to fight the Ballybay fight, when we have no doubt of success."[76] To intimidate his enemies, Lawless began to exaggerate the number of his followers as he approached Ulster. These propaganda efforts were greatly augmented by the paranoia of many Monaghan Protestants. Several informants reported that Lawless had left Carrickmacross for Ballybay with ten thousand to fifteen thousand followers. A comparatively sober police estimate placed the number at about two hundred.[77]

Lawless's aggressive tactics were perfectly consistent with the philosophy and goals of his mission. Both O'Connell and his energetic lieutenant believed that the Orange faction that opposed Catholic emancipation in Ulster lacked both depth and conviction. By issuing a public challenge to his opponents at Ballybay, Lawless was sure that he could achieve a significant public relations victory, for he felt certain that the few "bigots and bloodhounds" who made up the Brunswick movement would never stand up in public to the full might of his followers. Like O'Connell before him, Lawless proved to be quite wrong about the nature of his opposition.[78]

Lawless's challenge created an immediate sensation in Ballybay. Local Protestant activists quickly put out a call for the Protestants of Monaghan to step forward to defend Ballybay against "Honest Jack" Lawless and his followers. The chief local Orange leader was an innkeeper named Sam Gray. Widely known for his staunch loyalism, Gray long had been the Orange district master in the Ballybay region.[79] Upon hearing of Lawless's intended visit, Gray lost no time in organizing loyalist opposition. By 23 September an estimated four thousand men had poured into Ballybay to protect the town from invasion. Gray and his associates quickly readied themselves for combat. No detail was overlooked; incoming roads were decorated with orange and purple arches. The stage was set for a major confrontation in Ballybay.

As Lawless and his rapidly growing retinue approached, Maj.-Gen. William Thornton grew quite worried. Riding into town at about four o'clock on 23 September, the fever pitch of Protestant preparations alarmed Thornton. It was his job to keep the peace in Ballybay. Put simply, Thornton did not have adequate resources to perform his task; he only had about one hundred soldiers at his disposal. Clearly, this was a time for diplomacy. As a considerable body of armed loyalists positioned themselves along the Carrickmacross road, Thornton galloped off to talk to John Lawless.

Thornton found Lawless moving slowly toward town along the Carrickmacross road. An immense crowd had gathered behind his carriage and rather inflated estimates of its numbers ranged from 10,000 to 15,000, to Lawless's preposterous claim of 250,000. Receiving word of the hostile reception awaiting him in Ballybay, Lawless quickly halted the progress of his entourage. When General Thornton arrived, he had no trouble persuading Lawless to reroute his party to a nearby Catholic church. Although the vast majority of his followers wanted to accept Sam Gray's challenge and press on into town, Lawless demurred; they would regroup instead at the Catholic chapel on Rockcorry Road, about one and a half miles outside of Ballybay. Greatly relieved, Thornton rode back to town, assuring the waiting loyalists that Jack Lawless would not be coming to Ballybay.[80] A major sectarian riot had been averted.

Thornton was unable to keep the two parties completely separated. As a body of armed loyalists headed home from Ballybay they ran headlong into a group of Catholics who had just left Rockcorry chapel. Words were exchanged, and two Catholic men were killed in the ensuing struggle.[81] Lawless's decision not to enter town had been prudent. Daniel O'Connell certainly thought so. While not particularly fond of the Belfast agitator, O'Connell countered those who believed that Lawless should have taken up Gray's challenge at Ballybay: "I think Mr. Lawless was quite right at Ballybay. If the chapel had been in town, he should have gone there at all hazards, but as it was not, he was quite right, and the people decidedly wrong."[82] With O'Connell's support, John Lawless would not be recalled from his northern mission.

Lawless remained in southeastern Monaghan for several days, staging public demonstrations and generating enthusiasm for the Catholic cause. Somewhat chastened by the Ballybay experience, Lawless worked hard to prevent the kind of confrontation that had occurred in that town, urging Monaghan Catholics not "to meet me on the road with flags and banners and laurels. I trust that you will not commit so great an error. The fault we blame in others, we should not commit ourselves."[83] While Lawless was toning down his rhetoric, it became apparent that he had not learned the lessons of Ballybay; it was territory—not talk—that mattered. At one of his rallies he announced that he soon would be visiting Armagh city. This news created a predictable uproar in Armagh, where a large crowd of loyalists poured into the city to block "Honest Jack's" visit. Catholic leaders in Armagh quickly sent Lawless word advising him not to visit. Heeding their advice, Lawless backed down.[84]

Upon receiving word of Lawless's decision, hard-line Protestants gathered in Armagh city, marching in full regalia to the sound of fife and drum. The *Belfast Newsletter* exulted in Lawless's retreat: "Jack has now got a taste of the Protestant spirit of the North, and he will be consulting his own interest and the quiet of the country, if he makes his exit out of it as quickly as possible."[85] John Lawless soon took this advice. Blocked by the strength and fervor of plebeian loyalism in south Ulster, Lawless kept his mission in the safer border counties for several weeks before returning to Dublin.

The importance of the events at Ballybay often has been overlooked by Irish historians. Put simply, Ireland narrowly avoided a massive upswing in communal violence in September 1828. Had Lawless and his followers entered Ballybay, a major sectarian riot would have ensued. With party feeling already up, such a partisan bloodbath easily could have triggered widespread clashes between Catholics and Protestants throughout the north of Ireland. The Catholic politician and historian Thomas Wyse believed that Lawless's entry into Ballybay could have sparked a civil war: "A defeat of the crowd who accompanied him would have been followed up by a carnage; the carnage, by a massacre of the Catholics of the north. Their brethren of the south would not have looked on—hundreds and thousands would have marched from Munster—a counter massacre—a Sicilian Vespers, perhaps would have taken place."[86] Wyse's scenario was certainly overwrought, but there can be little doubt that a sectarian battle at Ballybay would have been followed by a major escalation in party violence throughout Ulster—an event that would have had a significant impact on the passage of Catholic emancipation.

The Lawless mission of 1828 was a dramatic failure for the Catholic Association. Designed to raise support for the Catholic cause in Ulster, the mission did not even visit eight of the nine northern counties. Furthermore, the "invasion of Ulster" actually energized the ultra-Protestant campaign against Catholic emancipation. Within two weeks, Brunswick clubs had been founded in Carrickfergus, Downpatrick, Lifford, Lisburn, Moy, Omagh, Portadown, and Tanderagee.[87] By strengthening its enemies, the Lawless mission actually hurt the Catholic cause. Even the normally supportive *Northern Whig* bemoaned the effects of the mission: "The state of the country at the present crisis is truly awful. In the North a desperate and armed faction, released from a temporary check, exasperated by a partial rebuff, and thirsting for blood, are daily excited against their Catholic countrymen by the inflammatory harangues of men, whose conduct more resembles that of priests of Maalock, than Ministers of Jesus."[88] Clearly, "the invasion of Ulster" had not done much to advance Daniel O'Connell's oft-stated goal of uniting Irish men and women of different creeds.

The Lawless mission failed for one reason—it had been crafted by men who simply did not understand the sectarian realities of early nineteenth-century Ulster. The leaders of the Catholic Association believed that Protestant opposition to emancipation was both weak and elite-dominated. With this in mind, Lawless was supposed to draw his enemies out into the open, where they would be overpowered by the sheer weight of his supporters. The mission was certainly effective in bringing out its Orange opponents. In fact, by using ritualized demonstrations to lay claim to contested public spaces, the Lawless mission's tactics can be viewed as a rough parallel to the Orange Order's controversial celebration of the Twelfth of July. As anyone even vaguely familiar with Ulster well knew, such territorial intrusions quickly invited a vigorous response.

Opposition to Catholic emancipation among Ulster Protestants was neither weak nor elite-dominated. Angered by the idea of "Honest Jack" leading Irish Catholics into a space they considered Protestant, hard-line plebeian loyalists aggressively moved to block Lawless's progress. Fiercely determined and much better armed than their Catholic opponents, Sam Gray and his supporters were able to rebuff Lawless's advance into the north, in essence driving the Catholic Association back to the friendlier fields of the more homogeneous south.

On 4 November 1828, ultra-Protestants gathered in Dublin for the annual meeting of the Brunswick Constitutional Club. Participants loudly cheered the recent Orange victory, shouting "Bravo! Ballybay Forever!"[89] But Orange joy proved to be fleeting, for the hard-line Protestant sentiments aroused in part by the "invasion of Ulster" were manifestly unable to halt the passage of Catholic emancipation in April 1829. The Lawless mission was a foolish venture on the part of the Catholic Association, but it was not a fatal one. Daniel O'Connell and John Lawless certainly lost the battle at Ballybay, but they soon won the war.

The ultra-Protestant attempt to block Catholic emancipation's passage failed for a number of reasons. Two of these stand out as especially critical. First, hard-line loyalists did not run a particularly effective campaign. They were not without assets. This was especially true after September 1828, when the Suppression Act expired, allowing conservative Protestants to reconstitute the Orange Order. With its strong, traditional ties to plebeian loyalism, the Orange Order mobilized hard-core sentiment more effectively than the new and elite-oriented Brunswick clubs. As one group of Down Protestants declared at a Downpatrick meeting on 27 September 1828: "the Protestants of this country shall re-establish the Old Orange institution, as being best understood."[90] With Protestant Ireland under siege, Ulster loyalists flocked

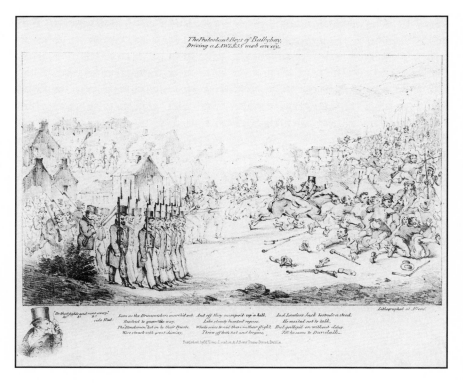

Collision in Ballybay, 1828. (F639—Loyalist Print of Ballybay Incident, courtesy of the National Library of Ireland.)

to the revived standard: by late 1828, Fermanagh alone claimed to have thirty-four thousand members.[91] By early 1829 the Orange movement was at its strongest point since the early nineteenth century.

The problem was not a lack of foot soldiers, but rather an absence of leadership. The Orange Order simply did not produce the kind of populist leader necessary to head a last-ditch resistance campaign. The events at Ballybay had shown the way; by organizing the forces of plebeian loyalism, Sam Gray had been able to face John Lawless down. With its ability to produce disruptive sectarian confrontations, the Orange Order had the power to make Ulster ungovernable, thus making it unlikely that emancipation would be passed. At the very least, such a campaign might have delayed the inevitable. But this kind of campaign required a charismatic and populist leader. In later years William Johnston of Ballykilbeg and Thomas Sloan stepped forward to put themselves at the head of popular Orange crusades of sectarian resistance.[92] In late 1828 and early 1829 aristocratic grandees like the Earl of Enniskillen and the Duke of Cumberland led Orange resistance to emancipation. Such figures were unlikely to lead such a violent and nakedly tribal campaign.

More importantly, the Orange Order's stance against emancipation had few allies in the British government. The Catholic Association's electoral successes between 1826 and 1828 had convinced many previous supporters of the Protestant cause in Ireland that Catholic emancipation had to be granted in order to maintain any semblance of political and social stability. Both the prime minister, the duke of Wellington, and his home secretary, Robert Peel, personified this transformation. Wellington was typically blunt: "I confess that what has moved me has been the Monaghan, the Louth, the Waterford, and the Clare elections. I see that we shall have to suffer from all the consequences of a practical democratic reform in parliament if we do not do something to remedy the evil; and if I could believe that the Irish nobility and gentry would recover their lost influence, the just influence of property, without making these concessions, I would not stir."[93] With few substantial parliamentary allies, ultra-Protestant resistance had little chance of success. After a passionate debate and rather bitter exchange between King George V and his chief ministers, the Roman Catholic Relief Act became law on 13 April 1829.[94]

Loyalist reaction to Wellington and Peel's advocacy of Catholic emancipation was predictably hostile. The *Dublin Evening Mail* was typically soft-spoken: "We tell him [the Duke of Wellington] there is a power in the empire, a power even in Ireland superior to him and to his policy—one that will not brook his measures, not submit to his encroachments—a power that will never prostrate itself before Popish domination. He may drive the Protestants into rebellion—he may banish them from their native land—and if he perseveres he will; but we tell him that he can never coerce them into passive submission to a measure which places their lives and their liberties, their institutions and their religion, at the mercy of a faction who thirst for their blood."[95] Ultra-Protestant anger did not fade quickly. As the Twelfth of July approached, the Grand Lodge of Ireland made it clear that the Orange Order planned to use the upcoming marching season to convey their displeasure to the British government and make a showing of Orange strength to the enemies of loyalty. A June 1829 circular expressed these sentiments quite clearly: "the same motive which induced the destruction of the constitution of 1688, in the late bill passed by parliament, exists still in undiminished force and will urge the enemies of Protestantism to avail themselves of events likely to arise from the processions on the 12th of July to crush the last supporters of Protestant loyalty in this country—the

Orangemen of Ireland."[96] The address went on to emphasize the need to take action to "preserve, unbroken, that compactness and strength now so necessary for the continuance of our existence."[97] Under siege once again, it declared that Ulster loyalists must unite to face the enemies now arrayed to destroy them. The conciliatory course charted by the Dublin Grand Lodge and its British allies throughout the 1820s clearly had failed. It was time for a new direction. This would not be a tranquil Twelfth of July.

Since April plebeian loyalists had responded to the passage of Catholic emancipation in their own time-honored fashion—by using processions to lay claim to disputed territory and assert their own partisan strength. In the village of Crossgar, County Down, the liberal magistrate William Sharman Crawford reported that informal processions were on the increase between May and July 1829, on one occasion triggering a melee in which one man was shot in the arm.[98] By no means was this an isolated incident. As Orangemen used such public festivals to assert their continued ascendancy in the face of the rising Catholic tide, sectarian tensions heightened throughout the north, resulting in an increased number of party clashes at provincial markets and fairs. On 4 July 1829 the *Dublin Evening Post* reported that sectarian passions in the north of Ireland had reached a dangerous level—with good reason. In May and June alone, Orange and Green parties battled in Belfast, Enniskillen, Lurgan, and Rosslea.[99] On 8 July police arrested fifty participants when a major sectarian riot broke out in the notoriously turbulent Seagoe parish in north Armagh.[100] With both parties preparing for communal confrontation, the Twelfth promised to be one of the most violent days in years.

On 13 July 1829 Orangemen assembled in full regalia all across Ulster. The Orange demonstrations that day were the largest and most widespread in the history of the organization. The loyalist strongholds of Portadown, Ballybay, and Caledon hosted the most impressive assemblages but processions were not confined to these areas. Substantial musters of angry Orangemen and their supporters also assembled in Armagh, Belfast, Tanderagee, Moira, Downpatrick, Banbridge, Maghera, Strabane, Newtownstewart, Clones, Stewartstown, Newry, Enniskillen, Magherafelt, Castledawson, Greyabbey, Glenavy, and Derriaghy.[101] The battle over Catholic emancipation seemingly lost, Ulster loyalists used this partisan festival to voice their displeasure over the broken Orange covenant. Nor was this a purely plebeian phenomenon. Prominent Orange leaders took active roles in organizing the 1829 celebrations. In Pettigo a highly respectable meeting of local "masters and officers" unanimously resolved to assemble as usual on the Twelfth because of the British government's capitulation to the "popish association."[102] Such a challenge would not go unanswered. With Catholic confidence surging in the wake of their famous victory, few processions would go unopposed in 1829. Sectarian riots were the inevitable result.

One of the largest party clashes occurred at Macken Hill—situated near Derrylin village, seven miles south of Enniskillen. Party relations in the Derrylin region had been notoriously bad for quite some time; the monthly market there had been canceled because of frequent sectarian combat. In early July allegations surfaced that Orangemen had sent out a challenge to the Ribbonmen of the area, a rumor that Orangemen hotly denied.[103] Whatever the truth of the allegation, both sides were quite prepared for the marching season. Outraged by the passage of Catholic emancipation, local Orangemen had marched through Enniskillen twice in the first two weeks of July. In the wake of these insults their Catholic opponents met several times in Enniskillen to organize an anti-Orange force for the upcoming Twelfth. A third procession would not go unopposed.[104]

On 13 July 1829, Orange lodges from various parts of Fermanagh and its neighboring counties gathered in the vicinity of Enniskillen to commemorate King William's victory at the Boyne. Determined to prevent an Orange celebration, a large number of Catholic men and women assembled in a nearby townland. While the majority of the Catholic muster hailed from the immediate area, some had traveled from the nearby counties of Cavan and Leitrim, including one sizable contingent from Swanlinbar in Cavan. Armed largely with pitchforks and scythes, the immense crowd positioned itself along the projected procession route. The Earl of Enniskillen, understandably alarmed by the appearance of a large Catholic army in his domain, rode out to persuade the crowd to disperse. Aided by a local parish priest, the Earl seemed to achieve a measure of success. Promising the crowd that he would reroute the upcoming procession, the Earl managed to convince them to disperse. Perhaps the day would pass in relative tranquillity after all.

At that moment, however, a local Orange lodge rode to the "rescue" of their noble leader. Joined by a second force of Orangemen from the Belturbet region of Cavan, the sudden Orange appearance shattered any hopes for the Earl's brokered truce. In the confusion a general melee quickly broke out between the well-armed Orangemen and the hostile crowd. The usual conflicting accounts obscure the exact origin of the conflict. By all accounts, a shot rang out in the midst of the contested field, triggering a murderous conflict. Orangemen claimed a Catholic had fired, members of the Catholic crowd declared the converse. But if the origins of the riot were unclear, the deadly results were unmistakable—four Orangemen and a larger number of Catholics were killed in the fighting.[105]

Similar scenes occurred in the Stewartstown region of east Tyrone, where Orangemen gathered in force to commemorate the Twelfth. After spending a "convivial" afternoon on the Desertcreat estate of Thomas Greer, the Grand Master of the Order in County Tyrone, district Orangemen reconvened in Stewartstown, from whence they returned to their homes. One Orange lodge, L.O.L. 158 from Coole, ran headlong into a large Catholic group near the village of Glenoe, one and a half miles outside of Stewartstown. Apparently the Catholic body had assembled there to defend Glenoe chapel, situated on the road between Stewartstown and Coole. After a brief diplomatic effort, general fighting broke out between the Orangemen and their Catholic foes.[106] Taking refuge in a nearby stone house, the Coole men, who included fourteen yeomen, fired out at their opponents with murderous effect, killing at least six men. Two Orange leaders were killed in the crossfire.[107] The latter immediately found themselves enshrined as martyrs for the Orange cause, loyal citizens who died defending their rights under crown and constitution. According to Sibbett, they were not the only heroes of the battle of Glenoe. Local Catholics raised an obelisk dedicated to their fallen at Glenoe chapel, remembering their sacrifice with the following dedication: "Old Tyrone—first in the field and last to leave. Glorious Glenoe will plant the tree of liberty as they have done in America, should blood manure its roots, that our friends may say when mourning over our graves: these heroes died for liberty rather than live like slaves—John O'Neil, and Hugh O'Neil, and John Ritchie. They heroically defended the church of God from Orange desecration on July 13, 1829. R.I.P."[108] With two such conflicting visions at play, there simply was no common ground.

Nor was the violence confined to the rural districts of mid and west Ulster. Serious party clashes occurred in or near Armagh city, Belfast, Clones, Greyabbey, Newry, and Strabane.[109] All in all, at least forty people died in the rioting that broke out all across Ulster on 13 July 1829. Orangeism's symbolic protest of Catholic emancipation had taken deadly effect.

Hard-line loyalists used the marching season of 1829 to convey messages to several constituencies. First and most important, Orange public processions aimed to display the continued strength and ascendant power of Ulster loyalism to its Catholic enemies. Although the anti-Catholic statutes of the Penal Age might not be on the books any longer, these festivals were designed to show northern Catholics that ascendancy and exclusivity were still the laws of the land. Orange musters across the north were impressive—an estimated fifty thousand Orangemen participated in well over twenty processions on 13 July 1829. But while the display was impressive, the Orange show of strength was indecisive. Very few Orange processions went unopposed; Ulster Catholics exhibited an unprecedented ability to assemble in strength to block the hated demonstrations in 1829. While the better-armed Orangemen nearly always had the advantage in such clashes, their Catholic antagonists now constituted a serious opponent. Ritual intimidation was no longer enough.

Orange demonstrations also endeavored to maintain the vitality and relevance of loyalist belief. When processionists routed such parades into the heart of Catholic enclaves, outbreaks of sectarian violence almost always ensued. Thus, in times of crisis Orange marchers could almost choreograph party riots, creating a situation where Catholic enemies could be portrayed as rebels. After all, by walking on the Twelfth, Protestants merely honored the memory of King William's victory; anyone who assailed an Orange procession could be portrayed as attacking the very legitimacy of British government in Ireland: the seventeenth-century settlement of church, king, and constitution. With their exclusivist notion of the Irish polity under heavy assault in 1829, this message resonated richly in the minds of many Ulster Protestants. The marching season thus brought more supporters into the Orange fold by reminding Ulster Protestants of the "truth" of loyalism's narrow historical vision.

Finally, Orange public display served to convey a message to a third party—the British government. Orangemen believed that they had been betrayed by the Duke of Wellington and Sir Robert Peel. British parliamentarians might be fooled by Catholic gestures of conciliation, but Ulster's Orangemen would never fall into that trap. If British politicians were not ready to defend the sacred constitution, the loyal Orangemen of Ulster would have to go it alone. Unfortunately for the Orangemen, such a message was not well-received in London. Within a few weeks of the bloody Twelfth of 1829, formerly sympathetic politicians like Sir Robert Peel and the Duke of Northumberland publicly condemned processions.[110] If Colonel Blacker had thought that 1821 was a particularly bad year for Ireland, 1829 proved to be the darkest in recent memory.

Given the sectarian brutalities involved in the 1798 rebellion and its frenzied aftermath, the years between 1800 and 1820 proved to be relatively quiet in Ulster. While communal antagonism did not diminish appreciably, outbreaks of sectarian violence were sporadic and small in scale. Only between 1811 and 1814, when the Catholic question resurfaced at the center of British and Irish politics, did party rioting become frequent and fatal. Peace returned after 1814, when the implicit threat of a formal national Catholic political organization was removed with the dissolution of Daniel O'Connell's Catholic Board. Secure in its ascendancy, the Orange Order increasingly became embroiled in a series of internal struggles over the nature of rules and regulations. By 1820 Ulster had reached something approaching tranquillity.

Things changed dramatically in the following decade. In the years after 1821 a series of antagonistic forces reanimated the spirit of Ulster loyalism, creating an environment ripe for sectarian violence. These events ranged from the advent of the "anti-Orange" Wellesley administration to the unprecedented agrarian violence of the Rockite movement in the south and west of Ireland. But although these factors played a part in triggering the loyalist revival of the 1820s, they paled in importance when compared to the remarkable rise of Daniel O'Connell and the Catholic Association. With O'Connell mobilizing the Irish Catholic masses for a final assault on the last vestiges of the Penal Laws, many Ulster Protestants felt under siege.

The parallels with the 1780s and early 1790s are striking. In that era a confluence of factors seemingly opened up the possibility of a radically different Irish society, one in which religious distinctions would be blurred, if not wholly eliminated. Mid-Ulster plebeian Protestants formed a series of defensive associations—groups that used violence and ritual forms of intimidation to preserve their ascendant position over the Ulster Catholic population. With the essential aid of war and rebellion, Orangemen and their allies were able to maintain their exclusively Protestant vision of the Irish polity, ushering in two decades of Orange hegemony in Ireland.

Hard-line Ulster loyalists reacted to the rise of the Catholic Association in similar fashion, using fairs and partisan festivals to assert their continued dominance. With Ulster Catholics increasingly unwilling to capitulate to the tried and true tactics of ritual intimidation, sectarian contention rose throughout the decade. The situation became particularly alarming following the general election of 1826, when pro-emancipation candidates contested and won parliamentary seats from Armagh to Waterford. After 1826 it was only a question of timing; Catholic emancipation now seemed inevitable. The prospects of major political reform created an atmosphere ripe for party violence, as both communities mobilized to attack or defend the status quo.

But if parallels existed between the sectarian violence of the late eighteenth century and that of the 1820s, there was at least one major difference. In the late eighteenth century plebeian Protestants had set the tempo of the Armagh troubles—forming defensive associations designed to over-whelm their Catholic enemies. While rank-and-file Orangemen certainly remained active throughout the 1820s, the full weight of uncompromising loyalism only awakened in September 1828, when John Lawless led the in-famous "invasion of Ulster." By this time it simply was too late, especially after Lawless wisely withdrew his forces back to friendly southern fields.

In the late eighteenth century, plebeian loyalists were able to recon-struct a cross-class Protestant alliance based on the defense of the sectarian moral economy. Their success in this era largely rested on the looming threat of revolution that existed throughout the 1790s. With the United Irishmen and Defenders conspiring to overturn Irish society, members of the Ulster gentry linked up with their lower-class brethren, giving plebeian loyalists a well-needed dose of legitimacy and protection. Daniel O'Connell's Catho-lic Association simply did not present the same kind of revolutionary threat. Put simply, the demand for the political rights enjoyed by other British citi-zens hardly compared with the Society of United Irishmen's goal of Irish po-litical independence. Most British politicians remained quite willing to go to war to keep Ireland within the British polity; by 1829 few would fight that same war to preserve an exclusively Protestant political system. But it was not only substance that counted; matters of style were also important. Keeping his remarkably disciplined campaign largely clear of Ulster's combustible at-mosphere, O'Connell simply did not provide his enemies with much mate-rial for the rousing anti-Catholic campaign needed to obstruct the passage of Catholic emancipation. In April 1829 the British government finally conceded the measure, and a revolutionary victory had been won.

Unable to slow down the passage of Catholic emancipation, Orangemen were reduced to ritual forms of protest. The largest such demonstration oc-curred on 13 July 1829, when Orangemen assembled across the north of Ire-land to protest the apostasy of the British government and to display their continued ascendancy over their Catholic enemies. With party feelings at their highest pitch since 1798, Orange demonstrations triggered widespread riot-ing in Ulster; at least forty people died in a series of bloody clashes that day. But this Orange display proved to be as ineffectual as it was provocative. The Orange show of strength was indecisive at best, and the communal violence that it incited only served to anger formerly sympathetic British politicians. The clock could no longer be turned back by such ritual displays. As Colonel Blacker had feared, the forces of conciliation had triumphed.

■ 4

Ritual and Sectarian Violence

The Orange processions forbade us to forget the past, and there was a
history transacted under our eyes of which it was impossible to be ignorant.
Charles Gavan Duffy, *My Life in Two Hemispheres*

On Friday, 19 November 1830, a substantial party of Orangemen marched
from Killyman parish toward Maghery, a small village situated on the southern shores of Lough Neagh.[1] The Killyman Boys were on their way to attend a lodge meeting in nearby Derryinver townland. Upon entering
Maghery, the Orange party found itself surrounded by the Catholic villagers, who listened quietly to several tunes played by the Orange band.
Apparently appreciative of this impromptu concert, the locals accompanied the party all the way to Bannfoot ferry. When the Orangemen boarded
the ferry to cross the river, the villagers returned to Maghery.

The lodge meeting that took place in Derryinver that night was a "black
sitting,"[2] a special type of gathering publicly disavowed by the Loyal Orange
Order. John Richardson of Killyman, a man of "very respectable appearance," chaired the meeting. Two basic groups made up the lodge: the
Killyman Boys from Killyman parish in County Tyrone and a large number
of the inhabitants of Derryinver. The latter were all tenants of the controversial Ulster politician Charles Brownlow.[3] The assembly lasted late into
the evening, and the men remained in Derryinver until the next day.

On Saturday morning the Killyman Boys returned through Maghery,
where the inhabitants asked the band to play some music. When the
Orangemen launched into a vigorous rendition of "The Protestant Boys," a
number of villagers attacked the offending party. The villagers routed the
Orangemen, breaking their drums and taking several of their hats. As the

retreating Killyman Boys returned home, they vowed that they would soon return to wreck Maghery. Two days later, they made good on that promise.

At daybreak on Monday a well-armed party assembled in Killyman parish and set out for Maghery. Observers estimated that the party carried twenty to twenty-five guns. When the Killyman Boys reached Verner's Bridge, a toll-bridge over the Blackwater River, they found the gate locked. Col. William Verner, a local commander of the yeomanry, a justice of the peace for Armagh and Tyrone, and a prominent Orange leader, lectured the party and told them that he would not let them pass through the toll-gate. Seemingly chastened, the Killyman Boys retired to the comforts of a local public house, where a lieutenant of the local yeomanry corps treated them to whiskey.

When the Orangemen returned to the toll-bridge an hour later, they found it wide open and proceeded on their way toward Maghery. Colonel Verner, upon hearing this, rushed toward the village with a small contingent of his Churchill yeomanry corps. Verner's force ran headlong into the Killyman party on the outskirts of Maghery, where he admonished them for their conduct and read the Riot Act. It had little effect. One of the Orangemen allegedly leveled a gun at Colonel Verner while a number of comrades crossed the field to attack Maghery. The wreckers smashed at least twenty houses, breaking windows, destroying doors, and breaking and burning articles of furniture. There is no written record of resistance. The Killyman Boys had obtained their revenge.[4]

The Maghery wreckings of 1830 offer a good illustration of the ritual-laden process that typically led to sectarian riots in nineteenth-century Ulster. Party processions and other partisan festivals all too often produced brutal and bloody clashes between Catholic and Protestant crowds. Scholars have long recognized the important relationship between public ritual and communal violence. One historian estimated that six of the fifteen largest riots in nineteenth-century Belfast stemmed directly from Orange processions.[5] But while academics generally concede the importance of these events, they have often failed to analyze this crucial relationship systematically, instead falling back upon the reductionist view that mere tribalism does not merit their attention.

This chapter aims to undermine that view, for while sectarian riots certainly were rooted in rather simple issues of power and dominance, the process which typically produced party fights was highly structured and laden with ritual. The relationship between partisan violence and public rite is a critical one, for by setting the stage for confrontation, both Orange and Green rituals performed many critical roles in shaping the style and substance of party violence. But it is more than this. An examination of the public and private rituals of the Orange Order and their Catholic adversaries also enables us to enter a world too often neglected—the popular attitudes and motivations of lower-class Ulster Catholics and Protestants, that is, the rioters themselves.

A number of scholars have noted the exaggerated emphasis placed on passwords, signs, and regalia by both the Orange Order and their Catholic opponents.[6] In many ways this ceremonial accent was a natural inheritance from the Freemasons, upon whom both parties modeled their organizations. But the attention given to elaborate displays of rites and regalia involved much more than a matter of simple inheritance. Orange and Ribbon rites played critical roles in lending coherence to sectarian belief.[7] More tangibly, these ceremonies helped to legitimize the violence often produced by partisan processions and celebrations. The rich processional life of nineteenth-century Ulster is particularly important here, for partisan marches played several critical roles in shaping the contours of sectarian conflict. On an ideological level, perhaps the most significant of these functions was the procession's ability to translate contemporary events into the simplified context of a monochrome historical narrative. By continually placing events in the reductionist contexts of "ascendancy" or "oppression," partisan marches and their trappings played an important role in maintaining the vitality of Ulster's two conflicting visions.

Of course, the relationship between ritual and sectarian violence clearly was more than an ideological one. These links can be seen on several different levels. First, by placing what might be merely local events into a broader historical narrative, public ceremonies like party processions helped to bridge the gap between local and national. This in turn allowed sectarian associations like the Orange Order to extend and strengthen organizational connections between local, provincial, and national levels. In an important essay on ethnic conflict and politics in India, Peter van der Veer has argued that Hindu public performances and the violence they produced played essential roles in the evolution of modern Hindu nationalism.[8] The same phenomenon was at work in Ulster; there is no doubt that sectarian festivals allowed both the Loyal Orange Order and its Catholic opponents to play disproportionately large roles in the evolution and formation of Ulster Unionism and Nationalism.

More directly, of course, Orange and Green public displays physically set the stage for partisan confrontation throughout the nineteenth century, triggering riots that resulted in far more fatalities than the more storied nationalist rebellions of the era. Both Orangemen and their Catholic opponents saw partisan festivals like the Twelfth of July and Saint Patrick's Day as a chance to show their strength. Thus, when south Down Catholics taunted Orangemen for avoiding Dolly's Brae in July 1848, loyalists felt that they had to march directly through the contested pass to retain their honor. Similarly, the Orangemen of east Tyrone and southeast Londonderry made an annual point of walking through the Catholic stronghold of Coalisland on the Twelfth.[9] Such marches served to lay ritual claim to contested territory. Not surprisingly, these processions proved particularly controversial in times of political crisis: Twelfth of July violence increased rather dramatically in the 1790s, late 1820s, and late 1860s.

But the violence produced by such provocative festivals was by no means confined to times of political crisis. By the middle of the nineteenth century the summer marching season was an annual headache for government administrators, requiring a massive deployment of police and military to the north merely to keep the peace. The long litany of partisan riots throughout the century is a testament to the futility of their efforts. After all, Ulster's yearly rites of violence could hardly be stopped by mere policemen.

Orangeism, Ritual, and Sectarian Violence

No event exemplifies the symbiotic relationship between public ritual and sectarian violence as well as the Orange Order's celebration of King William's seventeenth-century victories at Aughrim and the Boyne. Since 1796, Orange lodges throughout Ireland have commemorated these historic triumphs by marching through town centers and rural districts to the partisan sounds of fife and drum, brandishing orange banners and sashes on the Twelfth of July. By celebrating the military successes that ushered in the Penal Age in Ireland, these partisan festivals physically reconstructed ultra-Protestant belief in ritual form, hearkening back to an era when the loyalist's Manichaean vision of Protestant citizen and Catholic rebel remained unquestioned.

Orange processions gave rise to some of the largest riots of nineteenth-century Ireland. Testifying before the Select Committee on Orange Lodges in 1835, the Earl of Gosford, then Lord Lieutenant of County Armagh, lamented the destabilizing effect of those partisan festivals. In his view Armagh was usually a relatively tranquil county, "except when those party processions or party meetings take place, then there is drinking, and that leads to riots and retaliation."[10] The British government usually concurred with these sentiments, a fact reflected in its repeated attempts to ban party processions in Ireland throughout the century.

Political anthropologists have noted that one of the most important features of mass public ritual is its ability to convey messages to both participants and the audience.[11] Orange parades and public meetings certainly support this elementary notion. The first and most important message was one of simple power and ascendancy. Through the Twelfth of July celebration the Orange Order, an organization which included only a minority of Ulster Protestants until late in the nineteenth century, could dramatize a power that it often lacked in real terms. David Miller has translated the Orange procession's primary message as follows: "We are the majority here. If you disagree, come out and try to stop us and we will prove to you that there are more of us than there are of you."[12] Orange processions thus set the stage for two possible outcomes, both favorable to the marching Orangemen. First, Catholic opponents could attempt to stop the procession, an event that often resulted in pitched battles between Catholic and Protestant crowds. Since the Orangemen and their supporters generally possessed more firearms than their Catholic enemies, they typically won such clashes. If Catholics did not challenge the marchers, the Orangemen also won, for such a Catholic "capitulation" usually involved allowing the Orange procession to move through Catholic territory. This result, by far the more common of the two, confirmed the Orangeman's belief in his own superiority by allowing him to ritually represent his ascendancy through the public exhibition of territorial domination.

In assessing the efficacy of Orange processions, it is vital to note the paramount importance of religious geography in Ulster society. Northern men and women saw land in religious terms: Catholic and Protestant. As A.T.Q. Stewart has noted: "The Ulsterman carries the map of this religious geography in his mind almost from birth. He knows which villages, which roads and streets, are Catholic or Protestant, or 'mixed.'"[13] This was as true in the nineteenth century as it remains today. By marching through the center of Catholic enclaves, Orange processions conveyed a not so subtle reminder of who controlled power on the ground in Ulster. This message was often supplemented with ritual elements from the hard-line loyalist view of Irish history. On 12 July 1829, Sir Gerald Tyrell, a leading Armagh Orangeman, led a procession into Irish Street, a Catholic area of Armagh city. To underline his point (as if such a message needed underlining) Tyrell led the procession dressed as King William astride a white horse. During the riot that predictably followed such an exhibition, Orangemen threw stones at Catholic shops and homes, and Tyrell wounded several people with his sword."[14] As Orangeism's official historians have stated, "Where you could walk, you were dominant, and the other things followed."[15]

Orangemen and their supporters used orange arches and banners to mark off territory during the marching season. Activists often strung arches of orange lilies across main thoroughfares in an attempt to define public spaces as Orange territory. Such displays became especially contentious issues during times of heightened sectarian tension. As one would expect, this was particularly true when loyalists positioned Orange regalia near or within clearly defined Catholic territories. In the late 1860s and early 1870s a Protestant rector created a great sensation in the Ballyward district of County Down by placing an Orange flag on his church (despite the opposition of some of his own congregation and the local Presbyterian pastor), which was located near the informal border between Protestant and Catholic districts. In July 1869 only the strenuous exertions of the police and a local parish priest prevented offended Catholics from attacking the partisan exhibition.[16] For obvious reasons police generally were loath to remove such symbolic markers, feeling that attempts to remove the flags and banners created more trouble than they prevented.

The territorial imperative emerged in other areas of police strategy regarding party processions. Throughout the century, police who were unable to halt partisan parades effectively were forced to shield Orange marchers from Catholic crowds at certain points along planned routes. This is illustrated nicely by the actions of William Butler, a magistrate charged with preventing sectarian collisions in the Ballyward district in the late 1860s. On the Twelfth of July Butler repeatedly positioned detachments of police near Catholic townlands to keep Orange processionists separated from Catholic crowds at these potential flashpoints. Police were especially cautious in the Ballyward area because Orange lodges had studiously avoided Dolly's Brae since the tragic fight of 1849. When Orangemen returned to these townlands, they found the local population quite eager to respond to such a challenge to regional Catholic hegemony. Only the determined efforts of the police preserved the peace during the marching season in Ballyward.[17] One must take the underlying power of religious conceptions of geography (and sensitivity to violations of communal territorial boundaries) into account when examining plebeian loyalists' impassioned response to events such as John Lawless's invasion of Ulster in 1828 and Daniel O'Connell's Belfast visit to promote repeal of the Act of Union in 1843. Spatial issues became even more contentious as the century progressed. As people flooded into the crowded environs of Belfast in search of employment in its burgeoning linen factories and shipyards, a narrow ground became that much narrower.

It is a commonly held view that sectarian clashes were merely simplistic tribal affairs. This is incorrect. Far from being random and primal outbursts of violence, nineteenth-century sectarian conflicts generally emerged from carefully constructed ritual contexts and often were tied to local and national political life. This becomes especially obvious when we examine the intent behind Orange processions in some detail. Of course, such partisan parades performed several functions for participants. When the British government in Ireland failed to live up to the terms of the Orange covenant, processionists often used marches to dramatize their power on the ground and to voice their displeasure to the government. In times of political crisis Orange public ritual could thus play a magisterial role, as marchers used processions and meetings as a crude form of popular government.[18] This can be seen in the summer of 1829, when the Orange Order used the Twelfth of July celebrations to protest the passage of Catholic emancipation. Marches took place all across the province that day, triggering riots that killed over forty people.[19] The message was clear: ignorant politicians might have changed the law on the statute books, but things would not change on the ground in Ulster.

Of course, Irish Catholics were not the only recipients of these messages. Since any interference with Orange marches represented a clear violation of the loyalist conception of true Ulster Protestantism, magistrates and policemen who attempted to enforce the law against party processions quickly became special targets for abuse. In 1837 the government sent stipendiary magistrates and extra police into various districts of County Armagh in an attempt to preserve the peace on the Twelfth. At least one Orange leader, Col. William Blacker, clearly resented what he viewed as interference in Orange territory: "I find it impossible to believe that Government by their doings in regard to the 12th of July had any other object in view than to provoke the Protestants into some hostile demonstration."[20] Loyalist resentment at police and magisterial interference often seemed to exceed their traditional hatred of their Catholic enemies. After all, "their" police should not deny loyal Orangemen their right to express their superiority and dominance over Irish Catholics. At times this became quite dangerous. In 1870 three policemen went undercover to monitor a huge crowd that had gathered in full regalia near the town of Lisburn to protest the Party Processions Act. Unfortunately for the policemen, their disguises proved inadequate, and only the rapid intervention of an armed escort saved the men from the full fury of the attacking crowd, who were angered by this intrusion on their meeting space.[21] As William Johnston declared in 1864, "We, in Ulster, shall never endure tyranny in the name of law."[22] Johnston and his compatriots adhered to a higher law than the ever-changing policies of a heretical British government—true law, they reasoned, lay with the Orange covenant.

Orangemen also employed public rituals to set standards of behavior for Ulster Protestants. As previously noted, the ideology and attitudes of the Orange Order aimed to provide ideals for all Ulster Protestants, not just members of the organization. Men and women who defied these standards often found themselves subjected to public mock trials. Predictably, magistrates and policemen active in suppressing Orange processions were favorite targets for ritual punishment. Such trials often were quite explicit. On 12 July 1833, William Hancock, a liberal Protestant magistrate for Armagh and Down, arrested fourteen men for participating in an Orange march in Lurgan. At Hancock's order the chief constable marched the prisoners off to the county jail. The jury convicted only three of the men at the following assizes despite the spirited charge of the judge recommending a guilty verdict for all fourteen. Outside the courtroom a large crowd enthusiastically greeted the acquitted Orangemen with partisan music and regalia. The assemblage then marched to Lurgan, where they assembled in front of Hancock's residence. The exuberant crowd proceeded to break several windows and placed a lighted tar-barrel at his doorstep. A week later, a crowd in loyalist Tanderagee burned Hancock in effigy.[23] A not particularly talented Orange balladeer captured the episode in "The Anti-Boyne Water Act—a new ballad supposed to be written by one of Justice Handcuff's fourteen incarcerated Williamites."

> But Lurgan's enlightened Just Ass
> Would fain 'gainst each Orange defaults act
> He whetted his fangs but alas!
> Knaw's files with his anti-Boyne Water Act
> With a salmon placed just in his reach
> Need you ask me, pray, how would an otter act?
> Thus Handcuff the lad to impeach
> Made a plunge with his anti-Boyne Water Act.[24]

The message was quite clear; true Ulster Protestants should not assault the institution that protected their interests.

Thus far, our discussion has focused on the ways in which Orange public rituals conveyed messages to various Ulster constituencies. But partisan processions and meetings were much more than communication devices.

They also played several important roles within the Order itself. Three of these are particularly important. First, public rites enhanced members' identification with the Orange Order. Second, Orange processions reinforced the hard-line loyalist's exclusivist definition of loyalty, acting as a physical representation of ultra-Protestant belief. Finally, public ritual legitimized both the Order and the violence that its display often produced.

Mass public rituals like Orange festivals increase participants' identification with a group and reinforce opposition to the foes represented in the public demonstration. By providing members with a common emotional experience achieved through group participation, public processions and demonstrations can serve partisan organizations by forging bonds of solidarity without requiring uniformity of belief.[25] In short, participation in public rites can create a sense of esprit de corps, which in turn can help to paper over differences based on variables such as class, gender, occupation, or religious denomination. Regalia play an important role in contributing to this sense of solidarity, as songs, slogans, and uniforms help to create a common language for the potentially disparate social groups within an organization. Seen in this light, the Orange Order's extraordinary emphasis on signs, symbols, and passwords heralds a new importance. By reducing the potential for conflict within this cross-class association, partisan public rituals played a critical role in strengthening the social bonds of the Loyal Orange Order.

One of the central tenets of loyalist belief was the notion that Ulster Protestants needed to forget their differences if they were to successfully face their Catholic adversaries. Orange public ritual often embodied this idea; the Orange procession itself depicts a loyal Protestant community united against untrustworthy and rebellious Irish Catholics. This, among other things, explains the importance placed on the inclusion of respectable men and women and government figures in Orange festivals. When these figures would not come to the celebration, Orangemen often brought the celebration to them. Loyalists regularly directed procession routes to aristocratic estates, where participants then sought permission to march on their land. Lord Gosford described this practice in rich detail in 1796:

One party consisting of thirty companies with banners, flags, . . . parading thro' Portadown, Loughgall, and Rich-hill, came toward his place. They halted about half a mile from my house and sent on a courier to enquire whether I had any objection to their paying me a visit, and allowing them to march through my demesne.

Gosford agreed and they came,

marching in regular files by, two x two, with Orange cockades, unarmed, and by companies which were distinguished by numbers upon their flags. The party had one drum, and each company had a fife, and two or three men in front with painted wands in their hands who acted as commanders. . . .

The devices on the flags were chiefly portraits of King William, with mottos to his establishment of the Protestant religion, and on the reverse side of some of them I perceived a portrait of his present majesty with the crown placed before the motto, God Save the King.[26]

By ritually portraying a united Protestant front against their Catholic enemies, Orange public rites helped to reinforce one of the critical themes of loyalist belief—the need for communal solidarity.

But that was not all. By clearly delineating sectarian divisions, Orange parades also acted as ritual idealizations of other critical parts of ultra-Protestant ideology. For one thing, such rites left no room for doubt as to who was loyal and who was not. The procession itself was pure, untainted by traitors and rebels. In many ways, Orange processions reconstructed their vision of a happier era—the late seventeenth and early eighteenth centuries—when Irish life had been black and white; Protestant and Catholic, loyalist and rebel. This simple vision of loyalty and rebelliousness was expressed most explicitly at the Order's annual sham fight at Scarva, where loyalists ritually recreated the Battle of the Boyne. At the Scarva festival, Orangemen, led by King William astride a white horse, always defeated the forces of a craven King James, predictably mounted on a black horse. Simple duality ruled the day: loyal and rebellious; good and evil; Protestant and Catholic.[27] By ritually reconstructing this worldview, Orange processions and celebrations helped to maintain the relevance of a powerful view of Irish history.

Orange parades also played another critical role for the organization, often creating situations that brought legitimacy to processionists and the Order in general. Because of the paramount importance of sectarian geography in Ulster society, partisan marches were ideally suited to instigate party confrontation. Indeed, in times of political crisis procession leaders could almost choreograph sectarian riots, creating situations where Catholic enemies could be depicted as rebels (a very useful propaganda tool). After all, by walking on the Twelfth, Orangemen merely honored the memory of King William's historic victories. Anyone who assaulted such a procession was attacking the very cornerstone of British government in Ireland—the Constitutional Settlement of 1688–1691.

The ultra-Protestant response to the Macken fight of 1829 illustrates this point rather nicely. Following the battle, the *Fermanagh Reporter* intoned that "the spirit of Popery is not changed—as the same thirst for spilling Protestant blood, so notorious in 1641, 1688, and 1798, still, and with equal insatiableness, exists."[28] The newspaper proceeded to report that the Catholic rebels were now encamped on a nearby mountain, awaiting further reinforcements from the neighboring counties of Cavan and Leitrim. By transforming a crowd of country folk intent on blocking an offending partisan procession into a military regiment of a rebel army, the Orange procession (with the substantial aid of a sympathetic paper) legitimized the existence of the Order and the violence that its celebrations produced.

Marches often provided more tangible forms of legitimacy for Orangemen and their supporters. The active participation of religious and political leaders often served to lend Orange public rites a degree of respectability (not to mention a hint of state sponsorship) that they otherwise lacked. The presence of these figures helped to assure processionists that they were in the right in assuming their magisterial roles. Orangemen often went to rather astonishing lengths to include such men in their festivals. In an 1832 letter, Augusta Kiernan described an Orange meeting at Rathfriland, where Orangemen chaired a somewhat reluctant Lord Roden. After describing the procedure, in which the processionists hoisted Lord Roden into a chair and carried him two miles on their shoulders, she observed, "they made Lord Powerscourt walk on their heads, which he literally did. I hope Mr. O'Connell won't be allowed to walk figuratively on ours."[29]

Of course, Orangemen also had very pragmatic reasons for including such influential figures in their festivities. Since partisan processions were against the law throughout much of the nineteenth century, the participation of J.P.'s and magistrates gave marchers a very helpful insulation from later legal proceedings. This certainly was the case at Dolly's Brae in 1849, where Orange processionists heard speeches from three magistrates at Tollymore Park. The relationship was not all one-sided. By participating in Orange festivities, elite figures all but ensured themselves the support of the Orange rank and file.[30] But this was more than a cynical exchange of mutual interest. Elite participation provided the rank-and-file member with more than judicial protection—it gave sanction to his display and the violence that partisan festivals often produced.

Most of the ceremonies and symbols of Orange public ritual also reinforced and legitimized the ideology and collective action of the Order. The popular songs so prevalent at Orange festivities provide one example of this theme. Party tunes played a number of important roles in northern sectarian clashes. Orange songs, driven by the deafening sounds of the Lambeg drum and the shrill piping of the fife, proved to be one of the processionists' most effective weapons in drawing Catholic crowds into partisan conflict. But the songs did more than this. They also served to strengthen the Order's self-image as stalwart champion of Ulster Protestantism.

In his work on Irish political songs, George-Dennis Zimmerman identified five essential qualities in Orange songs and ballads.[31] Two of these categories are particularly important for our purposes: the historical narratives of Orange songs and their emphasis on mystery and ritual. Most Orange ballads commemorated either the historic victories or savage persecutions of Irish Protestants. Two verses from a turn-of-the-century Orange song illustrate these themes particularly well:

If you should wish from history's page this statement true
Go read the blood-stained annals of 1642
And 'Scullabogue' and 'Wexford Bridge' in 1798
Have proved that time does but increase their fierce and hearty hate

. . . Then hurra! Hurra! for church and state and for our gentlemen
Up! With the gallant Orange flag; Down! With the guilty green
And as ye tread on each traitorous head, let the cry for each Defender
Be, 'Our glorious Constitution, Our Faith, and No Surrender!'"[32]

Despite its rather halting rhyming scheme, this song's lyrics touch on several of the central themes of the sectarian moral economy: Irish Catholics' historic and unchanging revanchism; the need for Protestant vigilance and unity; and an implicit call for partisan paternalism. Finally, by celebrating the Orange Order's role as the last defender of true Protestantism in Ireland, this song, like almost all Orange songs, reinforced the legitimacy of its anti-Catholic attitudes and behavior.

Partisan songs also played a role in heading off the potential for class conflict within the order by stressing the need for Protestant unity in the face of constant Catholic conspiracy. The language employed here was not solely concerned with the supposed lessons of Irish history. Orange songs were replete with biblical imagery, placing the Ulster experience within the millennial context of the Book of Exodus. The loyalist use of the Israelite myth was hardly exceptional. In her award-winning book *Britons*, Linda Colley has shown that the idea of Britain as Israel played an important role in the formation of a British patriotism.[33] Given Ulster Protestantism's historic besieged predicament, the explicit parallels that loyalists drew between themselves and the ancient Israelites should not be particularly surprising. Orange songs often featured comparisons between ancient Israel and Ulster. Songs like "When Pharaoh Reign'd" and "Moses and William" were important parts of the Orangemen's early nineteenth-century repertoire.[34] Of course, this theme typically found a more general form of expression. The impending deliverance from doom is one of the central themes of Orange music: "Always bear it in your mind, when you receive the word and sign, it was instituted by divine, to free us all from slavery."[35] Of course, not all songs contained such overt millennial and biblical references. But even the most secular Orange tunes focused on the deliverance from evil, thus combining two of the most powerful forces in Ulster Protestant popular culture—the Bible and the constant threat posed by Irish Catholics. Because they reached such a wide audience,[36] Orange songs proved to be one of the most effective vehicles for maintaining the power and relevance of loyalist ideology.

Colorful banners, arches, and sashes also abounded at Orange festivals and processions. Predictably, these symbols often commemorated the great dates of Ultra-Protestantism's folk memory: 1641, 1689, 1690, and all that. By ritually consecrating a monochrome interpretation of Irish history, Orange regalia reinforced and justified the aims and behavior of the Order. During the marching season Orangemen and their supporters often strung arches across urban streets or rural lanes. Colorful bunches of orange and purple ribbons often adorned these arches. More lavish constructions were not unknown. On 12 August 1829 several lodges from the Pettigo region in western Fermanagh celebrated the anniversary of the relief of Derry by suspending an equestrian statue of King William from a purple and orange arch. A local Orange band provided musical entertainment, and the Orangemen spent the afternoon "in the greatest conviviality."[37] On another occasion Orangemen put up an arch in the center of the Down village of Crossgar despite the protestations of the local magistrate, William Sharman Crawford. When the Orangemen refused to take the arch down, the local police constable decided that it would be imprudent to take action. Crawford apparently thought otherwise, arresting the leaders and lecturing the Orangemen about the evils of "partyism."[38] These arches represented more than simple territorial markers; they also symbolically constructed an interpretation of Irish history that legitimized the Orange Order's sectarianism. By placing contemporary events into the context of their own selective historical narrative, loyalists used public rituals to justify the existence and behavior of partisan organizations like the Loyal Orange Order.

Private rituals played many of these same roles. Like most secret (or in this case, not so secret) societies, the Orange Order's meetings and internal procedures were highly ritualized in structure and content. These private rites performed a series of important functions for the organization. Elaborate ceremonies increased the cohesiveness of the organization by providing individuals with a common panoply of symbols. Although different members of the Order certainly attached varying meanings to these symbols, they did provide members with a broad ritual language with which they could construct Orange ideology.[39] This belief system rested on a particular view of Irish history that members continually reconstructed within this symbolic context. Like their public counterparts, private rites played a key role in reinforcing and legitimizing this ideology and the collective action based on it. These functions can be clearly seen in two forms of private ritual: the organization's initiation rites and the prayers that opened and closed lodge meetings.

The form and content of Orange initiation ceremonies did not radically change between 1800 and 1835.[40] (The Order did drop its oath in an effort to maintain legal status in the mid-1820s).[41] Like so much of the organizational framework of the early Order, these rites were modeled closely on the secret rituals administered within Freemason lodges.[42] Two Orangemen sponsored a prospective member by vowing that he was a true Protestant and loyal subject. If deemed suitable, the new brother received an orange sash to symbolize the successful completion of his initiation into the Orange Order. While it may seem trivial, the physical process of going through these rituals was important, engendering a sense of solidarity or brotherhood.

After the new member passed through this first stage, the chaplain of the Order gave a scriptural reading. The text serves as an excellent example of the diffuse millenarianism so prevalent within prefamine Irish popular culture.[43] The biblical imagery that dominates these prayers comes from the Book of Exodus, which neatly fits into the siege mentality so central to Orange political culture. The concept of deliverance even found its way into Orange passwords. Testifying before the Select Committee on the State of Ireland in 1825, the Rev. Holt Waring indicated that one Orange password system involved the following exchange: "Whither do you go? To the Promised Land. How do you expect to get there? By the benefit of a password. . . ." The password that Waring knew was Migdol, a reference to the original campsite of the Israelites.[44]

In his analysis of the relationship between millenarianism and rural agitation in the south and west of Ireland, James Donnelly found that anti-Protestant millenarianism served to reduce the level of class conflict between Catholic rural laborers and larger tenant farmers participating in the Rockite movement of the early 1820s.[45] Although the anti-Catholic millennial imagery of Orange ritual was not as explicit as Pastorini's prophecies, it certainly promoted communal solidarity within the various social groups that made up the Orange movement, reinforcing what Elaine McFarland has termed the ecumenical theology of Orangeism (i.e., all Protestants are welcome).[46] Finally, by contrasting the embattled truth of Irish Protestantism with the savage and rebellious history of Irish Catholicism, millennial rites legitimized the survival of a vigilant Protestant organization capable of putting down the inevitable Catholic insurgents.

This same imagery pervaded the prayers that opened and closed lodge meetings. Not surprisingly, the texts of these prayers generally focused on the notion of protecting king, church, and constitution from conspiracy: "we yield thee thanks for so miraculously bringing to light and frustrating the secret and horrible designs of our enemies, plotted and intended to have been executed against our gracious king, our happy constitution, and the true religion established by our glorious deliver, William the Third, Prince of Orange."[47] The prayers appealed to a potent vision of Irish history by reinforcing the powerful folk memory of the bloody sectarian massacres of the 1640s and 1790s. Of course, such appeals were hardly an Orange preserve. The Order used notions of the barbaric slaughter at Scullabogue in 1798 in the same manner that nationalists kindled Irish Catholic passions in postfamine Ireland with images of the body-strewn streets of Skibbereen. Although these visions did not command anything like universal allegiance among Ulster Protestants until late in the nineteenth century, they did promote unity within the Orange Order itself.

Images of Catholic conspiracy pervaded every corner of Orange political culture. Many loyalists professed knowledge of a Ribbon oath that vowed to exterminate the Irish Protestant population. In his history of Orangeism, R.M. Sibbett focused on the vicious conclusion of this supposed oath: "I swear to fight knee deep in Orange blood—the crying of children, the moaning of women, or the groaning of men will not daunt me for the restoration and continuation of the long-promised liberty of the Catholic church."[48] This quotation, repeated ad nauseam in Orange histories and correspondence, says much more about the imagination and psyche of Orange historians and landowners than it does about nineteenth-century realities, for as we shall see, Ribbon oaths were much more mundane and certainly less bloodthirsty than these writers would have us believe. But as so often occurs, it is perception rather than reality that mattered. For although no formal conspiracy to massacre the Protestant population existed, Orange private rituals, grounded in the belief that such a conspiracy prevailed among the Irish Catholic population, reinforced traditional anti-Catholic feelings within the Order. Rites rooted in this common ground provided the organization with greater solidarity and helped to justify its own chosen role as the security guard of true Irish Protestantism.

"Ribbonism" and Ritual

Symbols and rituals also played a prominent role in the lives of those Ulster Catholics dedicated to opposing the Orange Order's activities. Recent scholarship has noted the inordinate amount of energy expended by Ribbonmen in creating elaborate password and sign systems.[49] Though reliable information about the internal life of these partisan associations is notoriously scarce, their public displays do provide an opportunity to examine the role played by such rites in Ulster Catholic life. Not surprisingly, these rituals served many of the same functions as those of their Orange antagonists.

Although Ulster Catholics had no exact equivalent for the Orange Order's Twelfth of July celebration, they did use certain festive occasions for the purposes of public display. Throughout the century both Saint Patrick's Day (17 March) and Our Lady's Day (15 August) gave northern Catholic activists a chance to march in partisan parades. While both of these festivals were held on days that celebrated Catholic religious figures, these were not religious rites per se. Obviously, this does not mean that religion had no part in these ritualistic struggles over the control of public spaces. After all, the restoration of the Catholic church to its rightful place in Irish society constituted one of the central tenets of Irish Catholic political culture. But there was nothing particularly Catholic about these marches. For Ulster Catholics, these processions represented a conscious attempt to counter the loyalists' processional tradition. In many ways they were simply a Green version of the Orange Order's ritualistic assertions of secular power and territorial control on the Twelfth of July. As was so often the case, Ulster Catholics copied the public rites of their communal adversaries in an effort to counter the insults of Orange hegemony.

Of the two festival days mentioned above, Saint Patrick's Day marches were far more important in the early decades of the nineteenth century. To commemorate Ireland's patron saint, northern Catholics often paraded through the center of towns and villages in rural Ulster, playing partisan music and brandishing green and white banners. Like Orange processions, these marches derived much of their efficacy from the paramount importance of religious geography in Ulster society. When processionists marched through the center of a fair or townland, they typically were laying down a challenge to their Orange opponents, attempting to intimidate them through a ritual display of strength. The message of power was not particularly subtle. On 17 March 1849 two hundred Ribbonmen walked by William Beers's residence at Brook Cottage, County Down. According to Beers, a county magistrate and a leading Orangeman, the processionists halted outside his home and fired fifty shots over the heads of Beers and his family.[50] No one was harmed, but a clear message had been sent. It is easy to see why one early nineteenth-century observer viewed Saint Patrick's Day as simply an instance for the Catholic mob to "show their strength and sow the seed of disloyalty."[51]

If such processions aspired to parallel Orange celebrations of the Twelfth of July, they started from a position of great disadvantage. Put simply, northern Catholic sectarian associations lacked the power and organization of their Orange adversaries. Most Catholic processionists had to be content to exhibit their strength in Catholic-dominated or peripheral locations, far from the strongholds of the Orange heartland. Belfast Catholics did not march on Saint Patrick's Day until late in the nineteenth century. Of course, this does not mean that rural parades did not secure Orange attention. For rural Ulster's loyalist inhabitants, these marches merely highlighted the government's unwillingness to support its own loyal subjects. After one Saint Patrick's Day march in 1841, the Protestant residents of Creggan parish in south Armagh were so upset with the government's inaction that they petitioned the Lord Lieutenant: "That we have been greatly annoyed for some time past, and particularly so on Saint Patrick's Day last, with party processions of the so-called Teetotal Medal Men walking in military order with flags, sashes, and music; we are also threatened with a grand display on the Easter holidays coming."[52] At a time when the government explicitly had denied the Orangemen his right to march on the Twelfth of July, government violations of the terms of the Orange covenant struck a sensitive nerve with Ulster's loyalist population.

Like their Orange foes, Catholic activists used arches and flags to mark their territory. Partisan regalia often did more than delineate the lines of religious geography. In times of political controversy partisan markers were put up to challenge Orange foes. In one such instance Catholics from the Lawrencetown area of County Down threw a line with green leaves attached across a road that Orange party would have to take to reach the annual sham fight at Scarva. An alert J.P. prevented the inevitable clash by pulling down the arch before the Orange party arrived.[53] Although most territorial markers were essentially the Green equivalent of Orange regalia, some nationalist symbols reflected a more elaborate ideological background. This was especially true in the 1790s, when the Defenders imported symbols and ideas from the French Revolution.[54]

Northern Catholic secret societies also used rituals and public ceremonies to set standards of behavior within the Ulster Catholic community. Violators of these ideals often found themselves subjected to verbal and physical abuse. Because of their public opposition to Ribbonism, parish priests commonly were targeted for such ritual sanction. On 12 July 1829 a body of east Tyrone Catholics lay in wait for their Orange foes near Coalisland. The crowd hoisted a large green flag overhead to symbolize their defiance. When a priest attempted to reduce the tension by taking the flag down, he was abused and sent away by his parishioners.[55] Catholic activists used flags and other regalia in their battle to counter Orange hegemony. Much like the liberal Protestants who attempted to curb Orange activities, Catholics who opposed these communal rites often faced a ritualized form of justice.

Of course, such public rites did much more than convey opposition to Orangemen and parish priests. Like the rituals of the Orange Order, Ribbon ceremonies reveal parts of a belief system that members used to legitimize their actions. Not surprisingly, the interpretation of Irish history presented in these ritual displays differed fundamentally from the mythic chronicle portrayed in Orange festivals. In its reductionist narrative context, this imagery focused on the central theme of a nascent form of Irish nationalism: the historic dispossession of the Irish Catholic church and its adherents.

Popular partisan music illustrates these themes rather nicely. Like their Orange antagonists, Catholic marchers used party songs as weapons of provocation. The Catholic community possessed a wide repertoire of songs to publicly challenge loyalists. One popular tune was "The White Cockade":

No more the cuckoo hails the spring,
The woods no more with staunch-hounds ring;
The song from the glen, so sweet before,
Is hushed since Charles has left our shore.
The prince is gone; but soon will come

With trumpet sound and beat of drum;
Then up with a shout and out with blade
Hurrah for the Right and the White Cockade![56]

The impending return of the Stuart prince was a favorite subject for Catholic balladeers. But the general theme of restoration is more important than the particular Jacobite call. Rebel songs often yearned for the return of a deliverer who would lead the Irish peasantry to victory. This triumph would then usher in the mythical glorious days that Ireland had supposedly enjoyed before the devastating events of the seventeenth century.[57] In a public arena such songs proved to be as provocative as their Orange counterparts. On 15 May 1829 a sectarian riot broke out at a fair in Ballyjamesduff, County Cavan. The *Belfast Newsletter* reported that the clash originated in a dispute over a balladeer's rendition of "King O'Connell" and other political songs.[58] These rather millenarian songs had obvious political implications for Ulster Protestants and so proved to be very effective provocation devices.

Catholic processions also featured lavish and often exotic regalia. Although the symbols exhibited at such occasions were not as consistent as those of their Orange enemies, most of these parades presented a fairly coherent set of images. Many of these were obvious counters to Orange regalia—green and white flags and sashes. Some decorations were more elaborate, however. In early July 1828 a large concourse of "Ribbonmen" marched through the town of Castleshane, County Monaghan. At the head of the procession leaders carried a flag adorned with "treasonous phrases" on both sides.[59] On Saint Patrick's Day in 1834 an estimated four hundred to five hundred men assembled at Plumb's Bridge in Tyrone to march through the center of the town fair. According to one constable's report, a number of the "Ribandmen" were armed with short arms resembling carbines. He went on to provide a rich description of the march. Apparently, the processionists walked with four banners decorated in green and white. Each of the flags had a harp on one side and a man's profile on the reverse.[60] Like Orange regalia, the flags and banners displayed on Saint Patrick's Day symbolically reconstructed a particular view of Irish history, paying homage to Catholic heroes like Hugh O'Neill and Patrick Sarsfield. Such displays helped to keep the language of Irish nationalism alive in the early nineteenth century; a kind of symbolic bridge between 1798 and 1848.

Ribbonmen often distinguished themselves by wearing ornaments in their hats. On 17 March 1826 a large crowd marched through the town of Portglenone adorned with green and white flowers in their hats. According to a rather overheated *Enniskillen Chronicle* report, these decorations bore a close resemblance to "the artificial hats worn by ladies."[61] In Ulster's tense atmosphere of ritual confrontation even headgear could prove contentious. On two separate occasions in the late 1820s loyalists instigated riots by plucking consecrated palm sprigs from the hats of Catholic churchgoers.[62]

Private meetings and ceremonies were also highly ritualized in structure and content. Because of the shadowy nature of these secret sectarian societies, it is very difficult to gain a clear picture of the roles played by rituals and symbols employed outside the public arena. William Carleton's writings provide one of the best sources for the private world of these Ulster Catholic activists. Growing up in the border counties of south Ulster, Carleton's early exposure to the bloody clashes between Orangemen and their Catholic foes seems to have made a substantial impression, for he later wrote extensively on the evils of both Protestant and Catholic sectarian associations.[63] Although these fictional accounts of partisan conflict make good reading, the rich anecdotes of his autobiography provide the most insight into Ribbonism's private rites.

In 1814 William Carleton attended school in County Monaghan. Even at this early date Monaghan seems to have been a notoriously Ribbon county.[64] Carleton joined the local Ribbon society soon after arriving in the area, his initial hesitation greatly diminished by the effects of two glasses of poteen. Several young men directed the initiation ceremony, making Carleton take the Ribbon oath and learn the organization's passwords and signs (collectively known as "the goods"). The goods were replete with the vivid (if rather bizarre) millennial phraseology that Daniel O'Connell put to such effect in the political world of prefamine Ireland:

What age are we in?
The end of the fifth.
What's the hour?
Very near the right one.
Isn't it come yet?
The hour has come, but not the man.
When will he come?
He is within sight.[65]

On one level such obscure phrases merely created a kind of private language for members of the organization, lending mystery and authority to its typically rather mundane affairs. But it is more than that. While not nearly as explicit as Pastorini's prophecies, the language employed in the goods also reflected the diffuse millenarianism so pervasive in both Catholic and Protestant popular culture in prefamine Ireland.

A brief glance at Ribbon initiation oaths illustrates several of these same themes. Texts of these oaths are available in several sources, ranging from Carleton's autobiography to police records held in the modern archives of Belfast, Dublin, and London.[66] The form and content of these texts are remarkably consistent. A Ribbon candidate typically swore to uphold a list of ten to fifteen principles outlined in the initiation oath. Although some dealt with national politics and religious issues, a substantial proportion of the clauses focused on more materialistic issues like preferential dealing. This led the Sligo magistrate John O'Brien to cynically conclude in 1841 that whatever the Ribbon system's anti-Orange origins, "it has latterly been kept up by interested persons, principally for the sake of making money."[67] Such statements were especially apt in the late 1830s and early 1840s. With Orangeism formally checked by government regulation, some Ulster Ribbon societies seem to have become little more than criminal gangs.

But it would be wrong to conclude our discussions of the roles played by public and private ritual in this world on such a cynical and reductionist note. As Garvin and others have noted, the Ribbonmen played a vital role in preserving Defenderism's rich symbolic culture for the use of late Irish nationalists. By continually employing these potent symbols in their rites and ceremonies, these northern Catholic activists played an important role in maintaining the relevance and power of Irish nationalist discourse.

But the importance of Ribbon rituals should not be relegated to such an ethereal (if important) plane. They also played several pragmatic roles within this shadowy world. Perhaps the most important of these concerned the sense of solidarity that these rites reinforced within the Ulster Catholic activist community. One of the most critical features of any secret society is the sense of belonging that it gives to its adherents. This certainly was true of the Ribbonmen, whose members often spoke wistfully of the sense of brotherhood engendered in the smoky backrooms of otherwise obscure rural pubs in the Ulster borderlands. Ribbon rites contributed to this sense of cohesiveness by creating a ritualized language for the organization and thus adding a weighty air of mystery and importance to its proceedings. By allowing members to pose as traditional defenders of the faith (even though parish priests consistently opposed Ribbonism), public and private ritual helped to justify the aims and behavior of these determined opponents of all things orange.

This chapter has focused on the many roles played by ritual in nineteenth-century Ulster's habitual outbreaks of communal violence. We should be careful, however, in making too much of the ritualized nature of sectarian rioting. Even the most sensitive historian can fall into this trap. Natalie Zemon Davis made this mistake in her pioneering study, "The Rites of Violence": "Much of the religious riot is timed to ritual, and the violence seems often a curious continuation of the rite."[68] The implied links between ritual and violence here are far too static. The relationship between ritual and violence is much more dynamic than this statement implies.[69] This should not be surprising. After all, violence typically is not a one-way street.

Orange and Ribbon rites are better viewed as playing integral roles in setting the stage for partisan confrontation, both physically and ideologically. Processions acted as ritual assertions of the two conflicting visions that dominated northern political culture. Party violence often careened out of these structures, following torturous paths that no one could have planned. This became especially true in the second half of the nineteenth century, when urban-based industry came to dominate Ulster society. Ritualized confrontations proved especially deadly within the increasingly constricted confines of Victorian Belfast, triggering month-long sectarian riots that devastated entire neighborhoods in 1857, 1864, 1872, and 1886.

But one brief point remains before we move on to examine the relationship between urbanization and sectarian violence. Scholars are becoming increasingly aware of the vital role played by symbols and rituals within the world of popular politics. Perhaps it is here that Orange and Ribbon rites made their most dramatic impact on northern society. Through their processions and other public festivals, Orangemen and their Catholic opponents played roles totally disproportionate to their numbers within both northern communities. Both the public and private rites of these sectarian associations were grounded in antithetical but interlocked reductionist views of the Irish past and present. By continually translating contemporary events into the contexts of two such simplistic narratives, Orange and Ribbon rituals played critical roles in maintaining the vitality of two monochrome views of the Irish experience—in effect, acting as a kind of ritualized history lesson. This has been noted with regard to Ribbonism, whose preservation of a set of symbols for the use of later Irish nationalists has been seen as one of its more important attributes.[70] Orangeism also played this role of symbolic curator. In this light the Orange Order should be understood as the caretaker (and maker) of the ultra-Protestant myth system. This function became especially important in the formative years of modern Ulster politics in the late nineteenth century. In the 1880s, Protestant politicians confronted with the threat of Irish Home Rule were able to call upon a powerful array of symbols to mobilize opposition to Home Rule legislation. Some of these phrases and arguments were the very ones kept in nineteenth-century political dialogue by the vigorous efforts of the rank-and-file members of the Orange Order. This was just as true on the other side of the communal divide. The rituals and symbols which nationalist and unionist politicians used to forge a "new" political order resonated with particular power because they had been kept in the public sphere by the rituals of both the Loyal Orange Order and their Catholic opponents. The importance of such an inheritance should not be taken lightly.

◼ 5

Urbanization and Sectarian Rioting in Mid-Victorian Ulster

The town is a social form in which the essential properties of larger systems of social relations are grossly concentrated and intensified.

Phillip Abrams

Writing to an aristocratic colleague in 1858, Thomas Larcom, the ubiquitous under secretary of the late 1850s and 1860s (his Orange opponents derisively termed him "Government Larcom"), described the chronically tense nature of communal relations in mid-Victorian Belfast in the following terms: "The near-equality of the rival creeds in the lower classes will be a cause of turbulence for some time to come, but it will die out at last there as it has done elsewhere."[1] While many of Larcom's more cynical colleagues did not share his Whiggish optimism, none could challenge the validity of his analysis of contemporary conditions. By the early 1860s Belfast had become nearly as famous for its sectarian riots as it was for its textile and shipbuilding industries.

Of course, northern party battles continued apace outside of Belfast's urban environment. Major sectarian clashes at Dolly's Brae in 1849 and Derrymacash in 1860 more than upheld rural Ulster's honor and reputation for such behavior. By the middle of the century, however, sectarian riots increasingly were seen as a major urban problem. Belfast rioters acquired a particularly unsavory reputation. As one veteran official commented: "A Dublin mob is a concourse of gentlemen in comparison with that of Belfast. I've known them both well for the last thirty years, and I can frankly and honestly say a more unmitigated set of rowdies and ruffians never existed in any clime than the Belfast mob. There is a low morality and ferocity about them quite appalling. Their demoniac yells and imprecations outstrip anything you ever dreamt of in the degradation of human nature."[2] After 1840 it was increasingly the city of Belfast, and to a lesser extent Derry, that acted as the primary "cockpits of community conflict" in Ulster.[3] Major riots occurred in Belfast in 1857, 1864, 1872, and 1886, while party clashes rocked Derry in 1869 and 1883. But it was not just these high points of communal violence that shook Ulster's major urban centers. After 1843 some form of party rioting occurred on an annual basis in the city of Belfast. By midcentury sectarian violence in Ulster had become a largely urban phenomenon.

The shift of communal conflict from the countryside to the city was closely tied to the changing nature of Ulster society. On one level the change in fighting venues merely reflected the increasingly industrial and urban character of northern life. Ulster's transformation form a rural to an urban-based society was especially marked in the second half of the century, when Belfast's great textile and shipbuilding industries drove the economic life of the entire province forward.[4] The pace of urbanization in late nineteenth-century Ulster was truly astonishing. In 1861 only 20 percent of the population of the six Ulster counties that were to become Northern Ireland lived in towns of more than fifteen hundred people; by 1911 this figure had increased to 48 percent.[5] Of course, by 1861, the urbanization of Ulster society was well under way. This can be seen by examining Belfast's population growth, as illustrated here in Table 3.

Table 3. Population Growth, Belfast, 1801–1881

Year	Population	% Increase
1801	19,000	——
1811	27,832	46.5
1821	37,277	33.9
1831	53,287	43.0
1841	70,447	32.2
1851	87,062	23.6
1861	121,602	39.7
1871	174,412	43.4
1881	208,122	19.3

Source: Ian Budge and Cornelius O'Leary, Belfast: Approach to Crisis (London: Macmillan Press, 1973), 29.

While impressive enough on its own, Belfast's population growth is even more striking when placed within a broader context. In 1782, Belfast was

Table 4. Catholics in Belfast, 1784–1881

Year	Number of Catholics	% of Population
1784	1,092	8
1808	4,000	16
1834	19,712	32
1861	41,406	33.9
1871	55,575	31.9
1881	59,975	28.8

Source: Ian Budge and Cornelius O'Leary, *Belfast: Approach to Crisis* (London: Macmillan Press, 1973), 32.

the sixth largest city in Ireland, ranking below Dublin, Cork, Limerick, Galway, and Waterford. By the middle of the century only Dublin surpassed Belfast in total population, and all of Belfast's southern competitors lagged far behind in terms of industrial production. But Belfast's population increase was not just remarkable within an Irish context. It also had the highest growth rate of any major urban center in the British Isles between 1821 and 1901.

But it was not just the rate of population increase that made Belfast an increasingly likely arena for outbreaks of sectarian violence. Put simply, it was the nature as much as the number of migrants that led to a potentially explosive situation. As the nineteenth century progressed, Ulster Catholics flooded into Belfast, drawn by jobs created by the city's rapidly expanding industrial base (see Table 4). The influx of Catholic migrants truly transformed Belfast's social and religious composition, challenging long-standing Protestant dominance within the city. Not surprisingly, the growth of a substantial Catholic minority fundamentally altered communal relations in Belfast. Indeed, most nineteenth-century analysts believed that it was the mass migration of unskilled Catholic workers into the northern capital that lay at the heart of Belfast's "age of riots."[6]

Most Irish historians have paid little attention to the party riots of mid-Victorian Belfast. Those scholars who have looked at the evolution of sectarian conflict in the northern capital generally have agreed that Catholic migration constituted the primary cause of the disintegration of communal relations in the city.[7] According to this view, the substantial Catholic migration from the 1830s onward reawakened Belfast Protestantism's traditional siege mentality. This in turn created a situation where each group attempted to assert its power by dominating urban territory—a process that led to the deterioration of communal relations and regular outbreaks of sectarian rioting.[8]

This interpretation essentially puts forth a two-phase approach to the study of party conflict in nineteenth-century Belfast. In the first stage, which lasted from 1780 to roughly 1830, Belfast enjoyed relatively harmonious communal relations, existing as a kind of "Northern Athens" renowned for its civic liberalism and religious tolerance. Most scholars wishing to distinguish this initial period from the ensuing era of violence have stressed the high levels of financial support given by Belfast Protestants for the foundation of Catholic churches in the northern capital. Protestant subscriptions often were quite substantial. When Catholic leaders raised Saint Patrick's chapel in Donegall Street between 1811 and 1815, Protestants contributed approximately thirty percent of the total cost.[9] While the value of using such subscriptions as evidence of cordial communal relations is problematic at best, many scholars have stated that such donations symbolized the tranquil state of Belfast before 1830.

In the view of Andrew Boyd and Sybil Baker, two of the most well-known analysts of Belfast sectarianism, this era of relative calm ended in the 1830s, when large numbers of Ulster men and women migrated to Belfast from the countryside—folk who brought their passionate rural sectarianism to the northern metropolis. Sybil Baker puts it succinctly, if a bit melodramatically: "For all these people there were only two shades in the spectrum of Ulster's society and politics—Orange and Green."[10] With the appearance of the rural masses Belfast entered a new phase characterized by habitual party conflict—an era nicely initiated by the election riots of 1832.

If this two-phase framework is broadly correct, it errs in painting too simplistic a picture of sectarian relations in early nineteenth-century Belfast. Two problems are especially important. First, scholars would do well to remember Arthur Young's classic admonition that the nature of Irish communal relations cannot be gauged accurately by counting the number of Protestants willing to subscribe to the foundation of Catholic churches: "I must be free to own that when I have heard gentlemen who have favoured the laws as they now stand, urge the dangerous tenets of the Church of Rome, quote the cruelties which have disgraced that religion in Ireland . . . , I could not but smile to see subscriptions handed about for building a mass house."[11] Without dwelling overlong on this point, it is certain that even at the height of the so-called ecumenical age of the early nineteenth century, Belfast Protestant elite subscriptions for Catholic church construction did not represent any type of "union of hearts" between plebeian urban Protestants and Catholics.

This point is closely related to the second critical error made by Boyd and Baker. Both assert that Catholic and Protestant rural migrants brought sectarian violence to Belfast in the 1830s. This simply is not true. Major riots between the Orange and Green occurred as early as 1813, and Belfast rested on the threshold of sectarian conflict throughout the political controversies of the 1820s.[12] By failing to take into account outbreaks of party violence in Belfast before the 1830s, Boyd and Baker present a model of the evolution of Belfast communal relations that is far too reductionist for our purposes.

This does not diminish the importance of Catholic migration to the northern capital. The formation of a substantial Catholic minority there was an essential precondition for the deterioration of communal relations in Belfast. But Catholic migration itself was not the primary cause of Belfast's annual decline into bouts of sectarian violence. The political scientists Ian Budge and Cornelius O'Leary recognized as much in their excellent book on the historic background of the current troubles, *Belfast: Approach to Crisis*. After all, they argue, the Catholic percentage of Belfast's population reached its apex in the early 1830s, long before the onset of the real "age of riots." Other forces must have been at work. Searching for another explanatory factor, Budge and O'Leary can only conclude that previous scholarship seriously underestimated the provocative nature of the Orange Order's processional tradition.[13]

While Budge and O'Leary deserve credit for examining party violence in the era before 1830, their brief explanation also fails to convince. Orangeism certainly constituted another important piece of the puzzle, but it was not the fundamental cause of the habitual sectarian rioting that disturbed mid-Victorian Belfast. Although Orangemen certainly helped perpetuate the communal divide, sectarian division produced Orangeism, not vice versa. Again, this does not diminish the Orange Order's many contributions to partisan rioting in Belfast; both Catholic migration and loyalist provocations were essential ingredients in the mix from which Belfast sectarian violence emerged, but neither constituted the precipitating factor.

In order to reach the ultimate roots of Belfast's sectarian violence, one must look past tangible factors like Catholic migration and Orangeism to the more ethereal realm of beliefs and attitudes. Put simply, the underlying factor in the habitual outbreak of sectarian rioting was the continuing power of Ulster's two conflicting visions of how Irish society should be structured. As stated throughout this study, hard-line loyalists fervently believed that Ulster Protestants had a historic right to a special and ascendant position vis-à-vis the Irish Catholic population. On the other side of the communal chasm, Irish Catholics aimed to break this long-standing mold, trying to win back what they viewed as their historic rights. These are hardly revelatory statements, but too often historians have left this basic notion as implicit, seeing sectarian conflict in the north of Ireland as "natural" and "rooted deep in Irish history." It is the survival of these two passionately held belief systems that lies at the root of the seemingly endemic party violence that plagued Belfast after 1850.

With this idea firmly in place, one can examine the other essential ingredients of urban sectarian conflict. The most important factor is undoubtedly the formation of a sizable Catholic minority in Belfast. But it is not simply a question of numbers. The mere existence of a substantial Catholic enclave in Belfast did not trigger sectarian conflict—it was the changing nature of that Catholic population that made the crucial difference. As the century progressed, Irish Catholics became increasingly assertive in both national and street politics, actively campaigning for Catholic emancipation, the repeal of the Act of Union, an end to Orange processions, the disestablishment of the Church of Ireland, and substantial land reform measures—all issues designed to erode the ascendant position of Irish Protestants. In short, Catholics now regularly refused to play the subordinate role written for them.

The Belfast Riot of 1813 provides an excellent illustration of the mounting confidence of the Catholic community. The riot originated when a Catholic crowd gathered to oppose an Orange procession through the city center of the Twelfth of July. In the ensuing decades Daniel O'Connell's crusades for Catholic emancipation and Repeal both reflected and added to Irish Catholics' growing self-assurance. This in turn created a reaction among the various hard-line communities of Belfast Protestantism, giving confrontational partisan organizations and individuals a larger stage on which to act. Again, it was not simply the formation of a sizable Belfast Catholic minority that led to endemic communal conflict in that city. Rather, it was the fact that Belfast Catholics increasingly proved unwilling to submit to the loyalists' provocative exhibitions.

These factors have been touched on elsewhere.[14] What has not been adequately documented are the ways in which the urban environment itself played a critical enabling role in structuring the process of sectarian violence in mid-Victorian Belfast. In an important essay on British urban history Phillip Abrams noted that cities both concentrated and intensified essential characteristics of societal relations.[15] Both Belfast and Derry's nineteenth-century experiences speak to the truth of Abrams' model. Belfast in particular provided an almost perfect environment for the kind of ritualized partisan conflict that characterized nineteenth-century sectarian violence in Ulster. With its urban proletariat neatly packed into the Catholic

Pound and Protestant Sandy Row, Belfast activists could easily manufacture the kind of provocative incidents that led to widespread and prolonged bouts of communal rioting. And that was not all the city provided. Belfast even acted as a kind of arms dealer for partisan violence: "as a medium for replying to such points in the preacher's discourse as were not altogether acceptable to their ears, these cobble pavements could scarcely be surpassed."[16] In more ways than one, the city proved central to the style and content of partisan riots.

This environmental focus is particularly important after the 1820s, when broader societal trends made spatial issues more contentious. Multiple factors were at work here; popular politicization, industrialization, and urbanization all transformed northern political culture in the mid-Victorian era. Although the traditional structures of rural authority and exclusive politics retained more influence than is often asserted, these dynamic forces altered political relationships to such an extent that it is really impossible to speak of a sectarian moral economy after 1830. This does not mean, of course, that plebeian loyalists or their Catholic opponents discarded core beliefs about the need for communal defense or restoration. In fact, in many ways the degree of cultural continuity in the face of dynamic societal change remains the most remarkable aspect of the nineteenth-century Ulster experience. Still, the reforms that brought about the gradual inclusion of the male population into the political nation did have a measurable impact on the style and structure of sectarian violence.

Both the popular politicization accelerated by O'Connell's crusade for Catholic emancipation and, more directly, the creation of a representative system of popular electoral politics that gave the right to vote to more and more of the traditional antagonists of sectarian combat put even greater emphasis on spatial issues. In an era of mass politics, dominance now depended less on who owned land than who inhabited and controlled territory. In short, it is no accident that Belfast's "Age of Riots" coincided with the forces of industrialization, urbanization, and democratization.

Belfast's sectarian clashes left several important legacies. On the most basic level, of course, the northern capital had its dead, and they far outnumbered the martyrs from the storied nationalist rebellions of 1803, 1848, and 1867. More broadly, by keeping denominational division at the heart of public politics, habitual outbreaks of Catholic/Protestant violence played a key role in the formation of modern Ulster's polarized political culture. This had a dramatic impact on virtually every corner of northern life, ranging from the segregated housing that characterizes the North's urban environment to this day to the formation of the uniquely divided political system that emerged in the late nineteenth century. Despite (or perhaps because of) their obvious centrality to the evolution of sectarian conflict in Ulster, Belfast's nineteenth-century tradition of communal rioting remains largely unexamined. By analyzing the complex relationship between sectarian ideology, popular politics, and the urban environment, this chapter aims to begin the process of closing this disturbing gap.

"No Pure Breath of Heaven Ever Enters Here"

In 1782, the city of Belfast had about 13,000 inhabitants; a century later, it housed a population of over 200,000. Such rapid growth obviously had a tremendous impact on every facet of Belfast life. A comprehensive examination of the nature of nineteenth-century urbanization in Belfast lies far beyond the range of this study.[17] Rather, this chapter is concerned with analyzing those aspects of the urbanization process in Belfast (and to a lesser extent, Derry) that created an environment ripe for sectarian violence. But before examining the forces behind party riots in mid nineteenth-century Belfast, we must first explore the nature of this new urban battleground.

To most observers the city of Belfast was a synonym for progress in Ireland, a shining example of a thriving English town in a remote corner of a backward island. Samuel Carter Hall, an English visitor to Belfast, spoke for many when he stated, "it was something new to perceive, rising above the houses numerous tall and thin chimneys indicative of industry, occupation, commerce, and prosperity. . . . The pleasant and cheery impression we received was increased as we trod the streets; there was so much bustle; such an 'aspect' of business . . . , making us for the moment believe we were in a clean Manchester."[18] But English tourists were not the only ones impressed by Belfast's industrious appearance. Declaring his fervent opposition to Repeal at a great Conservative meeting in Belfast on 21 January 1841, the Rev. Henry Cooke cried: "Look at Belfast, and be a Repealer—if you can."[19] Although nationalist politicians tended to be more circumspect about Belfast, many were struck by Ulster's industrial capital. While uncharacteristically positive for a nationalist, the Young Ireland leader Thomas Francis Meagher's impressions of Belfast certainly echo Cooke's: "Your fate has been as singular as that of Robinson Crusoe and your ingenuity in making the most of a desert island has been no less remarkable."[20] With flourishing textile factories and bustling port facilities, even its most severe critics conceded that Belfast appeared to be a veritable model of urban accomplishment in Ireland.

Of course, there was another side to the story. The massive population

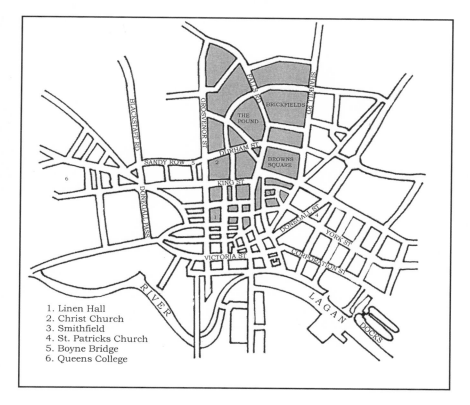

Belfast, circa 1870.

1. Linen Hall
2. Christ Church
3. Smithfield
4. St. Patricks Church
5. Boyne Bridge
6. Queens College

movement from rural Ulster to the urban metropolis created a housing and sanitation crisis in Belfast—an emergency that brought unprecedented challenges to the initiative and resources of local and city officials. Attracted by jobs created in textiles and, later, shipbuilding, men and women moved to Belfast from all across the north, creating deplorable housing conditions that matched any urban slum throughout the British Isles. Two talented social investigators, Dr. Andrew Malcolm, a physician long active in providing for the Belfast poor, and the Rev. William O'Hanlon, a minister of the Congregationalist Church in Upper Donegall Street between September 1849 and October 1854, documented this darker side of Belfast's urbanization process in two separate reports in 1852 and 1853.[21] Taken together, these two reports provide a number of rich insights into the lives of mid-Victorian Belfast's lower-class inhabitants.

Malcolm and O'Hanlon each found that the Belfast poor endured living conditions that were both congested and squalid. Above all, lower-class residents lived in a very constricted physical environment. Malcolm noted that the majority of the Belfast poor lived in two-story houses with two seven-by-ten-foot rooms per family. Such accommodations were "manifestly insufficient" for ten people; Malcolm reported that it was not uncommon for up to twenty people to sleep in such apartments.[22] Walking through poverty-stricken Brady's Row near the city center, O'Hanlon described the dilapidated character of several such homes: "Here my companion and myself fixed upon two houses as specimens of the whole. In one of these we found that seven persons live and sleep in the same room—their beds, if such they may be called, lying upon the floor. The desolation and wretchedness of this apartment—without windows and open in all directions—it is utterly impossible to describe."[23] Focusing his attention on sanitation, Malcolm painted a similar portrait of the industrializing city: "In Ballymacarrett the rain from the clouds and the sewage from the dwelling are at liberty to make their own intersections and channels without any interference on the part of man."[24] Of course, working conditions were not much better. Unskilled men, women, and children generally toiled long, dreary hours in west Belfast's dangerously unregulated textile factories. Such appalling conditions had a dramatic impact on the life expectancy of the Belfast poor. In the decade preceding 1841 approximately forty-five percent of all deaths in Belfast resulted from various "epidemic, endemic, and contagious" diseases.[25]

Of course, nearly every urban and industrial center in the British Isles faced similar problems. Even in Ireland, Belfast hardly stood alone. If anything, conditions for the Dublin poor were much worse than those of their Belfast compatriots. Furthermore, some working-class districts in Belfast provided much better living conditions. Both Malcolm and O'Hanlon found Sandy Row and other more suburban districts much more amenable to healthy living. But the overall tenor of these two reports remains clear—the vast majority of Belfast's poor lived in crowded and unsuitable housing with little sanitation.

But it was not only inner-city housing that was congested. Most city inhabitants lived their entire lives in extremely constricted physical spaces. Urban streets were narrow and open public spaces rare. People literally lived right on top of one another.[26] Spatial issues had an important impact on communal relations in Belfast. The open spaces that provided a kind of protective buffer zone between rural Catholics and Protestants were simply nonexistent in this new urban environment. Such compressed spaces produced conditions ripe for sectarian conflict, making it easier for partisan activists to manufacture and maintain prolonged sectarian riots.

As stated earlier, these developments were not unique to Belfast. Similar urban slums sprouted up in the nineteenth century in a plethora of industrial cities throughout the British Isles.[27] What made this urban environment somewhat atypical was the segregated nature of its urban districts. Building on existing settlement patterns, Belfast Catholics and Protestants quickly created and maintained tightly knit working-class neighborhoods that remained nearly pure in their religious affiliation.[28]

Catholic settlement in Belfast traditionally had centered on Hercules Street, a district located just west of the city center. Butcher shops dominated this major thoroughfare—men who slaughtered their livestock for the Smithfield markets. While the markets certainly provided sustenance for the region's rapidly growing population, the fact that butchers regularly killed their animals on the premises certainly contributed mightily to the street's unhealthy and unsavory reputation.[29] As Catholics flooded in from rural Ulster to work in west Belfast's textile mills, Catholic urban settlement moved southwest from this traditional base, pushing across Smithfield toward the Lower Falls Road. This working-class district, collectively known as the Pound, was almost entirely Catholic by midcentury.[30] The growth of the Pound created a great deal of consternation in the Protestant areas of west Belfast, as the new Catholic inhabitants competed for both territorial control and unskilled jobs with their Protestant brethren. It was here that many of the party battles would be fought.

The growth of the Catholic Pound encroached upon two traditional areas of Protestant working-class settlement, Sandy Row and the Shankill Road. These districts were home to the Protestant weavers of west Belfast, famous for their hard-core loyalism. In many ways the geographic proximity between these communal enclaves continually reinforced the hard-line partisan ideologies present within west Belfast's proletarian districts. Conflict zones developed wherever the Catholic and Protestant neighborhoods came into contact. Both Durham Street, which ran directly from Sandy Row through the center of the Pound, and Brown Square, which existed as a militant Protestant island in the midst of a rising Catholic sea, provided a number of potential battlegrounds for party warfare. For all their notoriety, however, the Smithfield area achieved the preeminent reputation as an arena for conflict. Indeed, Smithfield's standing was already firm in 1853, when O'Hanlon reported: "We penetrated Smithfield court, which is not unworthy of its patronymic. This is, we learned on the spot, the battleground of the whole neighborhood; and wrathful pugilists resort thither, even from the most distant parts of town, to settle their disputes after their own fashion, undisturbed by impertinent policemen."[31] Located on the edge of a frontier zone, this region would be one of the major theaters of communal warfare throughout the second half of the century.

Two other enclaves deserve mention before we move on to analyze the relationship between these segregated neighborhoods and the seemingly endemic sectarian violence of mid to late nineteenth-century Belfast. Another critical region of Catholic settlement lay at Cromac, where Catholic navvies ensconced themselves around the middle of the century. The navvies, brought in for harbor and railroad construction in the late 1830s and the 1840s, provided the traditionally overmatched Belfast Catholic community with an unprecedented amount of muscle. As others have noted, the appearance of such a tight-knit and effective fighting force temporarily tipped the balance of power toward the Belfast Catholics in this era, forcing loyalists to reorganize under the guise of the Belfast Protestant Operatives' Society and later the reconstituted Orange Order.[32]

The Cromac navvies eventually found their foil in north Belfast, where the dramatic growth of shipbuilding and engineering in the 1860s and 1870s created a staunch neighborhood of skilled Protestant workers—a group quite willing to fight to maintain their high status within northern industry. North Belfast's ship carpenters became particularly famous for their loyalist activism, acting as an effective counterweight to the muscle of the Catholic navvies. Skilled Protestant shipyard workers would be involved in a majority of the most heated battles of the late nineteenth century. These then, were some of the major religious and occupational neighborhoods of mid-Victorian Belfast.

But how did the existence of such segregated enclaves affect the prosecution of sectarian violence in the northern metropolis? There has been very little serious discussion about the relationship between this segregated urban environment and outbreaks of sectarian violence. Most scholars simply have assumed that the physical separation of Belfast's Catholic and Protestant working classes reinforced the sectarian divide by allowing both communities to maintain traditional prejudices with relative ease. The work that has been done on residential segregation has concentrated on Northern Ireland's contemporary troubles. While this study has studiously avoided using data from contemporary Northern Ireland to examine conditions in nineteenth-century Ulster, the recent literature on residential segregation does provide a series of important insights into the crucial relationship between communal settlement patterns and sectarian violence.

Frederick W. Boal, a geographer at Queens University, Belfast, pioneered work in this field. Examining conditions along the Falls/Shankill divide in 1967–1968, Boal found that residential segregation provided a series of functions for the area's inhabitants.[33] First, by strictly regulating day-to-day social contact, urban segregation helped to preserve each community's distinctive beliefs and way of life. More directly for our purposes, Catholic/Protestant separation provided both communities with ready bases for ethnic self-defense. Finally, segregated districts furnished the more aggressive members of the community with a safe base from which to attack their enemies.[34] Using Boal's work as a model, John Darby argues that tight residential segregation, with its ritual flashpoints, local battlegrounds, and intense local pride, was a prerequisite for the sectarian riots that have characterized Northern Ireland since 1969.[35] Although recent scholarship has added the critical caveat that segregation has also prevented a number of the "sharper penalties of community conflict,"[36] the integral role played by the highly segregated urban environments of Belfast and Derry in shaping the contours of twentieth-century sectarian violence is now rightly recognized throughout the voluminous literature on the current troubles.

Each of these ideas is just as applicable to the mid-Victorian age as it is to the late twentieth century. Using the models employed by both Boal and Darby, we can begin to examine the critical relationship between the residential segregation of west Belfast's working-class districts and the sectarian rioting that occurred repeatedly throughout the second half of the nineteenth century.

Several themes emerge from such an analysis. First and foremost, the constricted and segregated urban environment of both Belfast and Derry provided a nearly perfect arena for the predominant vehicle of sectarian conflict in nineteenth-century Ulster—the party procession. As shown throughout this study, partisan public displays triggered the vast majority of substantial communal riots throughout the century. By clearly demarcating Catholic or Protestant territory, the segregated urban environment made it much easier for activists to provoke party conflict. In times of political controversy all one had to do to start a riot was to route an Orange procession through a particularly sensitive neighborhood or to put up a green arch over a street contingent to a Protestant residential area. Such ritual invasions played a catalytic role in the infamous Belfast riots of 1857, 1864, 1872, and in a major riot in Derry in 1869. In Belfast's denominationally divided and compressed environment, both hard-line loyalists and their Catholic adversaries had a perfectly constructed arena for triggering repeated bouts of communal rioting.

Local history and working-class folk memories also played a key part in the prosecution of sectarian riots. When combined with urban segregation, local sensitivities to symbolic assaults made it much easier for party activists to trigger sectarian conflict. As time passed, the frontier zones and former battlegrounds of west Belfast achieved a certain status as party flashpoints. Because of their prominence in partisan battles past and present, areas like Durham Street, the Brickfields, Brown Square, and Cullingtree Road became especially sensitive localities in this communal contest for territorial control. This kind of geographical hypersensitivity made it much more difficult to keep the peace.

Of course, geography was not the only variable involved here. The city's churches, schools, and even graveyards provided both Protestant and Catholic crowds with a vast array of symbolic targets. Rioters knew that assaults on these cultural and spiritual touchstones would evoke a response from their party adversaries. In the wake of a major party riot that broke out in Durham Street of the Twelfth of July in 1852,[37] a loyalist mob marched out to wreak vengeance on the Catholic cemetery at Friar's Bush near Stranmillis. When the crowd reached its destination, it began to attack the cemetery itself, throwing stones at grave diggers' homes and firing shots into the sacred burial ground. Before dispersing, the Protestant crowd even threatened to pull down the cemetery's cross and demolish its gravestones.[38] Twelve years later, a loyalist procession returned to the cemetery, bearing an effigy of Daniel O'Connell. Things did not end so quietly that year, as the situation deteriorated into the month-long destruction of the 1864 riots. Such symbolic assaults were certainly not new in Ulster. Churches in the province's many sectarian frontier zones had suffered throughout the century. The crowded confines of west Belfast, however, made such ritual destruction both easier and more effective.

Finally, although it is undoubtedly true that working-class segregation reduced the level of day-to-day conflict that would have arisen in a more integrated residential area, the divided nature of the urban environment certainly contributed to the continuing relevance and vitality of the irreconcilable worldviews that dominated northern political culture. By creating communally pure urban districts, segregation discouraged those day-to-day social contacts that might have been expected to erode such diametrically opposed attitudes. Mixed housing, interdenominational marriage, and even Catholic/Protestant employment situations all remained relatively rare in nineteenth-century Belfast. In short, mid- and late-Victorian Belfast had very few, if any, truly mixed proletarian spheres, public or private. Aided by an increasingly contentious political climate and the formation of a constricted and segregated urban setting, the two conflicting visions that had dominated Ulster life throughout the century also reigned supreme in the new urban centers of the north.

The Sepoys of Sandy Row and the Pound: Urban Riots, 1832–1869

Most government administrators in mid-Victorian Ireland must have sympathized with Lord Naas's angry outburst in 1858: "With the help of God we'll put down these riots if it entails the necessity of quartering a policeman or a soldier in half the houses in Belfast."[39] The outbreak of party riots in Belfast provided an annual headache for Dublin Castle's leading officials. In particular, the Orange Order's celebration of the Twelfth of July required intricate security arrangements that involved the large-scale movement of magistrates and troops from all over Ireland, and not just for Belfast. In 1869 Dublin Castle deployed forty-eight magistrates and twenty-six hundred policemen throughout the north of Ireland for the Twelfth festivities.[40] It is no wonder that administrators became alternatively frustrated and obsessed with party conflict in Ulster. With the exceptions of the threats posed by the Land League and the Irish Republican Brotherhood, Ulster's increasingly brutal sectarian riots provided the greatest challenge to public order within the relative tranquillity of postfamine Ireland.

A number of different factors triggered sectarian clashes during the high age of urban riots. Party processions and other forms of ritualized public exhibition were by far the premier catalyst, providing the primary impetus for major clashes in 1813, 1843, 1864, and 1872. Amazingly, the famous 1864 riots were initiated by a nationalist procession in Dublin, one hundred miles south of Belfast's increasingly narrow ground. The second most common cause was nakedly political: contested elections produced substantial party riots in 1832 and 1835. As we shall see, even royal visits could cause problems; Prince Arthur's visit to Derry led to a major riot in 1869. But political events did not touch off all major sectarian riots. Perhaps the most famous partisan battle of the century, the Belfast riots of 1857, were triggered by the provocative and controversial public sermons of Protestant preachers.

If the specific events that initiated these riots seem wide-ranging, at least two common trends run through the origins of all of these partisan conflicts. First, the major sectarian riots of nineteenth-century Belfast and

Derry all emerged from set-piece confrontations. None of these clashes were spontaneous; all originated in some form of partisan celebration or public meeting. Second, a perceived threat to the status quo lay underneath the outbreak of each of these communal riots. This typically centered on political developments, as Catholic nationalists worked to erode Protestant control of local and national politics. But political matters did not stand alone; political forces often were fused with economic and territorial issues into a more generalized and powerful sense of threat. In a broad sense the increasing level of Catholic political agitation, combined with the rapid growth of the Pound, led many Protestants to the belief that they were being overwhelmed by a Catholic tide.[41] The Orange ritual displays that so often gave rise to sectarian rioting were a way of reminding the growing Belfast Catholic population just who remained in the ascendant. As Orangeism's official historians have stated, "Where you could walk, you were dominant, and the other things followed."[42]

This same process can be seen in the general aims of the rioters. On a basic level, of course, these riots were simple contests of partisan strength—attempts to gain the upper hand in the struggle for communal ascendancy in Belfast. But that was not the whole story. Riots often emerged from protests of particularly egregious violations of communal codes of conduct. This is certainly what occurred in 1864, when loyalists, angered by the government's decision to allow a nationalist procession in Dublin while maintaining the ban on all Orange public celebrations, attacked a train carrying Belfast Catholics who had attended the Dublin festivities—an assault that led to a month-long bout of party violence in Belfast. Finally, both communities used sectarian riots to enforce residential segregation in Belfast, especially after 1857. In each of the clashes of the mid-Victorian era rioters concentrated a particular fury on those households that were unlucky enough to live on the wrong side of the sectarian fence. If mixed proletarian neighborhoods had been rare before 1850, they were even more so by 1872. Sectarian riots had seen to that, ensuring that Belfast's working-class districts would not be tainted by the dangers of mixed settlement.

One central thread runs through both the diverse events that triggered urban sectarian riots and the aims of the rioters themselves: riots between loyalists and their Catholic opponents originated in the perception that the central tenets of their antagonistic worldviews had been violated or were in serious danger of being transgressed. In this situation hard-line members of each community rallied to attack or defend the status quo. The remainder of this chapter uses this framework to examine three major party riots in close detail: the Belfast riots of 1843 and 1857 and the Derry riot of 1869.

Repeal Repulsed? The Belfast Riots of 1843

The Belfast riots of 1843 must be viewed within the broader context of two events: Daniel O'Connell's movement to repeal the Act of Union and the surge of Catholic migration into west Belfast in the late 1830s and early 1840s. By 1843 O'Connell's Repeal campaign had reached the apex of its power. Monster meetings throughout Leinster and Munster regularly attracted hundreds and thousands of supporters.[43] With such immense public demonstrations of power behind it, the Repeal tide seemed unstoppable. Like Catholic emancipation, Repeal had radical implications for Ulster's sectarian balance of power. On a national level, at least, the wind definitely seemed to be blowing in a Catholic direction.

This trend in national political life was echoed on a local level in Belfast. Here, Catholic migration from rural Ulster had a definite impact on the city's communal relations. With Catholic settlement expanding south and west from its traditional base on Hercules Street, the new Catholic immigrants posed a definite threat to Protestant control of proletarian west Belfast. This became especially apparent after the 1830s, when Catholic navvies were brought in to work on the massive harbor and railroad projects needed to cater to the city's rapidly expanding industrial base. The navvies largely settled in the Cromac district, providing the Catholic community with a militant fighting force.

When this demographic trend combined with the surge of Repeal politics in 1843, Belfast loyalists responded in the way they always had—they formed a Protestant defensive association. With the Orange Order banned since 1835, activists needed to create a legal organization to mobilize loyalist strength in the face of the Catholic threat. This defect was soon amended by the Rev. Tresham Gregg, who brought together a large concourse of staunch loyalists to form the Belfast Protestant Operatives' Society at the Exchange Rooms on 3 April 1843.[44] Belfast loyalism now had an instrument to oppose the growing Catholic tide.

As the spring of 1843 progressed, sectarian tension mounted throughout the province. On 30 May a partisan confrontation deteriorated into a substantial riot near Dungannon, where Orange processionists wrecked several Catholic homes.[45] But loyalists made their real stand against their opponents within the city of Belfast. With support for Repeal advancing throughout the south of Ireland, communal violence would come to a head in the northern capital that summer. As always, the July marching season provided the occasion for a ritualistic test of party strength.

Things started quietly enough. With the organizational strength of the

Orange Order absent, no major procession occurred in Belfast. Of course, things were not perfectly quiet; Protestant youths marched with a fife and drum in Ballymacarrett and some teenagers engaged in stone-throwing flourishes in west Belfast.[46] But nothing approaching a major sectarian riot occurred. This relative tranquillity proved to be a false dawn, as both Catholic and Protestant mobs began to wreck houses on the edges of the Pound and Sandy Row the following evening. As the carnival of violence drew to a close that night, each side claimed to be afraid of what the other might do.[47]

If the loyalists of the newly organized Belfast Protestants Operatives' Society had been eager to put the Catholics of west Belfast in their proper place, the Pound's Catholic inhabitants seemed quite willing to take up the challenge. On the next evening the Pound mob put its numerical advantage to good use, driving the boys of Sandy Row from their traditional battle-field near Mulholland's Mill. The *Northern Whig's* report expressed the Catholic mob's newfound ascendancy in west Belfast quite bluntly: "The number of the Repeal party continued to increase vastly, and it became necessary for the Protestants to join with the police in order to protect the neighborhood and the police themselves."[48] Belfast Catholics later commemorated their victory by turning a funeral procession into a massive public demonstration for Repeal. Five thousand to six thousand people purportedly marched along west Belfast's sectarian frontier in a well-ordered display of Catholic strength.[49] Clearly, Belfast Catholics had won the day in July 1843.

The Belfast riots of 1843 provide an excellent example of the typical process that generated sectarian conflict in nineteenth-century Ulster. Both the success of the Repeal campaign and the movement of Ulster Catholics into the industrial heartland of west Belfast presented a fundamental challenge to the political and economic underpinnings of Protestant privilege. With the Orange Order in temporary abeyance, Belfast loyalists responded as ultra-Protestants had throughout the century, organizing a defensive association to put the offending Catholics in their place. In 1843 their efforts proved unsuccessful; increased levels of Catholic migration to Belfast in the 1830s and early 1840s temporarily had shifted the balance of power in the metropolis. This Catholic victory proved to be short-lived. Within a decade Orangemen and their loyalist supporters had regained their ascendant position in Belfast.[50]

Perceived threats to Ulster Protestant power triggered most of the substantial party riots of mid-Victorian Belfast. As shown throughout this study, loyalists typically used partisan festivals like the Twelfth of July to respond to these challenges. Accordingly, the Orangeman's "historic right" to walk lay at the heart of the origins of major riots in Belfast in both 1864 and 1872. But things were not always that straightforward. The infamous Belfast riots of 1857 illustrate just how complex such events could be.

The Word of God? The Belfast Riots of 1857

As the summer marching season opened in Belfast in 1857, few magistrates or policemen thought that it would be particularly problematic. To be sure, things would not be perfectly quiet. William Tracy, a resident magistrate who had lived in Belfast since 1849, could not remember a trouble-free Twelfth in the city. Moreover, party relations in 1857 seemed particularly tense. Hotly contested municipal elections in April had brought out stone-throwing crowds in Sandy Row and the Pound.[51] But on the whole, nothing seemed particularly unusual. Thomas Green, the chief constable of the Belfast night police, undoubtedly spoke for the vast majority of Belfast officials in 1857 when he stated: "I did not anticipate any riot supposing the parties could be kept in their own ground."[52] Sectarian animosity certainly remained, but the authorities were quietly confident in their ability to contain the two parties.

The events that led to the Belfast riots of 1857 occurred on the Twelfth of July at Christ Church, an Anglican church positioned precariously close to the city's major sectarian fault line. That morning, approximately three hundred men walked to Christ Church from Sandy Row. According to the testimony of one witness, each of the men marched with an orange lily in the buttonhole of his jacket. Once inside the church, the men added to the display by putting on orange sashes.[53] The men of Sandy Row joined the congregation at Christ Church that day—a huge assemblage that had come to hear the Rev. Thomas Drew deliver a special Twelfth of July sermon. Drew, who had been vicar of Christ Church since 1833, was renowned among hard-line Protestants for his ardent support of political Protestantism and his almost fanatical hatred of all things that smacked of Roman Catholicism. Drew's sermon that day did not undermine his anti-Catholic reputation. He began by giving a particularly emotional and graphic indictment of Roman Catholicism: "Of old time, lords of high degree, with their own hands, strained on the rack the delicate limbs of Protestant women; prelates dabbled in the gore of helpless victims; and the cells of the Pope's prisons were paved with the calcined bones of men and cemented with the gore of human hair!"[54] After whipping up his congregation with this emotive salvo of anti-Catholicism, Drew settled back into a more conventional Twelfth of July sermon, concentrating on the embattled history of Irish Protestantism and the need for vigilant Protestant unity in the face of the constant Irish Catholic threat.

If Drew's graphic language was noteworthy, such sermons were by no means rare. But in the already tense atmosphere of the marching season news of Drew's sermon and a rumor that the local police had escorted the Orange lodges to Christ Church moved rapidly through the Pound,[55] which mobilized quickly to confront the Sandy Row Orangemen outside Christ Church. While the police managed to keep the two parties apart on this particular occasion, the first stage of the deadly Belfast Riots of 1857 had begun.

Rioting first occurred in earnest on the evening of the next day. While the two mobs met at one of west Belfast's traditional battlegrounds—a strip of wasteland lying along Albert Street that divided the Pound from Sandy Row—both parties concentrated their energies on wrecking houses. Not surprisingly, those few Catholics and Protestants who lived in districts dominated by their communal enemies suffered the most.[56] Groups of Catholic and Protestant teenagers broke window panes and assaulted the houses of those unlucky enough to live on the wrong side of the sectarian divide. By most accounts, Protestants did the vast bulk of the damage, their primary focus being a series of houses in Quadrant Street owned by William Watson, a wealthy Catholic businessman.[57]

By 18 July the rioting had become more serious, with Orangemen arriving from the outlying loyalist districts of Lisburn and Newtownbreda to reinforce their brethren.[58] The two parties again met on the wasteland, with only the police keeping the Sandy Row mob from attacking the Pound itself. At one point a body of loyalists succeeded in breaking through police ranks and into the Pound. The Protestant party proceeded to assault houses in Quadrant Street again, making a large bonfire of the damaged shutters, doors, and window frames. After a lengthy delay, the police dispersed the loyalist mob, driving it back across the wasteland to Sandy Row.[59] While the two parties continued to fire gunshots at one another over the next few days, the first phase of the 1857 riots was now over.

Unlike past occasions, however, things did not end with July's violence. Although outbreaks of party violence had ceased temporarily, communal tensions remained precariously high throughout late July and August 1857. Two issues dominated discussion during this interim period: the formation of a Catholic gun club in west Belfast and the provocative public sermons of evangelical street preachers. These two issues kept communal relations on edge throughout the late summer and early fall of 1857.

The issue of a Catholic gun club arose on 6 August, when several hundred Catholic working men assembled at Smithfield Theatre to consider the best means for future self-defense. Members of the crowd argued that the July riots had shown that both the government and the police were unable or unwilling to protect the Catholic community from Orange outrages. In this situation the inhabitants of Catholic west Belfast had to look to themselves. "Arm for your self-defense!" became the common refrain of the assembly—thus, the gun club, where members pooled their limited resources to purchase arms from a willing local retailer. According to the chairman of the meeting, John Hacket, an associate editor with the Belfast Catholic newspaper, the *Ulsterman,* the gun club's object was merely "to meet Orange aggression that might occur in the future."[60]

There was nothing novel about the formation of Catholic gun clubs in 1857. In many ways they were merely a rough urban equivalent of the Defenders or the Ribbonmen, groups designed to counter Orange assertions of communal hegemony. But as previously noted, the arms issue always provoked a reaction in Ulster. A belief that the right to bear arms in Ireland should be limited to loyal Protestants lay at the center of loyalist belief. Newspaper reports about the growth of Catholic gun clubs provoked fear and consternation among working-class Belfast Protestants.

Alarmed by the prospect of more firearms flowing into the powder keg of west Belfast, the authorities responded to the formation of the gun clubs by clamping down on arms sales in Belfast, effectively limiting the ability to procure firearms. Although the authorities successfully regulated the growth of Catholic gun clubs in 1857, they were a sure sign that sectarian contention was accelerating in Belfast. Trouble still remained on the horizon. All that was needed was a new spark to set it off.

The issue that triggered renewed rioting centered on evangelical Protestant street preaching. Prior to July's party fights, the Belfast Parochial Mission, a Protestant organization set up to combat "spiritual destitution" in December 1856,[61] had planned a series of controversial public sermons beginning on 19 July. These sermons were to be delivered on the famous steps of the Customs House by various ministers of the Church of Ireland; well-known anti-Catholic controversialists led by Thomas Drew and the Rev. William McIlwaine. While the individual titles of the addresses seemed innocuous enough, the title of McIlwaine's Lent lectures on Popery, "Is Popery Christianity?" underlined the provocative anti-Catholicism of the series.[62]

Controversial open-air preaching certainly was not new to central Belfast's public spaces. Such sermons had occurred throughout the 1850s, rarely sparking extensive public outcry. But things were very different in the summer of 1857, as communal tension remained high in the aftermath of the July riots. In this volatile climate the Belfast authorities argued that such open-air sermons were "frought with danger to life and property" and should be delayed if not canceled.[63] McIlwaine reluctantly concurred and agreed to postpone his lecture series until the controversy subsided.

The strategy initially seemed to work, for McIlwaine's first public sermon on 9 August was met with relative indifference. Unfortunately, this tranquillity proved to be something of a false dawn. When one of McIlwaine's colleagues, Thomas Roe of east Belfast, attempted to deliver a similar lecture two weeks later, police arrested several men who had attempted to rush the podium.[64] Somewhat shaken by this violent reaction to its work, the Belfast Parochial Mission canceled the remainder of its public lecture series.[65]

But things did not end there. Many loyalists were outraged by the cancellation of the sermons, viewing McIlwaine's conciliatory gesture as a surrender to the "Romish mob."[66] They need not have worried. A loyalist defender soon emerged from the ultra-Protestant camp in Belfast, a fact reflected in the sarcastic tones of the *Belfast Daily Mercury:* "But although the episcopal clergy acted in this truly Christian spirit, they, in the opinion of some wonderfully wise men, by so doing, abandoned the Protestant cause, sacrificed Protestant principle, and imperiled Protestant rights—yet happily, a champion was found in such an hour of danger to rush to the rescue, and in his own person to vindicate the outraged rights of the Protestant community."[67] The new Protestant "champion" was the Rev. Hugh Hanna, a Presbyterian divine born in Dromara, County Down. Ordained as a minister in 1851, Hanna acquired a solid reputation as a true Protestant and militant anti-Catholic while ministering to his congregation in Berry Street. He now announced that he would pick up where the Belfast Parochial Mission had left off, declaring that he would preach on the Custom House steps on 6 September.[68] Testifying before a later commission of inquiry, Hanna defended his decision to take up street preaching: "Our most valuable rights have been obtained by conflict; and if we cannot maintain them without that, we must submit to the necessity."[69] The more conciliatory *Northern Whig* quickly got to the heart of the matter: "Our annual explosion of Orange ferocity and Roman Catholic reprisals is being converted into a weekly social meeting."[70]

On the night before Hanna's scheduled performance, communal tensions were heightened by a rumor that the hated Thomas Drew was to speak at the Custom House on the following day. A poster printed secretly at the offices of the *Ulsterman* was distributed throughout the Pound and other areas of central Belfast. The placard was a ringing Catholic call to arms.

DOWN WITH OPEN-AIR PREACHING! (DOWN WITH THE FANATIC DREW, THE SQUINTING DIVINE!) THE ENEMY OF TRANQUILLITY AND PEACE! Gather to the Custom House on Sunday at 3 o'clock and give the Orange bigot such a check that he will not attempt open-air preaching again. Catholics of Belfast, Down, and Antrim! We see by the public Placards that our religion is again to be assailed, our public walks Obstructed by that low and ruffianly system of Ranterism which has lately been got up by our evangelical neighbors for the sole purpose of giving annoyance to their Catholic neighbours. . . . We therefore call on all our Catholic neighbours and brethren to come and defend their rights.[71]

Although Drew was not actually scheduled to preach the next day, the belief that he was involved in the lecture series seemingly mobilized the Pound.[72] The sixth of September clearly was going to be a long day for the authorities.

On 6 September the Rev. Hugh Hanna began to preach in the rain to a large crowd outside the Seaman's Church in Corporation Square. In an attempt to placate the authorities Hanna had decided to hold his meeting away from the controversial steps of the Customs House. Despite the change in venue, those responsible for law and order clearly anticipated conflict. Several magistrates, the entire town police force, and a large body of the Irish Constabulary positioned themselves on the periphery of the crowd. This ready stance proved to be the correct one, for a large body of Catholics assembled outside the Customs House, where "Dr. Drew" was supposed to speak. When the Catholic crowd heard that Hanna was preaching in Corporation Square, the mob rushed down Donegall Quay toward the evangelical meeting.[73]

As the angry Catholic mob entered the square, individuals began to throw stones into the congregation listening to Hanna. At that point the balance suddenly shifted, as a body of Protestant shipwrights armed with trundles emerged from a nearby dockyard. Clearly, the police were not the only ones prepared for conflict. Violence spread quickly, as paving stones and shipbuilding tools flew back and forth between the two parties. While no deaths were reported to the authorities, rioting spread throughout central Belfast that afternoon and evening.[74]

There were no more substantial outbreaks of party conflict over the course of the next week. With a virtual army of police and troops at their disposal,[75] the authorities prevented pitched rioting in Belfast neighborhoods with relative ease. But unfortunately, things did not rest there. Throughout the week the "sepoys of Sandy Row and the Pound" used violence and intimidation to force Catholic and Protestant families from their midst. Things proved particularly difficult for the few remaining Catholic families living among the mills of Sandy Row: "Under the Dehli code of the Sandy Row mutineers a more open system was carried out; and as we have heard, 'notices to quit' were served by persons who used no disguise whatever. Several families of the Roman Catholic party were obliged to leave their houses on the edict of these self-constituted dictators; and where prompt obedience was not paid to the order, very summary proceedings followed."[76] While the troubles had calmed down by 17 September,[77] the denouement of the second phase of the Belfast riots had made one thing clear: housing, like all other aspects of life in west Belfast, was not free from the dictates of Ulster's conflicting visions. Communal purity must be maintained.

As one would expect, the Belfast riots of 1857 received a great deal of attention from both the Irish and the British press. In their search for an explanation, newspapers on both sides of the Irish Sea came up with a host of interpretations. Their analyses variously stressed the provocations of street preaching,[78] the aggressive nature of the "Popish mob,"[79] and the demographic pressure placed on Belfast by Ulster Catholic immigrants.[80] Perhaps the most interesting explanation offered for the riots came from the *Nation,* which blamed the clashes on the British government's efforts to generate religious hatred.[81] In their willful blindness to Ulster's sectarian realities, southern Irish nationalists were nothing if not consistent.

But if the Belfast riots of 1857 were somewhat more complex than the clashes of 1832, 1843, or 1852, they did share a similar framework or process with these earlier party conflicts. While Sub-constable Harris Bindon was undoubtedly right to point to spring elections as a critical factor in heightening sectarian tension in Belfast,[82] the triggering mechanism of both phases of the riots involved one singular factor—the sermons, private and public, of hard-line evangelical preachers.

These anti-Catholic diatribes proved to be particularly insulting to the Catholic community because they assaulted one of the touchstones of Irish Catholic political culture—the need to restore the Roman Catholic Church to its rightful position in Irish society. Of course, these particular sermons derived much of their provocative power from the explosive atmosphere in which they were delivered—the tumult of the annual marching seasons and the aftermath of the first phase of the 1857 riots. In many ways the critical element in the loyalist strategy of confrontation in the late summer and fall of 1857—open-air preaching—should be viewed as a religious variant on the usual Orange device of provocation, the party procession. Reverend Hanna's proposed lecture on the steps of the Customs House not only staked a claim to a sensitive central public space, it also threatened to insult one of the fundamental underpinnings of Irish Catholic identity, the Catholic church. With two of Ulster's central issues of contention in play, territory and religion, it is no wonder that Belfast Catholics responded in such numbers.

Once these events had set the stage for party confrontation, several other factors gave further shape to the Belfast riots of 1857. Above all, the city's compressed and largely segregated environment played a critical role in structuring and prolonging the riots. After partisan ritual display had initiated the first bouts of sectarian violence, the constricted urban arena made it easier to keep party feelings up over an extended time period. Three factors stand out here. First, information about provocative activities, whether true or not, traveled quickly through west Belfast's densely populated districts. Helped by the popular press's exaggerated reports, rumors about controversial open-air sermons or Catholic gun clubs helped to provide the impetus for the mobilization of partisan crowds. Second, the central district's condensed environment made the task of maintaining law and order very difficult. Policemen brought before the commission of inquiry repeatedly stressed how the narrow streets and alleys of Belfast made it incredibly difficult to apprehend suspected rioters.[83] Third, and perhaps most important, tight patterns of segregated proletarian settlement in Belfast helped to provide the riots with greater staying power. West Belfast had no real buffer zones; Catholic and Protestant districts pressed right up against one another, making it much easier for partisan activists to trigger sectarian confrontations. Such circumstances did not provide the spaces needed for party passions to dissipate.

Finally, Belfast's segregated working-class environment allowed party activists to implement their visions of communal purity on the ground. When rioting broke out, both Catholic and Protestant rioters focused much of their attention on assaulting the property and lives of those inhabitants who challenged the "black and white" views on communal relations that predominated within both proletarian communities. This seemed particularly important to the loyalists of Sandy Row, who not only intimidated and assaulted those few Catholics who resided around the mills of their district, but also wrecked the homes of the largely Protestant tenants of a wealthy Catholic landlord. Two issues were involved here: loyalists were not only issuing a warning to Protestants living in the wrong part of town; they were also symbolically attacking the right of any Ulster Catholic to achieve an ascendant economic position. But these bouts of "ethnic cleansing" were not limited to one side. Testimony given before the commission of inquiry that followed the riots clearly indicated that Protestants who resided and worked in the Pound regularly found themselves under siege by Catholic crowds eager to cleanse their districts of denominational diversity. Hard-line interpretations of partisan ideology demanded purity on both sides of the communal divide. Riots proved to be a very effective way of enforcing such sanctions.

Prince Arthur Comes to Derry

Belfast was not the only urban center plagued by sectarian rioting in mid-Victorian Ulster. The city of Derry also hosted several serious bouts of partisan contention. Derry's nineteenth-century experience faintly echoed that of its larger provincial cousin in a number of ways.[84] The growth of the shirt-making industry brought a substantial migration of rural Catholics into the traditionally Protestant city. Unlike Belfast, however, Catholics soon constituted a majority of the city population. From the early nineteenth century, settlement patterns in Derry also roughly mirrored those of Belfast. The city's overwhelmingly Protestant middle class moved to the Waterside, leaving proletarian Protestants in the Fountain district, surrounded by the working-class Catholic Bogside.

But if Derry's proletarian settlement patterns appeared similar to Belfast's segregated neighborhoods, Derry could not match Belfast's history of major sectarian riots. Although city authorities certainly welcomed this relative degree of tranquillity, few were foolish enough to view this as a reflection of anything approaching cordial communal relations. Rather, it pointed to the authorities' success in regulating party disturbances—an effort greatly aided by the city government's 1836 decision to ban Twelfth of July processions inside the city walls. While laws designed to restrict party exhibitions were certainly not enforced with perfect evenhandedness, they did help to reduce the number of ritual displays that led to rioting elsewhere. Unfortunately, Derry's relative peace was not destined to survive the 1860s.

Several factors converged in the late 1860s to accelerate the pace of sectarian contention. Three of these had particular impact in Ulster. The most important was undoubtedly the reemergence of Irish revolutionary nationalism on the national stage. Founded in 1858 by James Stephens, the Irish Republican Brotherhood (more popularly known as the Fenians) grew to become a real threat by the mid-1860s, mobilizing both Irishmen and like-minded Irish Americans in an effort to drive the British from Ireland. While Fenianism was not particularly strong in the north, the appearance of organized Irish Catholic nationalism anywhere on the island always raised sectarian passions throughout Ulster. This increased level of party tension certainly affected our second factor, which concerned William Johnston's decade-long campaign to repeal the Party Processions Act. Although this movement was not centered in Derry, it did touch a sensitive nerve among a Protestant population accustomed to the banning of Twelfth of July processions within the city.[85] Finally, William Gladstone's decision to disestablish the Church of Ireland further alienated many Ulster Protestants, adding yet another line to their growing list of grievances.

One thread runs through these factors: all three threatened to undermine the fundamental tenets of loyalist belief. In particular, many ultra-Protestants felt betrayed by the direction of British government policies in the late 1860s. Following the failed Fenian Rising of 1867, a rebellion which reinforced the hard-line loyalist view of the nature of Irish Catholic aspirations yet again, many Ulster Protestants were shocked to see the British government offering concessions to Irish Catholics—maintaining the ban on Orange celebrations and disestablishing the Church of Ireland. Not surprisingly, a strong current of anti-government feeling ran through Orange circles in this era. In April 1869 Derry activists would get a chance to register their feelings quite clearly.

Prince Arthur's visit to Ireland in April 1869 gave Ulster loyalists an occasion to express their disgust with the direction of British policy in Ireland. Ultra-Protestants did not wait long to exhibit their feelings of frustration. When the prince came to Trinity College, Dublin, in early April, angry students disrupted his visit with shouts of "groans for Maynooth" and rounds of Kentish fire.[86] It was an ominous sign for the royal visit.

Arthur's arrival in Derry on 28 April triggered a serious round of sectarian rioting in the city. Contention centered on the inner city, long considered sacred ground by those loyalists who annually commemorated the 1689 shutting of the gates and the relief of the siege of Derry with partisan festivals. Although such marches had been sporadic throughout the nineteenth century, the Apprentice Boys had revived the tradition in 1860, thus formally challenging the Party Emblems Act.[87] The right to hold a march, however, did not go both ways. When Liberal supporters attempted to march through the city center to celebrate the defeat of a petition lodged against Richard Dowse in February 1868, they found the city gates locked.[88]

To honor the presence of a member of the royal family, the Derry flute band, an association equated with the Liberal party (and thus Irish Catholics), marched to the city center playing the "national" anthem, "Patrick's Day." This violation of loyalist sacred space inflamed ultra-Protestant opinion, and a body of the Apprentice Boys and their hard-line supporters quickly positioned themselves in front of the Imperial Hotel, where Prince Arthur was staying. Calling up to the prince, the loyalist crowd shouted its fervent support for the queen, the prince, and the union of church and state while predictably deprecating Gladstone. Although the Protestant body alternated between shouts of support and condemnation, the Apprentice Boys flute band marched around the city center playing Orange songs.[89]

As the two flute bands engaged in this not-so-musical competition, Catholic and Protestant crowds coalesced in the city center. The two bodies hurled the traditional Ulster weapons of verbal abuse and stones at one another. Hoping to prevent a major sectarian riot in the royal presence, police positioned themselves between the two parties, desperately endeavoring to keep them apart.[91] Although they succeeded in keeping the crowds separated, their efforts were undermined by the panicked reactions of a few policemen, who fired shots into the crowd, killing three men. A major riot had narrowly been averted, but only at a tremendous human cost.[92]

Although the Derry riot of April 1869 was not comparable in scale to the Belfast riots of 1843 or 1857, the same framework that triggered and maintained those partisan conflicts lay at the heart of the fight inside the walled city. National and local political developments were critical in setting the stage for confrontation—in the late 1860s a series of events seemed to indicate to both Derry Protestants and Catholics that things were swinging in a Catholic direction. In this tense situation the activists of both communities attempted to use public demonstrations to assert their communal ideals of governance. Prince Arthur's arrival in Derry in April 1869 gave them their chance.

But it was not simply a struggle over conflicting visions. As in the Belfast riots detailed above, spatial issues lay at the center of controversy. In both of the Belfast clashes partisan contention within west Belfast's shared but segregated districts played a crucial role in sparking and maintaining widespread and lengthy sectarian riots. The situation was somewhat different in Derry. Here sectarian conflict revolved around a central civic space, one revered by loyalists involved in commemorating the great Protestant victories at Derry in the late seventeenth century. The celebration of a nationalist anthem, "Patrick's Day," within Derry's sacred city walls was a clear violation of loyalist belief. As such, it demanded a firm response. In the tense atmosphere of the late 1860s even the ritualized competition of flute bands could lead to deadly partisan violence.

While varying widely in scale and duration, the Belfast riots of 1843 and 1857 and the Derry riot of 1869 share a definite framework or process. In each case sectarian rioting was triggered by a perceived threat to one of the two antagonistic but interlocked worldviews that predominated throughout each city's segregated proletarian districts. Partisan activists of both communities responded by organizing set-piece confrontations in which each party engaged in a ritual-laden exhibition of the major tenets of its belief system. As repeatedly shown throughout this study, the party procession provided the most common vehicle for this kind of display, provoking some of the largest sectarian riots of nineteenth-century Ulster.

This was the same process that had structured party clashes in the north of Ireland throughout the century. What made conflicts in mid-Victorian Belfast and Derry different from their rural predecessors was the compressed nature of the urban environment. With its working-class population squeezed into shared but segregated industrial districts, Belfast in particular acted as a perfect laboratory for maintaining and intensifying partisan rivalries. In such close quarters hard-line activists could easily manufacture the kind of set-piece confrontations that often led to sectarian rioting. In many ways this new urban environment (reinforced by the gradual democratization of British and Irish politics) acted as a kind of pressure cooker, encapsulating and intensifying Ulster's traditional sectarian conflict.

But if this urban setting and its new political culture created a situation where party riots were both more frequent and extensive, the fundamental process of nineteenth-century Ulster's sectarian violence remained the same. Perceived threats to the ascendant position of Ulster Protestants continued to trigger most communal riots. Loyalists responded to such Catholic challenges by organizing and mobilizing their strength in Protestant defensive associations—the Protestant Operatives' Society, the revived Orange Order, or the Apprentice Boys—groups designed to use ritual displays of unity and power to put Catholics back in their rightful place. These exhibitions often led to party clashes—conflicts usually won by the better-armed and organized loyalists. If the new urban environment was dramatically different from the rolling hills of County Armagh, the process that produced sectarian violence was not.

■ 6

The Campaign to Repeal the Party Processions Act, 1860–1872

I hope you will take care that the Commission of Inquiry into the Conduct of the Constabulary during the visit of Prince Arthur to Londonderry is conducted with strict impartiality. I do not think it would be prudent to have it so conducted as to lead to the belief that the government wished to put down the Derry celebrations. To appear to desire this, just now, would seriously imperil the peace of Ulster—to attempt it would be to provoke civil war. I write this knowing intimately and thoroughly what I write, and the men you have to deal with.

William Johnston to Chichester Fortescue

On 12 July 1867 a crowd of twenty-five thousand to thirty thousand Orangemen and their supporters assembled near the seaside town of Bangor to protest against the British government's continued administration of the Party Processions Act.[1] Hard-line loyalists traveled from all over eastern Ulster that day, with many taking part in a massive Orange procession from Newtownards to Bangor. This imposing demonstration was the brainchild of William Johnston of Ballykilbeg, a relatively minor landowner in the Lecale district of south Down. Johnston had been active in Protestant politics since 1848, when he joined Ballydonnell Orange Lodge. Educated at Trinity College, Dublin, Johnston first tried his hand at journalism, publishing a series of loyalist tracts and a militant Protestant newspaper, the *Downshire Protestant*. But it was within the world of Orange popular politics that Johnston would make his name. A staunch Orangeman throughout his life, Johnston became a District Master in 1857 and held key posts within the Grand Orange Lodge of Ireland from the early 1850s onward. By the mid-1860s the independent and charismatic Johnston had become a driving force within the Orange Order in Ireland.[2] Johnston derived much of this power from his advocacy of plebeian demands to repeal the hated Party Processions Act. While this support got him into regular difficulties with an elite leadership eager to emphasize the Order's respectability,[3] it made Johnston a natural leader of the Orange rank and file.

Johnston only enhanced this reputation with his performance at Bangor that day. While introducing a memorial directed to the British prime minister, the Earl of Derby, he launched into an emotional defense of the Orange Order's historic right to march: "it afforded him a very great pleasure indeed to take part in so noble a demonstration of Orangemen and Protestants, who venerated the glorious 12th of July. . . . They had been trampled upon and trodden upon long enough, but they would hide their light under a bushel no longer. They would set their light upon the hill in Bangor, from which it would be seen fifty miles off."[4] In a sense he was correct. Two months later, British authorities charged Johnston and twenty-three other participants in the Bangor demonstration with violating the Party Processions Act. Johnston and two other men were convicted and sentenced to short terms of imprisonment. The light generated by Johnston's arrest and subsequent incarceration would prove visible from a distance far greater than fifty miles.

The Campaign to Repeal the Party Processions Act

The Bangor procession and demonstration of July 1867 constituted one of the high points in William Johnston's successful campaign to repeal the Party Processions Act. With the exception of a few Orange scholars,[5] Irish historians largely have ignored the campaign,[6] concentrating their analyses instead on the critical subjects of Fenianism and the nascent stirrings of constitutional nationalism and land agitation. While the historiographical emphasis on nationalist developments in Ireland is certainly understandable, it would be a mistake to overlook the importance of this loyalist movement of the late 1860s and early 1870s. Put simply, Johnston's successful campaign to regain the Orangeman's historic right to walk played a critical role in reanimating the system of cross-class Protestant collaboration that would later provide the essential foundation for Ulster unionism. With this alliance in place, Ulster Protestants would be ready to say no when Charles Stewart Parnell and his lieutenants organized the strength of Catholic Ireland into an unprecedented political force in the late 1870s and the 1880s.

The annual celebration of the Twelfth of July lay at the heart of Ulster Orangeism. As many historians have noted, the processional tradition was especially important to plebeian Orangemen and their supporters, who viewed the Twelfth festivities as a symbolic and territorial expression of their historic right to an ascendant position vis-à-vis Irish Catholics. The Orange elite's attitude toward processions had always been much more circumspect. The turbulent sectarianism of militant plebeian processionists and the sectarian riots that loyalist exhibitions often provoked were a constant source of acute embarrassment for aristocratic Orange leaders. Following the reconstitution of the Orange Order in the 1840s, figures like the Earl of Roden and the Earl of Enniskillen attempted to downplay the importance of party processions, concentrating on the respectable and loyal nature of Orangeism in Ireland.[7] Even William Johnston of Ballykilbeg, the future champion of the "right to walk," seemed to lack enthusiasm for the Twelfth of July celebration at times during the early 1850s.[8]

Not surprisingly, many Orange lodges simply ignored the wishes of their social betters, keeping alive the processional tradition on the Twelfth. In an attempt to curtail such partisan exhibitions and the sectarian rioting they often provoked, the British government had passed a series of Party Processions Acts throughout the nineteenth century. The most recent legislative attempt to curb processions had been passed in 1850, when a bill was rushed through parliament in the immediate aftermath of the bloody clash at Dolly's Brae, near Castlewellan, County Down.[9] Like other bills aimed at Orange marches, the Party Processions Act of 1850 was hardly an unqualified success. With the implementation of its provisions often left in the hands of local officials sympathetic to Orangeism,[10] there was a great deal of regional variation in the enforcement of the legislation. But if the law against party processions was not universally enforced, the government did arrest and imprison more than five hundred loyalists for violating its provisions between 1850 and 1867.[11]

Although the number of arrests made over this eighteen-year period looks impressive enough on paper, the fact that Orangemen across Ulster regularly ignored the provisions of the act underlines its failure to alter either the attitudes or behavior of plebeian processionists. Part of this could be put down to the way in which local officials administered the legislation on the ground. In enforcing its provisions, police generally attempted to find a middle ground between rigid adherence to the letter of the law and outright neglect. Two general principles dictated official enforcement of the legislation. First, police rarely intervened in predominately Protestant areas. As one magistrate in Kilrea, County Londonderry, admitted in 1869, it had long been accepted practice to allow Protestant celebrations in places like Coleraine, Kilrea, and Ballymoney, where intervention only stirred up trouble between offended loyalists and the generally outnumbered police.[12]

Even when arrests were made, typically only those processionists who had played leading roles in partisan demonstrations (especially organizers and musicians) were brought to trial.

Not surprisingly, this middle course simply offended both loyalists and their Catholic opponents. Directed by priests and other local leaders, Ulster Catholics angered by the often lax enforcement of the legislation repeatedly petitioned Dublin Castle for stricter administration of the law.[13] Conversely, the arrests that were made served only to irritate Orangemen, who considered the government's behavior a direct violation of their rights as Protestants. If the goal of the Party Processions Act had been to alter the behavior or the attitudes of rank-and-file Orangemen or their Catholic foes, it was a dramatic failure; hard-line plebeian loyalists kept the marching tradition alive despite the legal consequences. At the same time, the number of arrests made under its provisions was significant enough to trigger widespread anger among Orangemen and their supporters. With a sea of frustration lying just beneath the surface, conditions were ripe for a powerful movement against the hated legislation. All that was needed was an effective populist leader and the right opportunity. Events in the 1860s would provide enemies of the Party Processions Act with both these critical variables.

The first concrete challenge to the Party Processions Act occurred in the city of Derry in December 1860. Earlier in that year Lord Palmerston's government, reacting to a fatal affray at Derrymacash near Lurgan, had passed legislation to help curb partisan displays and the violence they provoked.[14] Entitled the Party Emblems Act, it made the following actions illegal:

1. The public exhibition of any banner, flag, party emblem, or symbol upon any building or place.
2. Giving willful permission for the public exhibition of any banner, flag, party emblem, or symbol upon said building or place.
3. Public meetings or parades.
4. The playing of music in any public street, road, or place.
5. The firing of cannons or firearms in any public street, road or place.[15]

The intent of the act seemed clear enough: the Party Emblems Act had been designed to give the authorities the flexibility to act against partisan demonstrations they deemed potentially dangerous. The first test came in Derry city in December 1860.

In 1860 Protestant activists decided to revive the Apprentice Boys' traditional celebration of the 1689 relief of Derry. But the Apprentice Boys were not the only busy party that year. The government, well aware of the planned festivities, dispatched two hundred constables to Derry to preserve the peace.[16] On 18 December the Apprentice Boys commemorated the loyalist holiday in style, marching through the city center adorned with crimson and white regalia dominated by the red hand of Ulster. The processionists made their way to the city's great cathedral, where they were met by William Johnston and the Rev. Thomas Drew, two of the central apostles of hard-line loyalism. Following divine services a large crowd cheered as Lundy's effigy was burned and fireworks burst overhead. The Derry commemoration was a dramatic victory for Johnston, Drew, and their local followers. No violence occurred and no arrests were made. If the government had intended to enforce the Party Emblems Act to the letter of the law, it certainly had failed to do so at Derry in 1860.[17]

Although the event underlined the government's unwillingness to use anti-marching legislation vigorously to ban party processions in the north of Ireland, the success of the day failed to spark an organized loyalist movement to repeal the hated legislation. While hard-line Ulster Protestants certainly remained frustrated with the supposed injustice of the Party Processions Act, they were not yet ready to challenge the British government. The pervasive sense of crisis needed to mobilize such an undertaking simply was not there in December 1860. It soon would be, however and the source of renewed loyalist anxiety was entirely predictable—Irish nationalism.

The early and mid-1860s saw the conspicuous rise of organized Irish nationalism on several levels. Undoubtedly the most worrisome of these from a loyalist perspective was the revival of physical force nationalism. Although the Irish Republican Brotherhood was not particularly strong in Ulster, the passion and support exhibited at the Fenian funeral of Terence Bellew McManus in November 1861 only underscored the need for Protestant unity in the face of a nationalist Catholic threat. But if the growth of Fenianism provided an important general backdrop for the dramatic revival of loyalist activity in the mid-1860s, it was a singular event that drew particular attention to the issue of party processions in Ireland. This occurred in August 1864, when nationalists celebrated in Dublin, and Belfast rioted in response.

From the outset, August 1864 promised to be an interesting month. In Dublin plans were well underway to celebrate the laying of the foundation stone for a new monument to Daniel O'Connell. On 6 August the *Nation* featured a prominent story about the upcoming "monster procession," detailing the elaborate route which the marchers would take through the streets of central Dublin to the future site of the monument on Sackville Street.

Organizers hoped that the pageantry and spectacle of this gala event would lend momentum to the cause of Irish constitutional nationalism.

As plans for the procession became public knowledge, Orangemen and their supporters reacted with vitriolic fury. In the previous three years nationalists had put on two massive public displays in Dublin. The British government's failure to block a third demonstration of disloyalty was viewed as tantamount to treason.[18] Newspapers were filled with angry letters, each intoning against the patent hypocrisy of a government which allowed nationalist processions to proceed while denying loyal Orangemen their customary right to march on the Twelfth of July.[19] One important correspondent disagreed with this line of reasoning. In a letter to the *Dublin Evening Mail,* William Johnston welcomed the government's decision to let the upcoming festival go ahead as planned. Noninterference was the correct policy, he insisted, in that it revealed the injustice of the government's one-sided administration of the Party Processions Act. Such flagrant hypocrisy could only help those trying to abolish the offensive legislation. In typically inflammatory fashion, Johnston proceeded to warn those who might try to obstruct future Orange processions: "For in spite of the diction of the judges and the well-meant advice of friends, it is felt to be intolerable that Protestants are to be imprisoned for doing what lord mayors and other dignitaries are free to do if the public processional display is of a nature antagonistic to Orangeism. We in Ulster shall never endure tyranny in the name of law."[20] These latter sentiments were certainly representative of feelings expressed within countless Orange lodges throughout the north of Ireland. As the day of the Dublin festivities approached, Belfast agitators planned a counter-demonstration to protest the O'Connell celebration.

Dublin's gala event finally took place on Monday, 8 August 1864. By all accounts it was a remarkable affair. The capital literally was draped in green; ribbons and banners adorned with harps, shamrocks, and the Irish wolfhound seemed omnipresent. Police estimated that approximately half a million people attended the celebration, having come to Dublin from all across Ireland. A rather large delegation of men and women traveled south from Belfast for the commemoration. The highlight of the day undoubtedly was the great procession through the streets of central Dublin. An estimated forty thousand people participated in the march.[21] The *Nation* exulted in the day's success: "It was a glorious scene. It was splendid in externals but infinitely more gratifying to the patriotic heart for the meaning which it conveyed. Ireland may be proud of the event. It will serve as a rebuke to the calumnies habitually uttered by her foes; it will ever be an honor to the character of her people."[22] While he was certainly less effusive in his praise, Thomas Larcom was also pleased; the day had passed with remarkably little disorder.[23] All in all, the Dublin festivities were a brilliant triumph for Irish constitutional nationalism.

At the end of the day the Belfast contingent boarded a train for their return trip home. When the Dublin train arrived in the northern capital, a hostile crowd of men and women from Sandy Row met the passengers at the station. As the train approached, makeshift bands launched into raucous renditions of "The Protestant Boys" and "Croppies Lie Down," while a number of people hurled stones at the train and its occupants. One section of the crowd marched in procession, burning an effigy of Daniel O'Connell. Only the determined efforts of the police prevented the Sandy Row men from moving down into the Catholic Pound, an event that surely would have triggered large-scale rioting and bloodshed. A heavy air of tension lay over Belfast that night.

The following day a crowd gathered in Sandy Row. The charred ashes of O'Connell's effigy were placed in a coffin, and a mock funeral procession set off to bury the remains at the cemetery at Friar's Bush. A man dressed as a priest led the march as it made its way toward Stranmillis. When the processionists arrived at the gate, they were greeted by an armed groundskeeper determined to prevent the insult of such a symbolic burial. After a brief period of taunting and shouting the crowd turned back toward Sandy Row. When they arrived at the Boyne Bridge, they set the coffin on fire. The effigy was then flung into the rather unsavory burial ground of the Blackstaff River.[24]

The next two days saw an acceleration of the pace of violence in Belfast. Egged on by exaggerated reports in the popular press, Sandy Row's ritual internment of O'Connell's effigy dramatically raised the pitch of sectarian tension throughout Belfast's working class districts.[25] Desperately short of professional personnel, the embattled police were unable to prevent violent clashes from occurring, and proletarian west Belfast soon was engaged in widespread sectarian rioting. The Belfast riots of 1864 had begun.[26] Violent street battles between Protestant and Catholic crowds continued throughout August and were halted only by the dispatch of a virtual army of police and military to Belfast.[27] The damage, however, already had been done. By the end of the month, at least twelve people were dead and untold harm had been done to Belfast property.

If Dublin's nationalist festival and the subsequent Belfast riots of 1864 had brought renewed attention to the issue of the Party Processions Act, it was a local issue in County Down that pushed William Johnston into the active leadership of a public campaign to repeal the legislation. This concerned the prosecution of eight Gilford millworkers at the County Down's spring and summer assizes of 1864. The event in question occurred on 14 July 1863, when the eight men had marched home from their jobs at a Gilford mill to the tunes of partisan music.[28] Charged with violating the provisions of the Party Procession Act, six of the eight defendants eventually were sentenced to three months imprisonment in the county jail in Downpatrick.[29] Predictably, the decision outraged Johnston, who immediately organized a petition to the lord lieutenant for the release of the "wronged" men.[30] While County Down's two MP's and fifteen magistrates signed the petition, Dublin Castle quickly rejected it out of hand.

One week later, an estimated forty thousand nationalists marched in procession through the streets of central Dublin. None were charged with violating the provisions of the Party Processions Act. As Johnston saw it, the government's decision to imprison loyal Protestant millworkers for walking in procession while allowing Catholic rebels to march in Dublin Castle's shadow was rank hypocrisy. More than anything, it was this sharp contrast that drove Johnston into the public fray. He had been sounding out County Down's Orange lodges since the spring of 1864, attempting to mobilize rank-and-file support within the Order for an assault on the one-sided administration of the Party Procession Act. Johnston redoubled his efforts in the wake of the events of the summer of 1864. As he stated, "the time for quiet endurance has gone by, and private remonstrances are useless."[31]

While Johnston's stance won him hearty approval among hard-line plebeian Orangemen desperate for activist gentry leadership, it won him few friends within the Orange Order's top ranks. It was not long before Johnston's populist course got him into trouble with the aristocratic grandees of the Grand Lodge. After touring many of the Orange lodges of County Down, Johnston attempted to organize a massive public demonstration at the Maze near Lisburn on 12 July 1865. At the meeting Johnston planned to draw up a petition for justice and liberty against the "penal acts of parliament." Johnston's proposal obviously struck a vibrant chord with many plebeian Orangemen. One resident magistrate reported that Orangemen from all across east Ulster were planning to attend the Maze meeting—a vast contingent that would no doubt include Belfast's notorious ship carpenters. According to this official, the demonstration was designed to "give them (militant loyalists) satisfaction for the O'Connell processsion, which they imagine was an insult to their feelings."[32]

The Maze demonstration was not to be, however. Most members of the Grand Lodge fervently opposed such a flagrant violation of the law and forced Johnston to cancel the meeting and apologize to the Grand Lodge for flouting their leadership. Johnston was predictably furious, declaring: "Let Orangemen indeed unite and augment their numbers. But let them not become flunkies or spaniels, to the disgust of all honest Protestants."[33] Not surprisingly, this letter only got Johnston into more trouble with his conservative superiors. Clearly, if Johnston was going to organize a great public campaign to repeal the Party Processions Act, he would have to do it without the initial support of the Grand Lodge.

To circumvent the disapprobation of both the government and his aristocratic brethren, Johnston decided to hold a demonstration on 12 July 1866 on his Ballykilbeg estate near Downpatrick. Hoping to generate enthusiasm for his cause, he invited both Belfast and Lecale Orangemen to commemorate the Twelfth on his land. Thomas Larcom expressed the government's disapproval with this course to Johnston in no uncertain terms. "His excellency had given strict orders to prevent the assembling of persons under such circumstances as are likely to lead to a breach of the peace, and the information received by his Excellency leaves no doubt that the proposed meeting is one which ought not be permitted to take place."[34] In one sense Larcom's fears proved to be unfounded. An estimated nine thousand Orangemen celebrated the Twelfth at Johnston's Ballykilbeg estate, but there were no disturbances or arrests.

For William Johnston the success of the Ballykilbeg meeting only confirmed his idea about the possibilities of raising a great Protestant campaign against the hated legislation. If the Orange elite was weak in its support, Johnston could depend on the plebeian ranks of the Order. This conviction was reaffirmed in 1867, when Johnston's campaign to repeal the Party Procession Act gained unprecedented levels of support from the main body of Ulster Orangemen.

The forces behind the growth of Orange activism in the summer of 1867 are not particularly difficult to understand. In early March of that year the depleted ranks of the Irish Republican Brotherhood attempted to trigger a general rising against the British government in parts of Leinster and Munster. While the Fenian Rising of 1867 was put down with relative ease, it reinforced the traditional loyalist call for pan-Protestant unity in the face of a renewed Catholic nationalist threat. As they had done throughout the century, plebeian loyalists would use the Twelfth that year to exhibit their unchanging loyalty.

Trying to capitalize on this renewal of hard-line spirit in 1867, Johnston organized a massive demonstration at Bangor on 12 July 1867 to highlight the injustice of the Party Processions Act. Between twenty-five thousand

and thirty thousand Orangemen and their supporters came to Bangor that day from all across the North. But Orange celebrations of the Twelfth in 1867 were by no means limited to Bangor. Sparked by the Fenian rising and Johnston's own agitation of the marching issue, Orangemen participated in partisan processions all across the province. Substantial marches and celebrations took place in Lisburn, Markethill, Portadown, Dromara, Scarva, Brookeborough, Derrygonnelly, Stewartstown, Pomeroy, and Coleraine.[35]

But if demonstrations took place across Ulster, it was the Bangor procession and meeting that captured public attention. Following the meeting, news spread quickly that the government intended to charge William Johnston and a number of other prominent participants with violating the terms of the Party Processions Act. Johnston's initial reaction was relatively muted: "We have been informed that the sessional crown prosecutor has been instructed to prosecute a number of persons who took a prominent part in the Orange demonstration at Bangor on the Twelfth of July. . . . May I venture to express a hope that it will not be attempted to revive in Ulster the feelings created by former governments."[36] Predictably, the government was not impressed with the logic of Johnston's argument. He and twenty-three other participants in the Bangor procession and demonstration were charged with violating the Party Processions Act.

By arresting Johnston, the government created a rather serious dilemma for itself. Although it wanted to enforce the law, it had no desire to create martyrs for the Orange cause. With this in mind, government officials told the Orange defendants that the prosecution would be dropped if they admitted their guilt.[37] This effort met with considerable success. When the case was brought before the Down assizes in the spring of 1868, twenty-one of the defendants pleaded guilty and were released on their own recognizance. Johnston, however, was not inclined to let the government off so easily. Not wanting to lend a degree of legitimacy to a law that they believed was tyrannical and unjust, Johnston and two others, William Mawhinney and Thomas Keatinge, pleaded not guilty to all charges.[38] Obviously guilty of violating the Party Processions Act, they were each sentenced to short terms of imprisonment ranging from one to two months.

William Johnston remained in the county jail at Downpatrick for nearly two months.[39] As many officials had feared, the government's actions had done Johnston a great service. His arrest and imprisonment created far more momentum for the movement against the Party Processions Act than any of his previous public demonstrations.[40] When he emerged from prison, Johnston was greeted with unbounded enthusiasm by plebeian Orangemen and other loyalist supporters. The reason for Johnston's overwhelming popu-

Table 5. Parliamentary Election Results, Belfast, 1868

William Johnston (I)	5,975
Thomas McClure(L)	4,202
Sir Charles Lanyon(C)	3,540
John Mulholland(C)	1,580

Source: Brian Walker, ed., *Parliamentary Election Results in Ireland, 1801-1922* (Dublin: Royal Irish Academy, 1978), 107.

larity was simple. By going to jail over the Orangeman's right to march, Johnston had exhibited a degree of commitment rarely seen among the Orange elite.[41] This was particularly important to Belfast's Orange artisans, who were "the most enthusiastic admirers of the imprisoned violator of the party procession act."[42] Johnston would soon get a chance to put his Belfast support to good use.

The general election of 1868 provided William Johnston with an opportunity to test the strength of popular loyalism. Prior to his imprisonment, Johnston had declared his candidacy for one of Belfast's two parliamentary seats. While he acknowledged the importance of other issues, Johnston largely stood on his record of populist Protestant activism. Predictably, he concentrated on the need to repeal the Party Processions Act.[43] Johnston's prison term only reinforced his Protestant credentials. Ironically, imprisonment actually improved Johnston's political base in Belfast. On 4 March 1868, a few days after Johnston began his prison term, a large concourse of Orange artisans met at Ulster Hall to declare their sympathy for the imprisoned loyalist leader. There they formed the Belfast Protestant Working Men's Association, a society dedicated to returning Johnston to parliament.[44] When he emerged from prison, he had already received the allegiance of the Protestant working classes of Belfast.

The extent of Johnston's support was revealed when the polls were closed in mid-November. Buoyed by Orange support and Liberal money, he raced home to an easy victory, followed by the Liberal candidate, Thomas McClure.[45] The result shocked the complacent world of Belfast parliamentary politics, long dominated by an aristocratic Conservative establishment. While McClure's election was an impressive accomplishment for a Liberal party that rarely bothered to contest elections in Conservative Belfast, the day belonged to Johnston.

The general election of 1868 has been analyzed in meticulous detail by Brian Walker in his groundbreaking study of late nineteenth-century Ulster politics. Walker found that "new presbyterian and working-class dissent had created for the Conservatives a difficult situation of which the Liberals were able to take advantage."[46] While this was true in a broad sense, the election results provide more than a strong hint that the Liberal Party's opportunity would be relatively short-lived in Belfast. Clearly, the Belfast electorate preferred Johnston's hard-line populist Protestantism to McClure's attempt to unite Catholic and Protestant under the Liberal banner. If anti-aristocratic feeling ruled the day in Belfast in November 1868, it still retained a distinctively Orange tinge.

Of course, Johnston's public campaign to repeal the Party Processions Act was not the sole or even primary force behind the revival of Orange activism in 1867–1868 so clearly expressed in his electoral triumph in Belfast. There were at least two other forces at work here. The first concerned the aforementioned resurgence of Irish revolutionary nationalism in 1867. Put simply, the Fenian Rising of that year clearly underscored the need for Protestant unity and loyalist assertiveness in the face of a renewed Catholic nationalist threat.

But if the growth of the Irish Republican Brotherhood and the Fenian Rising of 1867 helped to push many traditional loyalists into a more activist frame of mind, a more powerful threat came from an unanticipated direction—the British government. There was certainly nothing novel about the existence of friction between Ulster Conservatives and the British government in Ireland.[47] If such tension had existed before, however, it reached new heights in the wake of the general elections of 1868, for after the polls closed in November of that year, the Orangemen of Ulster faced a hostile Liberal government under the leadership of William Gladstone. This new government's Irish policy largely was directed by the belief that the failed 1867 Rising pointed to the need to take steps to conciliate nationalist Ireland—measures that included the disestablishment of the Church of Ireland and major land reform.[48] Needless to say, most Ulster Orangemen and their supporters viewed Gladstone's conciliatory course as nothing less than betrayal.

Gladstone's proposal to disestablish the Church of Ireland proved to be particularly important in mobilizing the forces of Ulster loyalism in opposition to his government. By attacking one of the central foundations of the ascendancy in Ireland, the campaign for disestablishment managed to animate substantial sections of two hitherto quiet social groups—the Orange aristocracy and the Anglican clergy. With their church under siege by a hostile government after 1868, members of the Orange elite played an increasingly activist role in Orange politics, hosting Twelfth of July festivities on their estates and organizing massive public demonstrations against various measures of the Liberal government.[49] Operating within a suddenly hostile political environment, Orange aristocrats increasingly echoed the plebeian call for Protestant solidarity at public meetings and demonstrations. The Fermanagh Orange leader, Henry Mervyn D'Arcy Irvine, made a typical plea for Protestant unity in 1869: "At the first great Protestant demonstration meeting held in Enniskillen in 1868, I had occasion to declare that the Orangemen of Ireland were all Protestants, and that the Protestants of Ireland were all Orangemen in principle."[50] Although aristocratic figures like Viscount Massarene and the Earl of Erne remained loath to join the populist Orange campaign to repeal the Public Processions Act, their public opposition to Liberal efforts to disestablish the Church of Ireland lent credibility and legitimacy to Johnston's campaign against the hated legislation.

But it was not only members of the Orange elite who involved themselves in popular agitation. Numerous police reports indicate that members of the Anglican clergy began to take a much more active role in public demonstrations against various aspects of government policy. In 1870 a resident magistrate from south Down remarked that "the Protestant clergymen are far more active than usual in keeping alive the Orange feeling, which seems to have gained strength since last year."[51] Clerical obduracy could occasionally reach astonishing levels. In the Ballyward district a local rector adamantly refused to take partisan flags down from his church during the marching season of 1870; he ignored the pleas of both the local magistrate and several Presbyterian clergymen.[52] Such partisan displays contributed greatly to mounting sectarian tension in the outlying districts and parishes of rural Ulster.

The increasing willingness of members of the Orange elite and clergy to take part in public demonstrations against the Liberal government strengthened the momentum behind William Johnston's crusade to repeal the Party Processions Act. Johnston himself was hardly idle, speaking at a series of Orange rallies across the province.[53] In many ways each of these loyalist campaigns against the various policies of the Liberal government acted to support each other; anti-Gladstone rallies became a regular feature of Ulster life between 1868 and 1872. Not surprisingly, the sudden surge in Orange public activism had a direct impact on communal relations in the province; with the status quo threatened, the pace of sectarian confrontation quickened dramatically.

As always, the Armagh-Down borderlands proved to be one of the most contentious regions in Ulster. Writing from Banbridge, Father John O'Brien reflected on the reasons behind the heightened level of party animosity in

1869: "The bad and excited state of feeling that exists here at present [is] partly on account of the disturbances that occurred in Banbridge in June, July, or August of last year, and partly on account of the Irish church question."[54] The disturbances to which Father O'Brien referred began on 31 May 1868, when he and two other members of the Order of Charity, a Catholic mission society, opened a two-week devotional exercise at the Catholic church on Dromore Street in Banbridge. The services attracted large numbers of Catholics, who passed through the church in order to take part in this special expression of Catholic piety.

Unfortunately, this event also drew the loyalists' attention. Upset at this overt expression of Catholicism in the center of Protestant Banbridge, Orangemen organized fife and drum parties throughout the first week of the devotions to intimidate the priests and their Catholic followers. On 4 and 6 June, Orange drumming parties came into conflict with police units attempting to protect the chapel and the priests within. When the loyalists found that they could not break through the police cordon, they retreated back to Banbridge, where they wrecked the windows and houses of much of the town's "respectable" Catholic population.[55] The unruly spirit of local loyalism did not subside quickly. When crown magistrates arrived in Banbridge in mid-August to preserve the peace on Our Lady's Day, they were "treated very much as the fathers of the Order of Charity had been."[56]

Of course, the increased level of sectarian conflict that characterized the period between 1868 and 1872 was not rooted in clashes over devotional exercises. Most partisan riots were triggered by the classic weapon of Ulster sectarianism—the party procession. Under siege once again, loyalists joined massive partisan celebrations to exhibit both their disapproval of the actions of the Liberal government and their continued ascendancy over Irish Catholics. A police report detailing the events of a meeting to commemorate the Twelfth of July at Crossgar, County Down, in 1872 makes the antigovernment feeling of political Protestantism quite clear. When approximately six thousand people arrived for the meeting, they were treated to "a band of orators, each and many of who employed language consisting for the most part of broad and bold assertion, unfounded in fact, calculated to bring the government of the country into contempt, and to keep the animosities of past generations."[57]

But if these massive public demonstrations drew the disapprobation of local policemen, it was the Orange processions of the Twelfth of July that provoked the majority of sectarian riots in these years. Orangemen and their loyalist supporters responded to their besieged predicament as they had throughout the century—by ritually asserting their power and perceived rights in party processions during the marching season. Sparked by William Johnston's energetic leadership and the supposed oppression of a Liberal government, Orangemen took to the streets en masse in July 1868, holding public processions and celebrations all across the province. Sizable loyalist demonstrations took place that month in Lisburn, Ballymacash, Ballymoney, Portadown, Tandragee, Annaghmore, Keady, Waringstown, Ballynahinch, Rathfriland, Randalstown, Newtownards, Bellaghy, Castledawson, and Monaghan town.[58]

Predictably, the surge in loyalist marching produced a reaction from the other side of the communal divide. We have seen that in a few instances Ulster Catholics drew up petitions to the government asking the authorities to put an end to provocative Orange processions. But many Catholics were unwilling to wait for government interference and decided to attempt to block the progress of Orange processions themselves. Fortunately, police and local Catholic leaders successfully kept the two parties apart at most potential flashpoints in 1868. Tragically, there were two exceptions to this rule. The first of these occurred in the Londonderry village of Desertmartin, where a party riot claimed the lives of two local Catholics. An Orange procession in Monaghan town triggered the other major clash of the day. Here, besieged Orange marchers fired into a crowd from the haven of a friendly pub, killing a Catholic farmer named Thomas Hughes.[59]

Of course, the sectarian violence of the marching season was not confined to the provocative processions of the Orange party. For some time Ulster Catholics had taken to emulating their loyalist enemies by marching in procession on Our Lady's Day, 15 August. Responding to the increased level of Orange activity in south Down in 1868, Newry Catholics decided to use that Catholic holiday to display their partisan resolve. On 15 August Catholic activists organized a drumming party of approximately fifty men on the County Down side of the Newry Canal. It soon became apparent that the Catholic party planned to march through the Orange districts on the canal's west side, where hard-line loyalists were making preparations to resist the Catholic advance. Fortunately, the police got wind of the plan and successfully blocked all attempts to invade the Orange districts on the Armagh side of town.[60]

With the status quo still under threat during 1869, sectarian contention continued apace. A series of anti-Gladstone demonstrations and the partisan riot that marred Prince Arthur's visit to Derry city showed that the party hostilities exhibited the previous year were not to be a passing phenomenon.[61] But if these events rightly reflected a marked increase of popular Protestant political feeling, the Twelfth of July would again drive the point home. In 1869 Ulster loyalists would make their stand.

Authorities in Dublin Castle were well aware of the dangers presented by the upcoming Twelfth celebration. A massive force of 48 magistrates and 2,368 police officers and constables was deployed throughout the province.[62] The government's precautions proved to be necessary, for Orangemen and their loyalist supporters turned out en masse in 1869. At least twenty-three major processions and demonstrations occurred throughout the province on 12 and 13 July.[63] The Orangemen of William Johnston's native county of Down were particularly active in 1869, holding at least ten demonstrations that weekend.[64] Given the enormous number of people involved, police efforts to keep the contending parties apart proved remarkably successful. There were, however, exceptions to this happy rule. Small-scale riots and affrays occurred in Belfast, Newry, and Pettigo, as well as in Muff Glen near Derry city. Unfortunately, one particular clash resulted in more than frayed tempers and a few broken heads; Orange celebrations triggered sectarian rioting in the loyalist heartland of northeast Armagh. It was here that party conflict had fatal results.

The trouble in County Armagh started on 1 July when a group of police constables attempted to put out a loyalist bonfire on the outskirts of Portadown. Upset at this interference with their celebration, the Protestant party hurled stones at the offending policemen, shouting "Down with Gladstone!" As the police retreated across a bridge, they fired several shots, killing a Protestant boy named Thomas Watson.[65] Predictably, this murder outraged local loyalist opinion; within two days a local newspaper, the hard-line *Portadown News and County Armagh Advertiser,* called for a full investigation into what it termed "firing on an unarmed crowd!"[66] An estimated ten thousand to twelve thousand mourners marched in Watson's funeral a few days later; the traditional trappings of Orange regalia dominated the procession.[67] With party feeling up, it was going to be a difficult Twelfth in the Orange heartland.

Ironically, the Twelfth of July itself was quiet in Portadown. Along with the vast majority of the Orangemen of north Armagh, Portadown loyalists traveled to massive rallies and demonstrations at Tanderagee and Killyman.[68] There were few serious disturbances in north Armagh that day. Given the trouble of the previous week, the police could be well satisfied with the relative tranquillity of the Twelfth. Unfortunately, such optimistic predictions proved to be premature. Party rioting shook north Armagh on the following day.

The trouble centered on Lurgan, where an Orange drumming party returning from the traditional sham fight at Scarva stopped outside a Catholic convent on Edward Street, shouting "No Surrender!" and other partisan epithets. Built in 1866, the convent had quickly become a party flashpoint, as local loyalists attempted to provoke the Catholic population by directing their drumming parties past this religious and symbolic center. As the Orange party hesitated in front of the convent, a Catholic crowd rapidly arrived to defend the holy building. A large proportion of the crowd consisted of women and girls, who attempted to drive the Orangemen off with a volley of stones. A reinforced troop of police arrived and successfully separated the warring parties. Peace seemed to be within reach. Unfortunately, the Orange party had other ideas. Moving away from the convent, the drumming band moved down into Falloon's Row, a nearby Catholic enclave. There, the Orange party went on a particularly vicious wrecking spree, breaking window panes and shattering furniture in a number of Catholic homes. Their work completed, the Orangemen marched off to their homes in Seagoe parish, a district well-known for its aggressive loyalism.[69]

The sheer scale of destruction involved in the Lurgan wreckings of 1869 prompted an immediate government inquiry. William Hancock, a long-time opponent of Orangeism in northeast Armagh, headed the inquiry. After collecting information from the various participants, Hancock laid the blame for the sectarian disturbances on two primary sources. Given Hancock's attitude toward party processions, the first of these was eminently predictable. In a public statement, he condemned the provocative behavior of the Orange processionists. The second factor that Hancock cited, however, is more interesting. It seems that prior to the party riots of 13 July the rector of Seagoe parish, the venerable Archdeacon James Saurin, had delivered an emotional anti-Catholic diatribe to his loyalist parishioners. Hancock found Saurin's behavior highly irresponsible and laid a heavy proportion of the blame on Saurin's instigation. Whatever the exact reason, the results of the Lurgan wreckings were quite clear. Falloon's Row lay in waste and eighty participants had been arrested.[70]

It was against this backdrop of increased sectarian contention that William Johnston initiated his parliamentary campaign for the repeal of the Party Processions Act. Supported by two Fermanagh Conservatives, Capt. M.E. Archdale and Viscount Crichton, Johnston introduced legislation to repeal the hated act in both 1869 and 1870. Speaking in the House of Commons prior to the second reading of his proposed legislation in March 1870, Johnston built his argument for repeal on two major points: the general ineffectiveness and partiality of its administration and the fact that it had not been enforced since 1867:

The act it proposed to abolish was passed in 1850 and admitted by all parties to have been eminently unsatisfactory in its working, besides having been administered with great partiality.... He must do the present government the justice to say that they by their action had condemned the Party Processions Act, for they had instituted no prosecution for its violation. He believed they were about to repeal the Ecclesiastical Titles Act on the ground that it had been allowed to remain a dead letter; and he submitted that this act so treated should not be allowed to remain on the statute books.[71]

Although Johnston's 1870 attempt received support from some very unlikely sources,[72] the government effectively blocked the bill's passage, arguing that "they were not prepared in the present condition of Ireland to do that which would appear to be a proclamation on their part that these party processions were harmless and inoffensive, and without danger to the peace and prosperity of Ireland."[73]

Ironically, the Party Processions Act was in reality a dead letter of Ireland. Since coming to office in 1868, the Liberal administration had not enforced its provisions, allowing Orange processionists to march with impunity on the Twelfth of July. As long as Orange marchers steered clear of sectarian clashes, they were free to commemorate the Protestant victory at the Boyne. This policy is well illustrated by instructions given by Undersecretary T.H. Burke to an inexperienced magistrate traveling north for the first time: "I was in hopes of seeing you on your way to the north, as this is the first time you have been sent there. I was anxious to impress upon you to act with great prudence and not to interfere unless absolutely necessary to prevent a breach of the peace. The constabulary can take down the names of any parties violating the Party Processions Act and apply for instructions as to whether any steps should be taken against them."[74] The fact that no Orangemen had been prosecuted for violating the terms of the act since 1867 was a clear indication of how assiduously the government wanted to avoid such confrontations.

There was one exception to the administration's laissez-faire approach to party processions—the city of Derry. Sectarian tension had been mounting in Derry since the election of 1868, when the Liberal party unseated the Conservative M.P., Lord Claud John Hamilton. Party hostility erupted in April 1869 when angry loyalists and their Catholic opponents marked Prince

Arthur's visit to Derry with a sectarian riot. With party feelings high in Derry,[75] the partisan celebrations of the Apprentice Boys became increasingly contentious in 1869 and 1870. In a desperate attempt to preserve the peace, the government sought to ban the celebrations in 1871, sending extra police and military to enforce the ban. This led to clashes between the police and the Apprentice Boys, who attempted to march in both August and December. The Party Processions Act clearly had not changed popular attitudes about marching in Ulster.

Angry at government interference with the Derry celebrations, William Johnston brought the matter up in the House of Commons in March 1872. To draw attention to the issue, Johnston proposed a motion condemning the government's recent intervention in Derry. His motion emphasized the now familiar theme that this legislation was administered with little regard for impartiality: "That the conduct of Her Majesty's government in prohibiting the Derry celebrations, while allowing party demonstrations in Dublin and Cork, evinced a spirit of partiality which in the opinion of this House is highly to be condemned."[76] Johnston's motion provoked a lengthy and rather tedious debate on the subject; a discussion dominated by well-worn arguments for and against the maintenance of the Party Processions Act in Ireland.

But then came an astonishing surprise. In the midst of the debate the chief secretary for Ireland, the Marquess of Hartington, stood up to respond to the motion and speech of William Johnston. After defending the government against Johnston's partiality charge, Hartington declared that the government was now ready to support Johnston's proposed repeal of the Party Processions Act. The reasoning behind Hartington's seeming change of heart was rather simple:

The government had never, during their tenure of office, instituted one single prosecution under that act. It had an injurious effect on the minds of people—because respect ought to be paid to law—when people were aware that an act existed on the statute book which was constantly violated and never enforced. Well, then, believing that the power the government possessed under the ordinary common law was sufficient, and that the maintenance of this act with the semblance of partiality on the statute book had an injurious effect, the government were prepared to propose to the House to repeal the Party Processions Act, and not to substitute any other enactment dealing with this particular class of demonstrations.[77]

In other words, the Liberal government believed that the repeal of the Party Processions Act was nothing more than symbolic. Since the authorities only prosecuted Orange processionists when their behavior threatened to disturb the peace, Hartington argued that Dublin Castle had no need for special legislation, especially when it aggravated the feelings of a substantial section of the Ulster population. With both Liberal and Conservative support Johnston's bill to repeal the Party Processions Act sailed through parliament unamended, receiving the royal assent on 27 June 1872.

But if the Marquess of Hartington believed that the repeal of the Party Processions Act was merely a symbolic gesture, loyalist reaction in Ulster proved just how important such symbols were to northern popular politics. Orangemen across the province rejoiced at the decision; their partisan rights had been saved again. While rank-and-file Orangemen were elated at their legal victory, the Orange elite made sure that things were kept under control for the upcoming Twelfth. In Portadown one policeman reported that local masters had gone so far as to limit the amount of alcohol consumed at the Orange festival.[78] Another constable summed up the 1872 marching season quite neatly: in gratitude for the repeal of the Party Processions Act, Orange leaders "will not this year permit anything of an aggressive character to be done by their body."[79]

The reassertion of gentry and elite leadership over plebeian Orangeism proved to be one of the critical by-products of William Johnston's campaign to repeal the Party Processions Act. William Gladstone's Liberal victory in 1868 was particularly important to this process. With Gladstone advocating a major measure of land reform and the disestablishment of the Church of Ireland, members of the Orange elite allied themselves with a broad populist campaign against the government. Disestablishment was particularly critical here, for it was the threat to the established church that pushed members of the clergy and gentry into a more activist stance. This shift was welcomed by plebeian loyalists, whose unwavering vision emphasized the necessity of Protestant unity in the face of a revanchist Catholic population. And this was critical, for Protestant Ulster would soon face its gravest threat yet. By revitalizing the cross-class Protestant alliance on which Orangeism was predicated, William Johnston's successful campaign to repeal the Party Processions Act played a critical role in setting the stage for the most important development of nineteenth-century Protestant politics—the formation of Ulster Unionism.

■ Conclusion

Sectarian Violence and the Formation of Modern Ulster Politics

> *The plain, the undeniable truth is that there are two antagonistic popula-*
> *tions, two different nations on Irish soil. To speak of one of them only, as is*
> *so often done, as the Irish people is a mischievous fallacy. . . . To put the one*
> *under the feet of the other, and that is what is meant by governing Ireland*
> *by an Irish legislature and according to Irish ideas, would be a shameful*
> *and cruel injustice. Whatever may be pretended, it never would, it never*
> *could, come to good. There is no community of feeling, and therefore can be*
> *no common citizenship between the two sections of the Irish people.*
>
> Thomas MacKnight, *Ulster As It Is*

In an important book on late nineteenth-century politics Brian Walker argues that the political, religious, and social divisions that have shaped Ulster's
modern history emerged in their modern form only in the period between
1868 and 1886. Looking closely at this formative period, he focuses on the
fortunes of the Liberal Party, which enjoyed a considerable measure of success between 1872 and 1883. While the Home Rule crisis of 1885–1886 destroyed the political independence of Ulster Liberalism, Walker cites its
strength as a poignant illustration of the existence of political alternatives
to the denominational politics that have characterized the twentieth-century Ulster experience. In his view this underlines the fact that the formalized political divide between nationalist and unionist in the north of Ireland
occurred in the crisis years of 1880–1886. Only by acknowledging the comparatively recent formation of modern Ulster politics can we "cope with
the real burden of our past."[1]

But if the formation of sectarian politics in Ulster was not inevitable, it was certainly always a likely outcome. As Walker himself notes, Ulster liberalism's electoral triumphs were directly tied to a single issue—tenant right. Frustrated by the inadequacies of the Irish Land Act of 1870, Presbyterian tenant farmers joined their Catholic brethren in supporting Liberal candidates in rural constituencies throughout the 1870s. Always tenuous, this Presbyterian-Catholic electoral alliance did not survive the Land Act of 1881, which satisfied most Presbyterian demands while leaving a number of Catholic grievances unresolved. This gap only widened when Charles Stewart Parnell redirected Irish Catholic political energies toward Home Rule, a shift that further alienated Ulster Presbyterian opinion. With agrarian interests divided and the constitutional question again at the center of political discourse, the Liberal party suddenly found itself without a substantial constituency in Ulster.[2] The Reform Act of 1884 only reinforced this trend, enfranchising rural laborers, small farmers, and urban workers, social groups that traditionally espoused the views of hard-line political Protestantism. By late 1885, Ulster liberals found that the middle ground that they had successfully cultivated in the 1870s had disappeared. From 1886 political and religious allegiances would rarely conflict in the north of Ireland.

The process which forged a formalized sectarian system of politics in the mid-1880s was the same process that had produced partisan contention and violence throughout the century. Catholic challenges to a status quo that gave Protestants an ascendant position vis-à-vis Irish Catholics consistently had produced a vehement reaction from plebeian loyalists. Orangemen and their allies typically responded to such threats with ritualized displays of strength, public exhibitions that provoked most of the sectarian riots of the century. The primary difference this time was one of scale. Building on the organizational foundation of the Irish National Land League, Charles Stewart Parnell headed a Catholic political movement of unprecedented size and scope in the mid-1880s. Combining this populist strength with brilliant parliamentary tactics, Parnell succeeded in pushing Irish Home Rule to the front of the Liberal agenda. With Prime Minister Gladstone's support, Home Rule suddenly seemed within reach. Predictably, this produced a response from hard-line loyalists in Ulster, where sectarian contention had been increasing in direct proportion to nationalist agitation throughout the late 1870s and early 1880s.[3]

Although Land League activity was more than enough to spark a substantial Orange renewal in the early 1880s,[4] it failed to forge anything like the pan-Protestant coalition for which hard-line loyalist ideologues were pressing. This should not be surprising. While Presbyterian tenant-farmers (particularly thick on the ground in northwest Ulster) certainly viewed the Land League's tactics and ultimate aspirations as extreme, they shared many of the League's intermediate goals, particularly the demand for the enactment of the famous three F's: fair rent, fixity of tenure, and free sale.

Conditions for the creation of an antinationalist Protestant movement began to emerge in 1883, when the newly formed Irish National League contested a by-election in County Monaghan. The Irish Parliamentary Party had hitherto largely steered clear of Ulster,[5] allowing the Liberal party to represent northern Catholic interests. This ended abruptly in 1883 when Timothy Healy, the controversial M.P. from County Wexford, contested the open Monaghan seat. In his campaign Healy stressed his excellent credentials on the land question, and with the considerable aid of both Parnell and the Catholic bishop of Clogher, Dr. James Donnelly, he won a narrow victory over his Conservative opponent.[6]

Healy's victory heralded the beginning of another "invasion of Ulster," as the Irish National League attempted to capture Ulster Catholic support by organizing a series of public demonstrations throughout northern border counties. These displays of nationalist strength predictably produced a series of Orange counterdemonstrations. The proximity of these rival meetings often gave rise to partisan confrontation; on several occasions only police action kept the two parties separated. The most serious of these near-affrays occurred in October 1883 near the Fermanagh border village of Rosslea, where Lord Rossmore, the grand master of the Orange Order in County Monaghan, organized a loyalist demonstration to counter a nationalist meeting occurring outside of town. Thomas Macknight, editor of the *Northern Whig,* captured the fever pitch of sectarian tension at Rosslea: "Lord Rossmore . . . was represented as saying, that the Nationalists on the hill were rebels and scavengers, whom the Orangemen could easily vanquish, and that the Brethren could also, if they thought fit, eat up the handful of soldiers in a few seconds."[7] The two parties exchanged both insults and gunfire, but the authorities managed to keep participants apart. Needless to say, the government did not take kindly to Lord Rossmore's inflammatory remarks and stripped him of his position as magistrate.

Although counterdemonstrations like the one at Rosslea brought renewed enthusiasm for hard-line loyalism among plebeian Orangemen desperate for activist gentry leadership, these confrontations still failed to create a true antinationalist Ulster Protestant coalition. Divisions between Liberals and Conservatives simply remained too wide to forge the Protestant unity sought by loyalist activists. In particular, most Liberals viewed the

Orange Order as a reactionary and divisive force in Ulster life, a sentiment nicely expressed by the Tyrone landowner Hugh de Feltenberg Montgomery: "The task that remains is to obliterate all remembrance of the old strife and civil war. . . . They and they alone are keeping alive the memory of the old strife and with it the old feeling of disaffection to the present settlement."[8] While it must be noted that Montgomery's statement was made in the comparative tranquillity of the early 1870s, such anti-Orange beliefs did not fade easily. Even with nationalist Ireland beginning to assert itself, Montgomery and other liberal-minded Protestants remained loath to ally themselves with their old Orange adversaries.

Two events transformed this situation in 1885 and 1886. First, Irish nationalists, capitalizing on the organizational structure of the Irish National League, the expanded post-1884 electorate, and continuing Protestant division, dramatically extended their political "invasion of Ulster," capturing seventeen of the province's thirty-three parliamentary seats. Significantly, the Liberal party failed to win a seat in Ulster in the general election of 1885.[9] Not surprisingly, Home Rule dominated the election. But while the results seem to herald the formalization of sectarian politics, they disguised the continued existence of significant divisions within the Protestant camp. Ulster liberalism was not quite dead yet. This can be seen by examining the role played by the Orange Order in the contest. Although Conservatives effectively used Orangeism to mobilize newly enfranchised laborers and workers in east Ulster, the Order proved to be a hindrance to Protestant politics in several contests, as a number of Liberals remained unwilling to sink their differences with the forces of hard-line loyalism.[10]

Needless to say, the nationalist triumph in the north came as a shock to many Ulster Protestants. In many ways the election was the first step in the crystallization of denominational politics. This was not just a matter of results. The year-long focus on constitutional issues had already pushed many Ulster Liberals toward the need for an antinationalist alliance.[11] This transition gained speed throughout the second half of 1885. At a meeting at Craigavad, County Down, on 5 November 1885, the Liberal leader Lord Hartington coined the term Liberal unionist, nicely underlining Liberal movement toward a pan-Protestant political front. According to Thomas MacKnight, "every Ulster Liberal regarded himself from that time as a Liberal unionist."[12]

But if the campaign's emphasis on constitutional matters had initiated Liberal Conservative discussion, it was the nationalist victory in the general election of 1885 that underscored the need for a united Protestant front. This shift was especially apparent in west Ulster, where activists formed the

THE LIVE SHELL.

(WHICH OF 'EM WILL THROW IT OVERBOARD?)

The Irish Question, 1886. (*Punch,* 30 January 1886.)

North West Loyalist Registration and Electoral Association to maximize Protestant electoral resources. The formal process by which Ulster unionism was born had begun.

But union was not to come easy. Throughout the early months of 1886 many Liberals continued to believe that William Gladstone would somehow resist the temptation of Irish Home Rule. The dream came crashing down on 8 April 1886, when the first home rule bill was introduced in the

House of Commons. The bill came as a tremendous blow to Ulster Liberals, who had hoped that it would at least include substantive provisions to protect the rights of the Protestant minority in Ireland. Thomas MacKnight's bitter reaction to Gladstone's conversion was indicative: "William Smith O'Brien was still the same man. He had not changed; Mr. Gladstone had."[13] The appearance of home rule legislation removed the final obstacle to the formal creation of a denominational system of politics in Ulster. On 30 April a large gathering of Ulster Liberals met at Belfast's Ulster Hall to declare their fervent opposition to home rule.[14] By July, when another general election was held, Protestant political divisions largely had been smoothed over (at least in public).[15] From 1886, Ulster politics would faithfully reflect the sectarian divide.

From the outset Orangemen and their hard-line loyalist supporters held a disproportionate influence within the unionist coalition that emerged from the crisis of 1885–1886. Two ideas help to explain Orange preponderance in the new movement. First, the Order's belief system was perfectly suited to the times. As shown throughout this study, loyalist ideology essentially was Manichaean in nature, calling for Protestant unity in the face of an unwavering Irish Catholic threat. Constructing their mythic narrative of Irish history around the tragic conflicts of the seventeenth century, loyalist activists had maintained the relevance of this belief system with repeated ritualized exhibitions of partisan strength. These displays provoked serious bouts of communal violence throughout the century—a fact that only reinforced the Orangeman's zero-sum view of Ulster society. With the very foundation of Irish Protestant society seemingly under siege by an unprecedented mobilization of Irish Catholic political strength in the mid-1880s, the loyalist call for Protestant unity behind its natural leaders suddenly seemed appropriate to wider sectors of the Protestant community.

Of course, Orangeism's role in the new unionist coalition transcended ideology. The movement also played a central part in reviving Protestant political fortunes. The Orange Order's political clout dramatically increased after 1884, when the Reform Act extended the franchise to agricultural laborers, small farmers, and the urban working class, exactly the social groups which constituted the backbone of Ulster Orangeism.[16] Conservative activists saw the political potential of such an organization as early as May 1885, when E.S. Finnigan, the full-time secretary of the County Down Constitutional Association, proposed to give the Orange Order a formal role in the Conservative electoral strategy:

It was proposed to form a large committee in each of the polling districts into which the county would be divided, this committee to be composed of the members of the present district committees together with the representatives of the agricultural labouring class and those who would have a vote as lodgers, employees, and servants. The Orange association would have a well-defined position. The district master and district officers, together with the master of each of the lodges in the district, would be appointed, or other brethren nominated by them, upon each committee.[17]

The Order accordingly played an integral role in several east Ulster campaigns in 1885, nominating and selecting candidates who supported the loyalist cause. With the constitutional crisis in full swing, the Order's role was extended in 1886. Political events in north Armagh illustrate this shift rather dramatically. In the general election of 1885, Orangeism had been a divisive issue in the district, dividing the Protestant vote and allowing the nationalist candidate to race home to victory. In 1886, north Armagh Protestants united to select the head of the Orange Order, Maj. Edward Saunderson, as the unionist candidate. Saunderson won in a landslide.

The creation of formal links between the Orange Order and the emerging Ulster unionist coalition brought distinct benefits to both organizations. As we have seen, Unionism profited from the Order's organizational structure, particularly critical in mobilizing the newly enfranchised proletarian classes. The Orange Order's intimate ties to Ulster Unionism ultimately transformed the organization, adding much-needed respectability to the Orange cause. In the decades after 1886 the social constitution of the Order expanded dramatically. With its anti-Catholic beliefs seemingly confirmed by the crisis of 1886, Orangeism began to move to the center of Ulster Protestantism, attracting long-reticent middle-class Protestants to the movement. By the early twentieth century, Orangeism lay at the heart of Ulster Unionism.

As if to confirm the formalization of denominational politics in Ulster, the summer of 1886 saw the worst sectarian riots of nineteenth-century Belfast. That party violence occurred in Belfast in 1886 came as no surprise. With the first home rule bill before parliament, communal tension increased throughout the late spring and early summer. What was surprising was the unprecedented extent and duration of the summer's rioting in Belfast. The fighting lasted three months, occurring over three relatively distinct phases.

The Belfast riots of 1886 began on 3 June, when a Catholic navvy working on the new Alexandra graving dock allegedly told a Protestant laborer that after home rule had passed "neither he nor any of his sort should get leave to work there or earn a loaf there or any other place."[18] A report of this incident reached the predominately Protestant workforce of Harland and Woolf on the following day.[19] At midday at least one hundred Protestant shipwrights gathered at Queen's Island and marched down to the mudflats to get their revenge. Using the tools of their trade as weapons, the shipwrights drove the Catholic workforce into the Lagan, where a young man named Curran drowned.[20]

Belfast nationalists used Curran's funeral on 6 June as a massive demonstration for home rule. Starting in Ballymacarrett, an estimated seven thousand men, women, and children walked in procession through the city. Although the police succeeded in separating the two parties, the funeral/demonstration kept party resentment near the boiling point. Clashes occurred all along the Shankill-Falls divide, where a loyalist mob attacked the works of a Catholic brick and oven manufacturer who employed several "home rulers" at his Grosvenor Street establishment. Excitement reached new heights on 8 June, when news of the rejection of the first home rule bill reached Belfast. The news produced a predictable reaction from Belfast loyalists. Accompanied by a seemingly ubiquitous fife-and-drum band, they drove Catholic workers out of their jobs at various Grosvenor Street enterprises.[21]

The rejection of home rule injected a new element into the riots. To celebrate the occasion, hard-line loyalists made plans to light a number of bonfires in the Shankill district. Unfortunately, one body of revelers decided to add to the festivities by wrecking a Catholic-owned spirits shop on Percy Street. Police responded to the rumored attack, only to find the shop destroyed and its contents consumed. Loyalists proceeded to stone the police, who responded by firing buckshot into the crowd, which one policeman described unkindly as the "lowest scum of the locality." The next three days saw accelerated confrontation between the police and Protestant crowds angry with interference in such loyal districts. Police-loyalist clashes reached their height on 9 June, when besieged policemen shot and killed seven members of a Protestant crowd.[22] The first stage of the riots ended on the following day. By 10 June, 850 additional policemen had been brought into the northern capital to quell the disturbances. Eight days had wrought havoc throughout west Belfast; at least eight people were dead and untold numbers injured. Local combatants did not have a monopoly on suffering. At least 126 constables had been injured in the line of duty. Peace had been bought at quite a price. The quiet would survive less than a month.

The second phase of the riots began in early July, sparked by the results of the general election held on the sixth of that month. The election itself proved to be relatively tranquil, no small feat given the level of communal violence that had characterized the city in early June. Trouble started on the following day, as nationalists discovered that they had won the parliamentary seat for west Belfast. Home rulers celebrated their victory throughout Catholic areas of the city, lighting bonfires and parading with bands. Unfortunately, one body of east Belfast Catholics disobeyed the mayor's edict to contain such festivities within the bounds of communal settlement. This brought a reaction from a group of plebeian loyalists in east Belfast, who paraded down Newtownards Road, throwing stones at the windows of St. Matthew's Catholic chapel. Small-scale clashes broke out along west Belfast's major fault line on the following day, but the presence of a company of infantry managed to contain the situation.[23] Tensions remained high, but the situation seemed to be under control.

This seemingly was confirmed on 12 July, when approximately ten thousand people participated in the Orange festivities. Such a display might have been expected to produce another round of widespread rioting, but nothing of the kind occurred on the Twelfth. Unfortunately, any semblance of peace was shattered the next day, when a nationalist crowd attacked an Orange band in Grosvenor Road. That evening saw renewed rioting, sparked by a nationalist invasion of the Shankill district. This territorial intrusion inevitably triggered rioting throughout west Belfast. The most serious clashes centered on the traditional battlegrounds of Durham Street, Killen Street, and Grosvenor Road. Not surprisingly, some of the heaviest fighting occurred between loyalist crowds and the police. The two groups exchanged shots on four separate occasions, killing two people.

Although the second phase of rioting concluded on the following day, it was not long before sectarian clashes broke out again. Ironically, a children's field trip initiated the final phase of the 1886 riots. Every summer, groups of Belfast's Protestant school children marched to railway centers accompanied by music and scriptural banners. Many Catholics understandably viewed these occasions as sectarian in nature, a kind of youth version of the Twelfth of July. In that summer's combustible atmosphere, such festivities were likely to stir up trouble.

This final phase of the riots began on 31 July, when the Rev. Hugh Hanna took his children on their annual excursion. The trouble started when a loyalist crowd met the children's group and "insisted upon playing some 40 or 50 of the children through the town."[24] As soon as the makeshift procession made its way down Donegall Street, it found itself engaged in a stone-throwing clash with a home rule crowd positioned across from Carrick Hill. The news that a Catholic mob had assailed the "children's parade" enraged plebeian loyalist opinion, triggering general rioting along the familiar Shankill-Falls divide. The final and most murderous phase of the 1886 riots had begun.

This time the rioting lasted more than a week, as both parties surged back and forth throughout west Belfast. Protestant crowds concentrated their attacks on public houses and spirits shops, businesses generally owned by Belfast Catholics. The drunken state of loyalist mobs undoubtedly intensified the August disturbances; on 7 August policemen reported that they had attempted to intimidate a loyalist crowd with gunfire, but that members of the "mob were so drunk and reckless that they paid little heed to it."[25] Police attempts to defend the shops only exacerbated bad relations between militant Protestants and the police. Magistrates were soon forced to use the military rather than police constables to maintain law and order in the Shankill district. While this undoubtedly wise move removed a central grievance from the situation, it did not end the rioting.

The worst day of violence occurred on 8 August, when a running series of vicious street battles claimed the lives of nine people. Fighting raged unimpeded for five hours on Caper Street, where two youths were mortally wounded in the rioting. Called into action to defend Catholic public houses from loyalist assault, police constables shot and killed six people that day. Rioting gradually subsided after the tumult of 8 August. Outbreaks of partisan violence did not stop entirely (four people were killed in clashes between 15 August and 19 September), but things slowly returned to normal. The final shots of the season were fired on 21 September. While casualty reports are always a bit suspect, at least thirty-one people died in Belfast's bloodiest summer on record.

The Belfast riots of 1886 illustrate many of the themes discussed throughout this study. In many ways the situation paralleled the summer of 1829. In 1829 ultra-Protestants had used the Twelfth celebration to protest the passage of Catholic emancipation; their displays triggered widespread rioting throughout the province. As in 1829, a perceived threat to the status quo precipitated the 1886 riots. Most plebeian loyalists viewed home rule in near-apocalyptic terms, as a plan that would put them "under the feet" of their nationalist enemies. Orangemen and their loyalist allies reacted to this threat as they had throughout the century, by asserting their strength in ritual-laden demonstrations, exhibitions that inevitably provoked sectarian riots in Belfast's combustible atmosphere that summer.

What made the 1886 riots particularly noteworthy was their duration and human cost. In part this reflected the issue at stake, for home rule threatened the very foundation of loyalist political culture. But other factors played a critical role in sustaining party clashes over a three-month period. The constricted and segregated urban environment was particularly crucial here, allowing militant activists to repeatedly manufacture the kind of set-piece confrontations that often had led to sectarian violence throughout the century. Lacking the buffer zones that regulated conflict in the countryside, west Belfast became a kind of laboratory for maintaining and intensifying communal violence. Once conflict started, it became very difficult to bring the heat down.

The years between 1886 and 1921 saw the crystallization of modern Ulster's joint political culture, a system of popular politics centered on two interlocked but antagonistic views of how Irish society should be structured. For all the discussion about two separate Irish nations, it is important to note that these conflicting visions were inextricably tied to one another. In many ways these were complementary political ideologies, each dependent on the opposition of the other. This was especially true of Ulster Protestants, who have been unable to forge a political culture that defines itself positively with any of the nations of the British Isles.[26]

The formalization of Ulster's joint political culture had major consequences for the evolution of northern politics. Unable to obtain an adequate sense of political community, Ulster unionism remained centered on the exclusivist tenets of loyalist ideology. This in turn defined the political options for Ulster Catholics, who remained arrayed against the imposition of Orange hegemony. Sectarian contention thus remained at the heart of this joint political culture, a fact that redounded to the benefit of hard-line Ulster Protestants. By defining the terms in which Ulster politics operated, loyalists ensured that the communal divide dominated both politics and public discourse. As long as loyalty remained the focus of discussion, Ulster Protestants would retain their ascendant position over the Catholic population.

The sectarian displays and riots detailed throughout this study played an integral part in the formation of this denominational system of politics. By continually replaying the traumatic events of the seventeenth century, party processions and the violence they produced maintained the vitality and relevance of a political discourse centered on sectarian division. But it was not just a question of keeping the divisions of the past alive. Partisan contention also helped to prevent the formation of alternative political arrangements. Brian Walker's study of the brief renaissance of Ulster liberalism in the 1870s illustrates this phenomenon perfectly. When political discussion shifted from the land question to the constitutional relationship between Ireland and Great Britain in the early 1880s, the Catholic/Presbyterian coalition that had pushed the Liberal Party to a position of prominence quickly disintegrated. Within months, Ulster politics consolidated around political parties centered on each of these conflicting visions. The natural order had returned. This study has analyzed the wide array of factors that led to sectarian rioting in nineteenth-century Ulster, focusing on the impact of national and local politics, demographic and economic trends, and notions of sectarian geography and territory. But if a number of different variables shaped the contours of communal conflict, one constant theme lay at the heart of partisan contention in the north of Ireland. Virtually every party riot in this period originated in a perceived threat to an Irish polity structured upon Protestant privilege. Specific issues and political forms changed with the times, but the ideological core of Ulster loyalism was not altered—Protestants must preserve their ascendant position vis-à-vis Irish Catholics. Sectarian violence revolved around the ritual display of this particular tenet of loyalist ideology (and critically the Catholic reaction to this display). In such an argument, there could be no middle ground.

In the early decades of the twentieth century the two irreconcilable worldviews detailed throughout this study emerged to form the basis of a system of politics and eventually a state. This was by no means inevitable. But given the depth of division involved, it was always the most likely outcome. Contention over these conflicting visions resonated in both Ulster communities with a power unmatched by any competing belief systems. By promoting sectarian division in the public arena through their ritual-laden public exhibitions and the riots they produced, plebeian loyalists and their Catholic adversaries played a critical role in maintaining the relevance and vitality of the antagonistic worldviews that gave rise to such conflict. Tragically, the narrow ground that they helped to construct has not widened perceptibly in the ensuing years.

Notes

Abbreviations

AM	Armagh County Museum, Armagh
NAI	National Archives of Ireland, Dublin
NLI	National Library of Ireland, Dublin
PRO	Public Record Office, London
PRONI	Public Record Office of Northern Ireland, Belfast
Rep. on Orange Lodges I	*Report from the select committee to inquire into the nature,character, extent, and tendency of Orange lodges, associations, or societies in Ireland, with min utes of evidence and appendix,* H.C. 1835 (377), XV.
Rep. on Orange Lodges III	*Report from the select committee to inquire into the nature,character, extent, and tendency of Orange lodges, associations, or societies in Ireland, with min utes of evidence and appendix,* H.C. 1835 (476), XVI.
SOC	State of the Country Papers
SOI evidence	*Report from the select committee of the House of Lords appointed to inquire into the state of Ireland,* H.L. 1825 (181), IX.
TCD	Trinity College, Dublin

Introduction: The Study of Sectarian Violence and Modern Ulster History

1. *Northern Whig,* 19 July 1849.

2. Evidence of Joseph Tabiteau, *Battle of Magheramayo. Report of the Evidence Taken Before the Government Commissioner, Walter Berwick, Esq., Q.C., at a Court Held in Castlewellan from 30th July to 4th August, and, by Adjournment, on Tuesday,*

18th September 1849 (Newry: James Henderson, 1849), 15. Hereafter cited as *Battle of Magheramayo.*

3. Ibid., 70.

4. Evidence of Major Arthur Wilkinson, *Battle of Magheramayo,* 4.

5. Ibid., 5.

6. See Thomas Redington to the Lord Chancellor, 6 Oct. 1849, PRO, H.O. 45/2603/94–110. For an angry ultra-Protestant response to their dismissal, see *Dublin Evening Packet,* 20 Oct. 1849.

7. Whyte, *Interpreting Northern Ireland,* viii.

8. For an excellent overview of the evolution of modern Ulster historiography, see Walker, "Historical Perspectives," in *Dancing to History's Tune,* 128–52.

9. For aspects of nineteenth-century Ulster, see Gibbon, *Origins;* Hepburn, *Past Apart;* Miller, *Queen's Rebels;* Henry Patterson, *Class Conflict;* Walker, *Ulster Politics;* and Wright, *Two Lands.* For a balanced overview, see Bardon, *History of Ulster.*

10. See Jarman, *Material Conflicts;* David Miller, *Peep O'Day Boys;* Smyth, *Men of No Property;* and Wright, *Two Lands.*

11. Stewart, *Narrow Ground,* 143–45.

12. Jarman, *Material Conflicts,* 11.

13. Walker, *Ulster Politics;* and Wright, *Two Lands.*

14. See Joseph Lee's heavy-handed treatment of Ulster unionism in his prizewinning book *Ireland, 1912–85.*

15. For an excellent introduction to the evolution of the idea of political culture, see Gendzel, "Political Culture," 225–50.

16. Thompson, "The Moral Economy of the English Crowd in the Eighteenth Century," 76–136; Davis, "Rites of Violence," 152–87.

17. Here I must acknowledge an intellectual debt to Suzanne Desan, whose work on Davis and Thompson provides an excellent introduction to the study of popular violence. See Desan, "Crowds, Community, and Ritual," 47–71. Also see Freitag, *Collective Action,* 3–18.

18. For an excellent introduction to the study of communal violence in northern India, see Freitag, *Collective Action.* See also Peter van der Veer, "Riots and Rituals: The Construction of Violence and Public Space in Hindu Nationalism," in Brass, *Riots and Pogroms,* 154–76.

19. Walker, *Ulster Politics,* 267.

1. Trouble in Armagh, 1784–1798

1. Edward Cooke to Lord Gosford, 7 July 1796, PRONI, Gosford Papers, D.1606/1/185A.

2. For contemporary condemnations of the Armagh magistracy, see Lord Camden to Thomas Pelham, 12 July 1796, PRONI, Calendar of Pelham Papers,

T.755/3/27; William Elliott to Thomas Pelham, 4 Aug. 1796, PRONI, Calendar of Pelham Papers, T.755/3/49; John Pollock to Robert Ross, 26 Aug. 1796, NAI, Rebellion Papers, 620/24/161; "J.W." to ——, 27 Aug. 1796, NAI, Rebellion Papers, 620/24/165 and —— to Edward Cooke, 14 July 1797, NAI, Rebellion Papers, 620/31/231.

3. The Armagh expulsions have been well-served by local historians. See Patrick Tohall, "Diamond Fight of 1795," 17–50; McEvoy, "Peep of Day Boys," 60–127; and Desmond O'Neill, "Ulster Migration to Mayo, 1795–1796," in Bernard O'Hara, ed., *Mayo: Aspects of Its Heritage* (Galway: The Archaeological, Historical, and Folklore Society, 1982), 84–87.

4. Among many recent accounts see Smyth, *Men of No Property,* 110–1; Nancy Curtin, *United Irishmen,* 150–52.

5. Senior, *Orangeism,* 1–21; Gibbon, *Origins of Ulster Unionism,* 155–92; Miller, *Peep O'Day Boys and Defenders;* Cullen, "Political Structures of the Defenders," 117–38.

6. Thompson, "Moral Economy," 76–136.

7. Ibid, 79.

8. For insightful critiques of Thompson's work, see Bohstedt, "Moral Economy"; and Desan, "Crowds, Community, and Ritual," 47–71. Before his death in 1995, Thompson issued a typically sardonic rejoinder to many of his critics. See "Moral Economy Reviewed," in his *Customs in Common,* 259–351. For an interesting application of this conceptual tool within Irish studies, see Bartlett, "End to Moral Economy."

9. Bardon, *Belfast,* 116.

10. A notable exception being the work of David Miller, whose *Queen's Rebels* is certainly one of the most creative and insightful monographs in Irish historical writing. In this work, Miller examines the evolution of Ulster loyalist ideology, focusing on the importance of traditional Scottish Presbyterian contractual thinking. It was this intellectual heritage, Miller argues, that primarily informed the notions of conditional allegiance that were (are?) so central to the often strained relationship between Ulster Protestants and the British Crown. For a similarly nuanced examination of nineteenth-century politics, see Wright, *Two Lands on One Soil.*

11. In using the term moral economy to describe aspects of communal relations in the north of Ireland, I am obviously expanding upon Thompson's more economic focus. My use of the idea originally was inspired by the work of James Scott, who employed this framework in his powerful study of patron-client relations in Southeast Asia. See Scott, *Moral Economy of the Peasant.*

12. I am emphatically not arguing that all Ulster Protestants had the same conceptions of their exclusive right to citizenship. There obviously was a wide range of opinion within the communities of Ulster Protestantism, including a rather small minority who were reluctantly willing to give Irish Catholics equal standing within the Irish polity.

13. In using the term mythic I do not mean to imply that this view of Irish

history is in any way false. Rather, myth is defined here as an extremely complex interplay of perceptions, beliefs and attitudes that shape fundamental concepts of cultural identity. For Ulster Protestants this "system" of beliefs rested in part on a view of Irish history that emphasized certain historical events: 1641, 1688–1691, and 1798. See Barnard, "The Uses of 23 October 1641 and Irish Protestant Celebrations"; Brown, *The Whole Protestant Community.* For a cautionary note, see Walker, "1641, 1689, 1690, and All That: The Unionist Sense of History." Finally, for a balanced reassessment of the threat posed by Jacobism in eighteenth-century Ireland, see Connolly, *Religion, Law, and Power,* 237–60.

14. For an excellent discussion of the real impact of penal legislation, see Connolly, *Religion, Law, and Power,* 262–313.

15. Historical proofs of Catholic revanchism were reinforced with a liberal dose of religious anti-Catholicism. For an interpretation of sectarian relations that focuses on religious aspects of the Ulster-Scot worldview, see Akenson, *God's Peoples,* 97–150.

16. Miller, *Queen's Rebels,* 53.

17. Elliott, "The Defenders in Ulster," 223.

18. Catholic relief acts were passed in 1778, 1782, 1792, and 1793. In addition, various Volunteer companies brought a very limited number of Catholics within their ranks after 1782. Two excellent monographs recently have been published on these critical political matters. For the politics of the Catholic question, see Bartlett, *The Rise and Fall of the Irish Nation,* and Malcomson, *John Foster: The Politics of the Anglo-Irish Ascendancy.* For groundbreaking insights into popular politics, see Smyth, *Men of No Property.*

19. For the growth of the Irish linen industry, see Gill, *The Rise of the Irish Linen Industry.*

20. Miller, "Armagh Troubles," 168.

21. Ibid., 181–86.

22. J. Byrne, *Impartial account.* There has been some controversy over the true identity of the author. Louis M. Cullen argues that Byrne was in fact Father James Quigley, an Armagh man active in the United Irishmen (Cullen, "Late Eighteenth-Century Politicisation in Ireland"). The late Armagh historian T.G.F. Paterson made a transcript of Byrne's manuscript that is housed at the Public Record Office of Northern Ireland (PRONI, T.1722). David Miller placed a full copy of the transcript at the heart of his indispensable collection of documents on the Armagh troubles. See Miller, *Peep O'Day Boys and Defenders.* Because of the greater accessibility of this latter work, all citations to Byrne's pamphlet will refer to Miller's publication.

23. For an excellent discussion of the complex relationship between the Volunteers and the Catholic question, see Bartlett, *Fall and Rise of the Irish Nation,* 103–20.

24. *Belfast Newsletter,* 15–19 Feb. 1782. The next several months saw a flurry of Ulster Volunteer meetings to support the sentiments expressed at Dungannon.

25. Ibid., 8–11 June 1784.

26. James Kelly, "Selected Documents," 279.

27. Miller, *Peep O'Day Boys and Defenders,* 10–15, 17–23, 25–37, 44–48, 53–63. See also Lord Gosford to Arthur Acheson, 8 Feb. 1788, PRONI, Gosford Papers, D.1606/125C.

28. Coyle, a manufacturer of cambric and muslin, reportedly employed 150 men and women in the Lurgan area (*Belfast Newsletter,* 25 Jan. 1796).

29. Fitzgerald was hanged for murder in 1786. He reportedly fought in twenty-six duels in his lifetime. A biographical sketch can be found in "George Robert Fitzgerald—Part I," in *Dublin University Magazine,* 16, no. 91 (July 1840), 17. See also James Kelly, *That Damn'd Thing Called Honour: Duelling in Ireland, 1570–1860* (Cork: Cork University Press, 1995).

30. *Belfast Newsletter,* 27–30 July 1784.

31. "A.B.," 3 July 1798, NAI, Rebellion Papers, 620/39/10; Miller, *Peep O'Day Boys and Defenders,* 25–37.

32. Miller, *Peep O'Day Boys and Defenders,* 17–23.

33. Ibid., 25–37.

34. Thomas Prentice to Lord Charlemont, 28 Nov. 1788, in James Caulfield, first earl of Charlemont, *The Manuscript and Correspondence of James, First Earl of Charlemont* (2 vols., London, comprising Historical Manuscripts Commission, *12th Report,* appendix, pt. 8, vol. 2, 79–81. Hereafter cited as *HMC Charlemont MSS.*

35. This is Byrne's phrase. For his narrative of the battle, see Miller, *Peep O'Day Boys and Defenders,* 57–59.

36. At least one more "Defender" died of wounds received that day. See Robert Livingstone to Lord Charlemont, 17 Dec. 1788, *HMC Charlemont MSS,* vol. 2, 83.

37. Another clash occurred at Lisnagade, County Down, in July 1789. Many more were prevented by the exertions of local gentlemen. See Miller, *Peep O'Day Boys and Defenders,* 57–59.

38. Smyth, *Men of No Property,* 51.

39. Miller, *Peep O'Day Boys and Defenders,* 93–97, 103–8. For an excellent secondary account, see Smyth, *Men of No Property,* 49–50.

40. The high sheriff and grand jury of Armagh made a declaration to this effect at the summer assizes of 1793. See *Belfast Newsletter,* 23–27 Aug. 1793.

41. Defenderism proved particularly successful in the north Leinster counties of Louth and Meath. See Smyth, *Men of No Property,* 100–120.

42. Evidence of James Christie, *Rep. on Orange Lodges I,* H.C. 1835 (377), XV, 379–80.

43. Gen. William Dalrymple to Thomas Pelham, 9 Aug. 1794, PRONI, Calendar of Pelham Papers, T.755/2/94–6.

44. Richard Abbot to ———, 17 June 1795, NAI, Rebellion Papers, 620/22/90. Abbot reported that much of the problem arose from the partiality of magistrates in the region. His other prescription for solving crisis was more interesting. Abbot recommended closing the local public houses run by Daniel Winter and a man

named Cullen. These pubs were points of general rendezvous for the parties and served as arenas for cockfights. Daniel Winter is the famous "Diamond Dan" of Orange lore.

45. There are a large number of sources for the Battle of Diamond. For contemporary press reports, see *Belfast Newsletter,* 21–25, 25–28 Sept. 1795. Transcripts of Col. William Blacker's description of the clash can be found in Belfast (PRONI, T.2595–4) and in Miller, *Peep O'Day Boys and Defenders,* 117–22. The original manuscripts are housed in the Armagh County Museum.

46. This fact is reflected by the sparse press coverage devoted to the clash in the *Belfast Newsletter* and the *Northern Star.*

47. For one of the innumerable Orange hagiographies of the heroes of the Diamond, see Col. Sir William Verner, *A Short History of the Battle of the Diamond.* Orangemen have not been the only ones to remember the Diamond. Collecting local folklore in Armagh in 1927, T.G.F. Paterson recorded the following remarks from one Laurence Cullen: "Some of the people killed at the Diamond were buried here. People are not long quit coming to say prayers for them." See AM, Paterson Collection, 12/53.

48. Accounts of the first meeting can be found in the transcripts of the Blacker manuscripts (PRONI, T.2595/4).

49. Col. R.H. Wallace, "History of the Orange Order: The Formative Years, 1795–1798," in Grand Orange Lodge of Ireland, *The Formation of the Orange Order: The Edited Papers of Colonel William Blacker and Colonel Robert H. Wallace* (Belfast: Grand Orange Lodge of Ireland Publications, 1994), 65.

50. Blacker Manuscripts, Armagh County Museum, Armagh, 2/20. Hereafter cited as Blacker MSS. Blacker lists Joseph Atkinson, the Verners of Church Hill, Viscount Northland of Dungannon, William Brownlow of Lurgan and Major Waring of Waringstown, County Down, as the principal members of the region's gentry who gave the Order early support.

51. Orange historians have been quick to challenge the assumption that members of the Orange Order had anything to do with the expulsions, claiming that the outrages occurred before Orangeism really took root in Ulster. While technically there may be some justice in this claim, in that these men had not formally joined a lodge at the time they were involved in the wreckings, there can be no doubt that these plebeian loyalists soon found a home within the Orange fold. For an Orange perspective on these events, see Aiken McClelland, *The Formation of the Orange Order* (Newcastle, Co. Down: Mourne Observer Ltd., 197–).

52. Blacker noted that the wreckers rarely used fire in these assaults: "Perhaps the perpetrators had an eye to their own interests as well as the executing of vengeance on public grounds, and contemplating occupation of the vacated holdings, were unwilling that they themselves or their friends be put to the expense of rebuilding sacked domiciles." See transcripts of the Blacker Manuscripts, PRONI, T.2595/4.

53. The nature and progress of the expulsions can be followed in the *Northern Star,* 24 Sept. 1795–17 July 1796.

54. For two press estimates, see *Northern Star,* 21–5 Dec. 1795, and *Dublin Evening Post,* 6 Oct. 1795. Predictably, Blacker states that these numbers have been greatly exaggerated, instead guessing that about 180 families were driven from mid-Ulster: "Too many, God knows, yet still far short of what it has suited the purposes of party since to assert." See Transcripts of Blacker Manuscripts, PRONI, T.2595/4. For the full range of estimates, see Tohall, "Diamond Fight of 1795," 17–50.

55. James Cuffe to Thomas Pelham, 25 Nov. 1796, NAI, Rebellion Papers, 620/26/95. Cuffe stated that he found the emigrants to be industrious and loyal. Another Mayo landlord, Lord Altamont, saw things very differently, stating that it was "by no means clear that they have come here with good intentions." Lord Altamont to ———, 17 Aug. 1796, NAI, Rebellion Papers, 620/24/122.

56. James Cuffe to ———, 22 Dec. 1796, NAI, Rebellion Papers, 620/26/145.

57. For a healthy sampling, see Lord Camden to Thomas Pelham, 12 July 1796, PRONI, Calendar of Pelham Papers, T.755/3/27; Capt. Robert Waddell to Robert Ross, 19 July 1796, NAI, Rebellion Papers, 620/24/33; Lord Camden to the Duke of Portland, NAI, Rebellion Papers, 620/18/11/1; and "J.W." to ———, 27 Aug. 1796, NAI, Rebellion Papers, 620/24/165.

58. William Elliot to Thomas Pelham, 4 Aug. 1796, PRONI, Calendar of Pelham Papers, T.755/3/49.

59. Lord Altamont to ———, 27 Nov. 1796, NAI, Rebellion Papers, 620/26/82; Abstract of Hon. Denis Browne's Returns of Catholics in Mayo Who Have Emigrated from the North, n.d., NAI, Rebellion Papers, 620/26/183.

60. James Cuffe to ———, 22 Dec. 1796, NAI, Rebellion Papers, 620/26/145. Parishes dominated by the names of Brownlow, Blacker, Richardson, Atkinson, and Verner featured prominently on this list.

61. Peter Gibbon's point in his *Origins of Ulster Unionism,* 40.

62. Thomas Knox to ———, 13 Aug. 1796, NAI, Rebellion Papers, 620/24/106. See also Charles Warburton to Thomas Pelham, 31 July 1797, NAI, Rebellion Papers, 620/31/292.

63. Colonel Blacker explicitly compared the raising of the yeomanry with that of the Volunteers. Not surprisingly, Blacker felt that the yeomanry were a much better tool, putting "loyalty" under the resident gentry and giving them military discipline, AM, Blacker MSS, 2/66–7. For an excellent essay on the yeomanry in Ulster, see Allan Blackstock, "The Social and Political Implications of the Raising of the Yeomanry in Ulster, 1796–8," in *United Irishmen,* 234–43.

64. For a general perspective, see Gen. John Knox to Thomas Pelham, 22 May 1797, PRONI, Calendar of Pelham Papers, T.755/5/67–9. In Armagh, Lord Charlemont attempted to raise a yeomanry corps composed of both "royalists and republican reformers." The loyalists refused to serve with the "men who three years ago erected the Tree of Liberty in Armagh Street." Although Charlemont, a figure of immense political importance, was allowed to raise his old Volunteer corps by manipulating the rules, the stand of Armagh loyalists shows just how determined

they were to maintain the purity of their corps. See Blackstock, "Social and Political Implications," 242–43.

65. Along with the prospects of regular pay, this explains the enthusiasm with which the raising of yeomanry corps was greeted in the north of Ireland. Blacker wrote that within days he was able to transmit a list of "1,000 good men and true" from the areas surrounding Lurgan, Portadown, and Tanderagee, AM, Blacker MSS, 2/66–7.

66. *Belfast Newsletter*, 14 July 1797. See also, AM, Blacker MSS, 2/208–9.

67. For Ulster depictions of Scullabogue and Wexford Bridge, see *Belfast Newsletter*, 24 July, 10 Aug. 1798, and 16 Aug. 1799.

2. The Orange Order and Catholic Resistance, 1795–1820

1. The Belfast riot of 1813 is documented in a wide variety of sources. For a full account of the riot and ensuing trials, see *Trial of the Belfast Orangemen* (Belfast: Joseph Smyth, 1813). For press accounts, see the *Belfast Newsletter*, 13 and 16 July 1813. See also General Michel to General Mackenzie, 13 July 1813, NAI, SOC, 1537/1.

2. The riot literature is far too extensive and diverse to detail here. For the seminal works of Rudé, Thompson, and Davis, see George Rudé, *The Crowd in History*; E.P. Thompson, "Moral Economy of the English Crowd," 76–136, and Natalie Zemon Davis, *Society and Culture.*

3. This view underlies much of the excellent work that has been done on secret societies in eighteenth- and nineteenth-century Ireland. See especially Beames, *Peasants and Power,* Donnelly, "The Whiteboy Movement of 1761–5," and Lee, "The Ribbonmen."

4. Garvin, "Defenders, Ribbonmen, and Others," 133–55.

5. Accounts of this first meeting can be found in the Transcripts of the Blacker Manuscripts (PRONI, T.2595/4). In addition, Orange historians have published several interesting anecdotal accounts. See Grand Orange Lodge of Ireland, *Formation of the Orange Order, 1795–8,* 25; and Sibbett, *Orangeism in Ireland,* 1: 230–1. For a solid academic account, see Senior, *Orangeism,* 18–9.

6. Such defensive associations almost certainly existed prior to the sectarian contention of the 1780s. Arthur Young, for example, makes reference to the Peep O'Day Boys in his famous *Tour of Ireland.* Arthur Young, *Tour of Ireland, 1776–79,* vol. 2, edited by Arthur Wollaston Hutton (London: George Bell & Sons, 1892), 55.

7. The Dyan Orange Boys claimed to have 138 members by early 1793. See *Belfast Newsletter*, 22 January 1793. Sloan, Wilson, and Dan Winter used Wilson's Orange Boys Society as a model for the Orange Order. The Order repaid this debt to the Dyan men by giving them the prestigious first warrant. Grand Orange Lodge of Ireland, *Formation of the Orange Order, 1795–8,* 25–27.

8. It is important to note that Sloan and Wilson were also Freemasons. While Freemasonry provided an important framework for the organizational structure

and rituals of the new movement, the Orange Boys Society and other plebeian defensive associations provided the basis for both its tactics and ideology.

9. This movement apparently originated on the estate of Col. William Blacker in Seagoe parish in Armagh. Grand Orange Lodge of Ireland, *Formation of the Orange Order, 1795–8*, 46–47. Rev. Waring, from the family estate at Waringstown, County Down, played a particularly critical role in mobilizing loyal forces in the Lurgan region. See also Senior, *Orangeism*, 45–47; and Sibbett, *Orangeism in Ireland*, 1:236–37.

10. Not wholly so, however. The creators of Orangeism took several specific steps that helped forge ties between themselves and the Protestant gentry. For example, James Sloan was chosen the first Master of the Order over Wilson or Winter because he had better connections to the local gentry and was less tainted with Peep O'Day Boy activities. In addition, Aiken McClelland cites a November 1834 story in *Dublin University Magazine* that relates that a captain of the Royal Dublin militia, John Giffard, played a prominent role in advising the original Orangemen to forego undisciplined musters and attempt to create better ties with local magistrates and gentlemen. See McClelland, *Formation of the Orange Order*, 7–8.

11. Transcripts of the Blacker Manuscripts, PRONI, T.2595/4.

12. For an excellent discussion of the renewal of the Protestant party in Ireland between 1795 and 1798, see Bartlett, *Fall and Rise of the Irish Nation*, 202–27.

13. Viscount Castlereagh to Thomas Pelham, 23 Aug. 1796, NAI, Rebellion Papers, 620/18/7/2.

14. Col. William Blacker's comments about the formation of the yeomanry are particularly interesting. Blacker compared the yeomanry favorably to the Volunteers (an important comparison), stating that the new corps placed loyalty more solidly under the leadership of the resident gentry. AM, Blacker MSS, 2/66–7.

15. Blacker, then a student at Trinity College, Dublin, recalled that Thomas Verner and J.C. Beresford were particularly active advocates for the Dublin lodges. According to Blacker, doctors proved reluctant to join the new organization but were more than made up for by the number of lawyers that flocked to the Orange standard. Transcripts of the Blacker Manuscripts, PRONI, T.2594/4. See also the evidence of William Verner, *Rep. on Orange Lodges III*, H.C. 1835 (476), XVI, 252.

16. Senior, *Orangeism*, 76.

17. L.M. Cullen and Kevin Whelan have engineered the reevaluation of the Wexford rebellion. For Cullen's perspective, see "The 1798 Rebellion in Wexford," and *The Emergence of Modern Ireland*, 210–33. For Whelan, see "The Religious Factor," "The Role of the Catholic Priest," and "Politicisation in County Wexford."

18. Grand Orange Lodge of Ireland, *Formation of the Orange Order, 1795–8*, 29.

19. Lodge 670 occupies a particularly prestigious place in Orange lore. Its first master, John Hyde, was present at the Battle of the Diamond. Moreover, the lodge met at Ballymagerney, located between Loughgall and the Diamond. See Grand Orange Lodge of Ireland, *Formation of the Orange Order, 1795–8*, 67.

20. Ibid., 67–68.

21. In an effort to convince the government of Orangeism's utility, several conservative supporters passed on more elegant copies of the new organization's principles. See Holt Waring to Edward Cooke, 4 July 1796, NAI, Rebellion Papers, 620/24/11. Although the principles espoused in the bylaws remained consistent, the rules and regulations were revised on numerous occasions in the first half of the nineteenth century. The rules typically were altered for two reasons: to clarify internal debates and to head off any attempt to declare Orangeism illegal. For the texts of the bylaws from 1799 to 1835, see Appendix, *Rep. on Orange Lodges I,* H.C. 1835 (377), XV, 2–34.

22. For a good overview, see Elliott, *Watchmen in Sion.*

23. Colley, *Britons,* 11–54.

24. Evidence of Rev. Mortimer O'Sullivan, *Rep. on Orange Lodges I,* H.C. 1935 (377), XV, 180–84.

25. There are innumerable examples of Tone's attitude toward Catholicism in his entertaining autobiography. See his *Life of Theobald Wolfe Tone . . . Written by Himself and Continued by his Son,* edited by R.B. O'Brien (2 vols., London: T. Fisher Unwin, 1893).

26. The events of 1641 long have been one of the most contentious issues in Irish history. Wildly inaccurate casualty estimates have been the norm—the Catholic massacre of helpless Protestant civilians forming a central motif of Ulster Protestant culture. Writing his history of Orangeism, Colonel Wallace claimed that one rebel officer had driven three hundred thousand Protestants into an old church and vowed to put them to death (Grand Orange Lodge of Ireland, *Formation of the Orange Order, 1795–8,* 69). Most scholars now believe that the thirty-three volumes of depositions, upon which the Protestant folk memory is primarily based, are essentially unreliable. That said, the fact remains that Catholics and Protestants achieved a level of violence only rivaled in Irish history by the sectarian barbarities of 1798. It is now believed that approximately four thousand Protestants were murdered in the initial assault and that the Protestant retaliatory attacks soon claimed a like number of Catholic lives. For a balanced discussion of the depositions as historical sources, see Perceval-Maxwell, "The Ulster Rising of 1641 and the Depositions," and Gillespie, "The End of an Era."

27. Brown, *Whole Protestant Community,* 8.

28. Walker, *Dancing to History's Tune,* 1–14.

29. The explicit reference to the 1641 massacres was subsequently removed from official Orange ritual. It was replaced with references to the great deliverer, William the Third, Prince of Orange, a much more respectable subject. See Appendix, *Rep. on Orange Lodges I,* H.C. 1835 (377), XV, 2–34.

30. For a detailed discussion of the importance of the processional tradition, see chapter 4.

31. M.W. Dewar, John Brown, and S.E. Long, *Orangeism: A New Historical Appreciation* (Belfast: T.H. Jordan Ltd., 1967), 118.

32. Grand Orange Lodge of Ireland, *Formation of the Orange Order, 1795–8,* 68.

33. For two innovative examinations of the importance of the covenantal mindset to Ulster Protestant culture, see Akenson, *God's Peoples*, 97–150, and Miller, *Queen's Rebels*.

34. Brig.-Gen. John Knox to Thomas Pelham, 19 April 1797, PRONI, Calendar of Pelham Papers, T.755/4/2/284–5.

35. When forced to defend Orange processions before the Select Committee on Orangeism in 1835, Orange leaders generally argued that making the marches illegal only served to sever the ties between lower-class Protestants (who would march anyway) and their natural leaders, the Protestant gentry. Evidence of Stewart Blacker, *Rep. on Orange Lodges I*, H.C. 1835 (377), XV, 144; Evidence of Lt.-Col. William Blacker, *Rep. on Orange Lodges III*, H.C. 1835 (476), XVI, 220. This argument for increased social control is exactly the same one made by the Armagh gentry in advocating the inclusion of the Peep O'Day Boys into the Irish Volunteers in 1788.

36. For an excellent discussion of the high politics of the Catholic question, see Bartlett, *Fall and Rise of the Irish Nation*, 244–67.

37. Appendix, *Rep. on Orange Lodges III*, H.C. 1835 (476), XVI, 145–8.

38. Evidence of Stewart Blacker, *Rep. on Orange Lodges I*, H.C. 1835 (377), XV, 101–2.

39. H.W. Kennedy to Alexander Marsden, 9 July 1802, NAI, Rebellion Papers, 620/62/59.

40. Sibbett, *Orangeism in Ireland*, 2: 107.

41. *The Charge of Judge Fletcher to the Grand Jury of the County Wexford, at the Summer Assizes, on Friday, 5 August 1814* (Dublin: Thomas Reilly, 1814), 7.

42. *A Brief Remonstrance to Mr. Justice Fletcher, Occasioned by his Charge to the Grand Jury of County Armagh, 12 March 1818* (Ballynahone, County Westmeath: Thady Maguire, 1818). At least one Ulster magistrate concurred with the content of Fletcher's speech, see William Hawkshaw to Lord Downshire, 17 March 1818, PRONI, Downshire Papers, D.671/C/12/197. For an Orange perspective on Fletcher's remarks, see Sibbett, *Orangeism in Ireland*, 2: 148–50.

43. See especially Lee, "The Ribbonmen," 26–35; Donnelly, "The Whiteboy Movement," 20–54, "The Rightboy Movement, 1785–8"; "Pastorini and Captain Rock"; Beames, *Peasants and Power;* and Lewis, *On Local Disturbances in Ireland.*

44. Clark and Donnelly, "The Unreaped Harvest," 419–33.

45. Lee, "Ribbonmen," 26–35; Garvin, "Defenders, Ribbonmen and Others," 133–55; and Michael R. Beames, "The Ribbon Societies."

46. Maj.-Gen. Robert Dalzell to Robert Peel, 30 Oct. 1816, NAI, SOC, 1756/11.

47. William Todd Jones to Lord Downshire, 23 January 1811, PRONI, Downshire Papers, D.671/C/12/66.

48. Evidence of Sir Frederick Stovin, *Rep. on Orange Lodges I*, H.C. 1835 (377), XV, 322.

49. Evidence of Mortimer O'Sullivan, ibid., 184.

50. Lee, "Ribbonmen," 26–28.

51. Garvin, "Defenders, Ribbonmen, and Others," 133–55. At least two prominent nineteenth-century commentators also believed the Ribbonmen had rather vague nationalist pretensions. See Sullivan, *A New Ireland,* 1: 70–77, and Davitt, *Fall of Feudalism in Ireland,* 40–43.

52. Garvin, "Defenders, Ribbonmen, and Others," 152–53.

53. Ibid., 133–47. See also Beames, "Ribbon Societies," 128–43.

54. It is interesting to note that Karl Marx came to a similar conclusion: "As to Ribbonism, its existence never depended upon secret conspirators. When, at the end of the eighteenth century, the Protestant Peep O'Day Boys combined to wage war against the Catholics in the north of Ireland, the opposing society of the Defenders sprang up. . . . When, at last, in our own days, the British government disavowed Orangeism, the Ribbon Society, having lost its condition of life, dissolved itself." Marx, "The Excitement in Ireland," 24 Dec. 1858, in Karl Marx and Frederick Engels, *Ireland and the Irish Question,* 89–90.

55. For an indictment of the treatment of women within Irish historical studies, see Ward, *The Missing Sex.* See also Fitzpatrick, "Women, Gender, and the Writing of Irish History," 267–73.

56. Stokes Report on Aughnacloy Riot, 19 December 1818, NAI, SOC, 1955/33. See also Capt. Edward Moore to Maj. Robert Marshall, 30 December 1818, NAI, SOC, 1955/39.

57. Capt. Edward Moore to Maj. Robert Marshall, 30 December 1818, NAI, SOC, 1955/39.

58. Stokes Report, 19 December 1818, NAI, SOC, 1955/37.

59. The history of Irish Freemasonry remains largely unwritten. See, in default of anything else, De Vere White, "The Freemasons." For Freemasonry in its Ulster context, see also Smyth, *Men of No Property,* 85–88; and Stewart, *A Deeper Silence,* 165–78. For an excellent overview of masonry's importance in eighteenth-century Europe, see Margaret Jacob, *Living the Enlightenment.*

60. Smyth, *Men of No Property,* 46. It is important to remember that the founders of the Loyal Orange Order were also Freemasons.

61. *Belfast Newsletter,* 15 June 1802.

62. Alexander Knox to Alexander Marsden, 19 June 1802, NAI, Rebellion Papers, 620/62/63.

63. Lord Londonderry to ———, 20 July 1802, NAI, Rebellion Papers, 620/62/39. See also Sibbett, *Orangeism in Ireland,* 2: 102–3.

64. George Porterfield to Lord Kilwarlin, 11 June 1803, NAI, Rebellion Papers, 620/66/181. Apparently, the Freemasons won the day at Dromore while the Orangemen were victorious at Fintona.

65. Not surprisingly, there seems to be a strong correlation between the decline of Catholic freemasonry and the Catholic Church's reconstruction of its diocesan infrastructure. Catholic mason lodges thus lingered longest in peripheral areas of Donegal and Tyrone, but even these aberrations soon succumbed to the dogma of the growing church.

66. Brig.-Gen. Palmer to Robert Peel, 6 Sept. 1813, NAI, SOC, 1544/75.

67. Sibbett, *Orangeism in Ireland*, 2: 106–7. Apparently, Patrick Duignean had angered Catholic militiamen by opposing the extension of the 1793 bill allowing Catholics in the Irish militia.

68. For a full discussion of the revival of Catholic politics in 1806–1811, see Bartlett, *Fall and Rise of the Irish Nation*, 298–303.

69. From Donegal to Down, plebeian Orangemen upped the provocation ante in 1811. Some Down magistrates expressed their exasperation with the rebellious spirit of these Orangemen at a public meeting in late 1811. For the response of one Orange supporter, see James Verner to Lord Downshire, 10 December 1811, PRONI, Downshire Papers, D.671/C/12/110. For a more general perspective, see Sibbett, *Orangeism in Ireland*, 2: 132.

70. Stewart to Dr. Vandeleur, 24 June 1811, NAI, SOC, 1383/41; Anon., 18 December 1811, NAI, SOC, 1383/6. The latter letter, from a Belfast informer, describes the nocturnal meetings of the Ribbonmen, "a new term for United Irishmen."

71. Carleton, *Autobiography*, 78.

72. The Ribbonmen were not confined to the south Ulster borderlands. Ribbon lodges existed in Dublin by 1820. In addition, the Ribbon societies split into two rival movements in the wake of the 1822 trials: the ironically named Northern Unionists in Ulster and the Dublin-based Irish Sons of Freedom. These two rivals existed side by side until an uneasy reconciliation was negotiated in 1838. See Thomas M. Ray to Daniel O'Connell, 15 Nov. 1837 (Public Record Office, London [hereafter cited as PRO], C.O. 904/7/73). For an account of the reunification meeting, see "A History of the Mission of Michael Young and Richard Jones to Belfast," 24 April 1838, NAI, Official Papers, 1838/133/32. Many of these critical documents can be found in *Report of the Trial Held at the Court-house, Green Street, on the 23rd, 24th, 25th and 29th days of June, 1840, of Richard Jones, who was charged with being a member of an illegal society, the members whereof did communicate with and were known to each other by secret signs and passwords* (Dublin: Hodges and Smith, 1840).

73. Evidence of John Dunn, *Minutes of evidence taken before the select committee appointed to inquire into the disturbances in Ireland, in the last session of Parliament, 13 May—18 June 1824* (hereafter cited as *SOI evidence*), H.C. 1825 (20), VII, 277.

74. Evidence of the Earl of Gosford, *Rep. on Orange Lodges I*, H.C. 1835 (377), XV, 250. For other assessments of the anti-Orange origins of Ribbonism, see Patrick Hynes to Thomas Drummond, 25 July 1839, PRO, C.O. 904/7/271; and Thomas M. Ray to Daniel O'Connell, 15 November 1837, PRO, C.O. 904/7/73.

75. Carleton, *Autobiography*, 78–79. See also Langston Heyland to Robert Peel, 28 Sept. 1813, NAI, SOC, 1537/2; Owen O'Neill to ———, 8 February 1816, NAI, SOC, 1765/61.

76. *Report of the Trial of Michael Keenan for Administering an Unlawful Oath* (Dublin: J. Exshaw, 1822), 42–43. For William Blacker's account of the 1822 arrests

in Armagh city, see AM, Blacker MSS, 6/193–7. For an overview of the events, see Information obtained of proceeding taken in reference to Ribbonism prior to September 1841, PRO, C.O. 904/8/299–300.

77. Carleton, *Autobiography*, 80.

78. W. Kemmis to Thomas Drummond, 19 Dec. 1839, PRO, C.O. 904/7/456–60.

79. M. Crofton to Edward Lucas, 8 February 1842, PRO, C.O. 904/9/92. For similar analyses of Ribbon leaders' social backgrounds, see Thomas R. Ray to Daniel O'Connell, 15 November 1837, PRO, C.O. 904/7/73; and Edmond Hile to ———, 31 January 1842, PRO, C.O. 904/9/68–9.

80. Garvin, "Defenders, Ribbonmen, and Others," 151.

81. Police report, 9 February 1842, PRO, C.O. 904/9/140.

82. Trial for Ribbonism of John Brady, Hugh O'Hare, John Rice, and Henry Hughes, 22 July 1842, PRO, C.O. 904/9/227.

83. For a particularly detailed look at the inner workings of later Ribbon societies, see Report of Inspector Mullins, PRO, C.O. 904/8/155–62. Mullins, a police spy, successfully infiltrated a Ribbon meeting in Swanlinbar, County Cavan.

84. *Report of the Trial of Michael Keenan*, 18.

85. F. Mansfield to Dublin Castle, 19 June 1811, NAI, SOC, 1383/38.

86. General Hart to Lieutenant MacManus, 18 June 1811, NAI, SOC, 1390/3.

87. F. Mansfield to Dublin Castle, 19 June 1811, NAI, SOC, 1383/38.

88. Rev. Arthur Kenny to the Protestant Inhabitants of that part of the County of Donegal, July 1811, NAI, SOC, 1383/42.

89. Rev. Arthur Kenny to Sir Charles Paxton, 16 July 1811, NAI, SOC, 1383/42. In the letter, Kenny hoped that Dublin Castle would attempt to persuade the Orangemen away from the marches. Paxton's response was typical: "Mr. Kenny means perfectly well but it is just impossible to stop the Orange Society unless you stop the Catholic meetings also."

90. See above for a detailed account of the 1813 riot in Belfast. Another clash over Orange processions had occurred in Armagh city in 1812. See James Iles to Dublin Castle, 31 July 1812, NAI, SOC, 1403/6.

91. *Trial of the Belfast Orangemen*, 20.

92. The term itself could have been taken from the Threshers, an agrarian movement active in the Irish midlands in 1806–1807. This is the term employed by Sibbett in his history of Orangeism. Sibbett, *Orangeism in Ireland*, 2: 122, 126–7. I have found another reference to the Thrashers involved in a sectarian fight in Armagh city in September 1813. This police report described the activities of a mob parading through the city streets shouting, "they were the Thrashers that could beat the Orangemen and Protestants and away with the yeomanry." See "Outrages in Armagh," Aug./Sept. 1813, NAI, SOC, 1537/14.

93. James Dawson to William Taylor, 8 January 1812, NAI, SOC, 1537/11.

94. *Belfast Newsletter*, 18 February 1812. Unable to ascertain the particular cause of the riot, the *Belfast Newsletter* blamed the clash on "the old one from which the parties took their appellations." See also Examination of the Riots at Ballynahinch,

n.d., NAI, SOC, 1403/16. For an Orange perspective, see Sibbett, *Orangeism in Ireland*, 2: 127.

95. Thompson was later arraigned for the murder at the Downpatrick Assizes but acquitted by a sympathetic jury.

96. Each of these riots occurred in public centers between Catholic crowds and Orangemen or members of the yeomanry. For the Killeter affray, see Maj.-Gen. John Burnet to Lieutenant-Colonel McDonald, 22 July 1812, NAI, SOC, 1403/27; Rev. John Wilkinson to ————, 22 July 1812, NAI, SOC, 1403/28; and General Burnet to Lt.-Col. Sir George Hart, 7 Aug. 1812, NAI, SOC, 1403/34. For Maghera, see John Graham, "A Journal of the Riots in the Neighborhood of Maghera, County Londonderry, from April 19 to July 26, 1813," 31 July 1813, NAI, SOC, 1537/29. For Garvagh, see McClelland, "The Battle of Garvagh." For Kilkeel, see *Belfast Newsletter*, 22 February 1814, and "Informations Regarding the Kilkeel Affray," 20–3 February 1814, NAI, SOC, 1565/38.

97. There was at least one police report that concurred with this notion. See "Outrages in Armagh," August/Sept. 1813, NAI, SOC, 1537/14.

98. In the wake of the Hilltown procession, William Paxton stated that Saint Patrick's Day provided the mob with an opportunity to "show their strength and sow the seed of disloyalty." William Paxton to William Gregory, 18 March 1816, NAI, SOC, 1765/43. For a similar assessment, see Langford Heyland to Robert Peel, 9 March 1814, NAI, SOC, 1565/15.

99. Dewar, Brown, and Long, *Orangeism*, 118.

100. In addition to the letters cited above, see William Chambers to Charles Grant, 11 March 1820, NAI, SOC, 2187/47; Bishop of Raphoe to Dublin Castle, 18 March 1820, NAI, SOC, 2187/14.

101. These internal disputes were known within the Orange Order as the Battle of the Orders. See Sibbett, *Orangeism in Ireland*, vol. 2, 157–58, 180–83; Senior, *Orangeism*, 194–95.

102. See above for Aughnacloy. For Crebilly, see Alex MaCarthur to E.A. MacNaughton, 30 June 1819, NAI, SOC, 2084/6. Accounts of the riots at Kilrea and Crebilly are included in Sibbett, *Orangeism in Ireland*, vol. 2, 173, 179–80.

103. Report on the State of the North, 1 May 1814, NAI, SOC, 1682/28.

104. Evidence of the Rev. Mortimer O'Sullivan, *Rep. on Orange Lodges I*, H.C. 1835 (377), XV, 41.

3. National Politics and Sectarian Violence, 1821–1829

1. AM, Blacker MSS, 6/161–71.

2. Pastorini's prophecies understandably worried Protestants living in outlying regions in Ulster. In December 1824 the Rev. George Prior reported that Protestants in Killybegs, County Donegal, were terrified by a report circulating "an old prophecy about to be fulfilled." Rev. George Prior to Dublin Castle, 17 Dec. 1824,

NAI, SOC, 2622/34. For an insightful examination of the Irish impact of Pastorini's prophecies, see Donnelly, "Pastorini and Captain Rock," 102–39.

3. For the emancipation campaign, see O'Ferrall, *Catholic Emancipation*. The definitive biography of O'Connell in this period is MacDonagh, *The Hereditary Bondsman*.

4. Sir George Hill to Dublin Castle, n.d., NAI, SOC, 2360/7.

5. See especially the interesting concluding discussion in O'Ferrall, *Catholic Emancipation*, 258–89.

6. Daniel O'Connell to Edward Dwyer, 14 April 1829, in M.R. O'Connell, ed., *The Correspondence of Daniel O'Connell*, 8 vols. (Dublin: Irish Manuscripts Commission, 1973), 4: 45–46. Hereafter cited as *Correspondence of Daniel O'Connell*.

7. For an important work that argues against the inevitability of tribal politics, see Walker, *Ulster Politics*.

8. Daniel O'Connell to Mary O'Connell, 23 Dec. 1822, in *Correspondence of Daniel O'Connell*, vol. 2, 414.

9. For the evolution of prefamine rules and regulations, see Appendix, *Rep. on Orange Lodges I*, H.C. 1835 (377), XV, 2–34.

10. Daniel O'Connell to Maurice O'Connell, 5 Jan. 1822, in *Correspondence of Daniel O'Connell*, vol. 2, 345–47.

11. *Freeman's Journal*, 13 July 1822.

12. For a detailed examination of the evolution of policing in Ireland, see Palmer, *Police and Protest in England and Ireland*. See also Broeker, *Rural Disorder and Police Reform*.

13. This bill also created stipendiary magistrates, salaried judicial officials designed to remain independent of local political factions. With the aid of the new Irish Constabulary, police reform advocates envisioned that stipendiary magistrates would weaken the partisan control of justice in Ireland, especially in the notoriously Orange courtrooms of Ulster. Although these reforms did not radically alter the balance of power on the ground, they did quickly reinforce Wellesley's bad reputation in Orange circles.

14. The Bottle and Rattle riot caused a sensation in the Dublin press. For varying perspectives on these events, see the *Dublin Evening Post, Freeman's Journal*, and *Dublin Evening Mail* throughout December 1822. Several suspects were charged with riot and conspiracy to riot, but the charges were thrown out (*Freeman's Journal*, 3 Jan. 1823). For an Orange perspective, see *A Full, Faithful, and Impartial Report of the Trials of Messrs. H. and M. Hambridge, W. Graham, George Graham, J. Forbes, and W. Brownlow for an Alleged Conspiracy to Assassinate His Excellency, the Marquess Wellesley, Lord Lieutenant of Ireland* (Dublin: J. Charles, 1823).

15. Robert Maxwell to Rev. Sir Harcourt Lees, 12 Dec. 1824, NAI, SOC, 2622/4.

16. Quoted in Sibbett, *Orangeism in Ireland*, vol. 2, 193.

17. Ibid.

18. Witness the warm welcome given to King George IV by O'Connell and the

Catholic hierarchy in August 1822. For an Orange perspective on these events, see Sibbett, *Orangeism in Ireland,* vol. 2, 182–83.

19. James Sinclair to Dublin Castle, 3 June 1822, NAI, SOC, 2360/26.

20. For a brief essay on the Ensor family and its Armagh connections, see Paterson, *Harvest Home,* 141–46.

21. George Ensor to Dublin Castle, 6 June 1824, NAI, SOC, 2622/3. See also George Ensor to Dublin Castle, 29 May 1824, NAI, SOC, 2622/3.

22. Most Irish newspapers of the period have relatively detailed accounts of the violent proceedings surrounding the Twelfth of July celebrations. For the riots in Armagh, Belfast, Dungannon, and Keady, see *Belfast Newsletter,* 15 and 18 July 1823, 20 July 1824, and 2 August 1825. For the trials stemming from the Newry riot, see *Enniskillen Chronicle,* 26 August 1824.

23. Luke Gibson to Thomas Burke, 28 July 1822, NAI, SOC, 2358/41.

24. Ensign H. Main to Major French, 27 May 1823, NAI, SOC, 2520/36.

25. Rev. J.S. Knox to Dublin Castle, 15 June 1823, NAI, SOC, 2520/37.

26. *Belfast Newsletter,* 20 June 1823. For various accounts of the riot, see Major-General Egerton to Lord Combermere, 18 June 1823, NAI, SOC, 2520/41; Rev. J.S. Knox to Dublin Castle, 15 June 1823, NAI, SOC, 2520/37; Ensign James Elliot to Lieutenant-Colonel Maclaine, 13–14 June 1823, NAI, SOC, 2520/38; Rev. J.S. Knox to Dublin Castle, 17 June 1823, NAI, SOC, 2520/40.

27. Partisan rivalries continued to haunt the eastern half of Londonderry for the remainder of the year. A major party riot broke out at Dungiven on 5 August 1823. Most commentators linked the Dungiven clash to the riot at Maghera. See Magistrates of Londonderry to Marquess Wellesley, 15 Aug. 1823, NAI, SOC, 2520/45; Lt. J. Donnelly to Maj. J. French, 6 Aug. 1823, NAI, SOC, 2520/46; and John Marshall to Maj. J. French, 8 Aug. 1823, NAI, SOC, 2520/47.

28. Maj.-Gen. Egerton to Lord Combermere, 18 June 1823, NAI, SOC, 2520/41.

29. *Belfast Newsletter,* 20 June 1823. Several of the Orange gunmen were brought to trial the following year at the Londonderry assizes. All were acquitted (*Belfast Newsletter,* 6 April 1824).

30. For a good discussion of the parliamentary problems faced by the Order, see Senior, *Orangeism,* 204–6.

31. Grand Lodge Address, 23 June 1823 (quoted in Sibbett, *Orangeism in Ireland,* vol. 2, 223).

32. The worst of these occurred at Cram, where Orangemen fired on their Catholic antagonists, killing one man (*Belfast Newsletter,* 18 July 1823).

33. It is interesting to note that the Orange historian Sibbett is rather contemptuous of the Orange leaders: "In too many cases they showed a disposition to support the institution when everything was going well with it, and when support of it served their own interests; but they were found wanting in the day of trial and difficulty." Implicit in this statement is the notion that the heart and soul of true Protestant principles resided with the rank and file, who needed to bring their more circumspect leaders along with them (Sibbett, *Orangeism in Ireland,* vol. 2, 269).

34. Although the secret, conditional oath of the Order was formally eliminated, prospective Orangemen were still required to take the oath of allegiance, the oath of supremacy, and the oath of abjuration before a civil magistrate. See Sibbett, *Orangeism in Ireland,* vol. 2, 227.

35. Grand Lodge Resolution, 21 May 1824, in *Report from the select committee of the House of Lords appointed to inquire into the state of Ireland,* H.L. 1825 (181), IX, 353.

36. For the trial following the Newry riots, see *Enniskillen Chronicle,* 28 Aug. 1824. For the Ballygawley riot, see *Belfast Newsletter,* 20 July 1824.

37. Evidence of Stewart Blacker, *Rep, on Orange Lodges I,* H.C. 1835 (377), XV, 144. Stewart Blacker, the Orange Order's assistant grand secretary for County Armagh in 1835, was Col. William Blacker's nephew.

38. Sibbett, *Orangeism in Ireland,* vol. 2, 266; Senior, *Orangeism,* 208.

39. Ironically, the Catholic Association dissolved itself on the same day (*Freeman's Journal,* 19 March 1825).

40. Declaration of the Grand Lodge of Ireland, 18 March 1825, *SOI evidence,* H.L. 1825 (181), IX, 354.

41. *Morning Chronicle,* 4 March 1825.

42. Draft of Petition, 1825, PRONI, D.1079/1.

43. In particular, Verner and Waring refuted some of the wilder conspiracy theories regarding the Orange Order, forcing parliamentary critics to focus on its members' "overexuberance of loyalty." Evidence of Col. William Verner and Rev. Holt Waring, *SOI evidence,* H.L. 1825 (181), IX, 326–58.

44. Evidence of Stewart Blacker, *Rep. on Orange Lodges I,* H.C. 1835 (377), XV, 109; Sibbett, *Orangeism in Ireland,* vol. 2, 286–88.

45. Printed Address of Benevolent and Religious Orange Institution of Ireland, 12 June 1826, NLI, Brunswick Papers, MS 5017.

46. Senior, *Orangeism,* 219.

47. Ibid., 215.

48. For the veto controversy, see Bartlett, *Fall and Rise of the Irish Nation,* 291–95, 307–8; Gerard O'Brien, "Beginning of the Veto Controversy in Ireland," 80–94.

49. The major confrontation between Lawless and O'Connell occurred at a Dublin meeting to consider the state of the Catholic cause on 8 June 1825. O'Connell routed Lawless and was drawn in triumph to Merrion Square (*Dublin Evening Post,* 9 June 1825).

50. The process that led to the formation of the New Catholic Association began at a meeting in Dublin in June 1825 (*Dublin Evening Post,* 25 June 1825). For an excellent discussion of the national political campaign in this later phase, see O'Ferrall, *Catholic Emancipation,* 114–289.

51. *Dublin Evening Mail,* 5 July 1826.

52. Because of the Catholic Association's triumph over the Beresford interest, Waterford typically is viewed as the most important electoral contest of 1826. See O'Ferrall, *Catholic Emancipation,* 121–33.

53. Brownlow was the first M.P. to declare himself an Orangeman in the House of Commons. See *Hansard's Parliamentary Debates,* Second Series, XI, 947.

54. *Morning Chronicle,* 20 April 1825. See also Daniel O'Connell to Mary O'Connell, 20 April 1825, *Correspondence of Daniel O'Connell,* vol. 3, 151.

55. This refers to Col. Robert Lundy, who advised the men and women of Derry to surrender when the Jacobite army approached the walled city in 1688.

56. *Belfast Newsletter,* 27 June 1826.

57. Papers donated by Crosslie, PRONI, T.1689/1/26. The text of the handbill can also be found in Sibbett, *Orangeism in Ireland,* vol. 2, 293.

58. Ibid.

59. *Belfast Newsletter,* 30 June 1826.

60. The Brownlow/Verner contest became symbolic of party division throughout Armagh. In 1828–1829 references to the election triggered sectarian riots in Armagh and Poyntzpass. See *Belfast Newsletter,* 22 April 1828; *Dublin Evening Post,* 9 Jan. 1829.

61. *Belfast Newsletter,* 30 June 1826.

62. O'Ferrall, *Catholic Emancipation,* 140–41. In addition, one of the other candidates, Alexander Saunderson, had relatively solid liberal credentials, which allowed some moderates to vote for him in good conscience. Saunderson in fact ended up voting for Catholic emancipation. For an interesting examination of the connections between the Saunderson family and the Cavan environment, see Jackson, *Colonel Edward Saunderson,* 7–23.

63. Compiled by the author from *Belfast Newsletter,* 1821–1829.

64. *Belfast Newsletter,* 4 July 1826.

65. Ibid., 11 July 1826.

66. Rev. Patrick A. Murray, quoted in Livingstone, *Monaghan Story,* 188–89.

67. For a detailed examination of the Clare election, see O'Ferrall, *Catholic Emancipation,* 189–201.

68. Declaratory Statement, 15 Aug. 1828, NLI, Brunswick Papers, MS 5017/1.

69. NLI, Brunswick Papers, MS 5017/49–54.

70. Ibid., MS 5017/38.

71. *Star of Brunswick,* 29 Nov. 1828.

72. The Catholic Association already had been remarkably successful in using similar tactics to suppress Catholic secret societies in southern counties.

73. Daniel O'Connell to Edward Dwyer, 22 Aug. 1828, in W.J. Fitzpatrick, ed., *Correspondence of the Liberator,* 2 vols., (London: J. Murray, 1988), vol. 2, 162.

74. Quoted in Livingstone, *Monaghan Story,* 191.

75. *Belfast Newsletter,* 23 Sept. 1828.

76. Information of Constable James Reynard, n.d., NAI, SOC, 2885/3.

77. Chief Constable E.A. Douglas to Maj. Thomas D'Arcy, 27 Oct. 1828, NAI, SOC, 2882/58.

78. The Ballybay confrontation is extremely well documented. For a particu-

larly detailed report, see Maj. Thomas D'Arcy to Francis Leveson-Gower, 8 Oct. 1828, NAI, SOC, 2885/19.

79. For details on Gray, see Sibbett, *Orangeism in Ireland,* vol. 2, 313–14; Livingstone, *Monaghan Story,* 190–91, 200–201.

80. Maj.-Gen. William Thornton to Dublin Castle, 23 Sept. 1828, NAI, SOC, 2885/5.

81. D'Arcy to Leveson-Gower, 8 Oct. 1828, NAI, SOC, 2885/19; *Belfast Newsletter,* 30 Sept. 1828. See also "Return of Party Outrages—Monaghan," Sept. 1828, NAI, SOC, 2882/55.

82. Daniel O'Connell to Edward Dwyer, 1 Oct. 1828, in *Correspondence of Daniel O'Connell,* vol. 3, 416.

83. Information of Rev. Charles McDermott, 25 Sept. 1828, PRONI, Clogher Diocesan Papers, DIO.[RC] 1/6/5.

84. Maj.-Gen. William Thornton to Earl of Wiltshire, 30 Sept. 1828, NAI, SOC, 2882/6; *Belfast Newsletter,* 3 Oct. 1828.

85. *Belfast Newsletter,* 30 Sept. 1828.

86. Quoted in O'Ferrall, *Catholic Emancipation,* 213.

87. *Northern Whig,* 9 Oct. 1828.

88. Ibid., 2 Oct. 1828.

89. See *A Full and Authentic Report of the Proceedings of the First Annual Meeting of the Brunswick Constitutional Club of Ireland, Held in the Rotunda on Tuesday, November 4th 1828,* 8.

90. Quoted in Sibbett, *Orangeism in Ireland,* vol. 2, 324.

91. Ibid.

92. Johnston's campaign to repeal the Party Processions Act is covered in chapter 6. For Sloan, see Patterson, *Class Conflict and Sectarianism,* 44–64.

93. Duke of Wellington to Robert Peel, 12 Sept. 1828, in Duke of Wellington, ed., *Despatches, Correspondence, and Memoranda,* vol. 5, 42–43.

94. The parliamentary politics of 1829 are ably handed in O'Ferrall, *Catholic Emancipation,* 234–57. For an Orange perspective on these events, see Sibbett, *Orangeism in Ireland,* vol. 2, 333–37.

95. *Dublin Evening Mail,* 6 Feb. 1829.

96. Address of Grand Lodge of Ireland, 8 June 1829, quoted in Sibbett, *Orangeism in Ireland,* vol. 2, 337.

97. Ibid.

98. Evidence of William Sharman Crawford, *Rep. on Orange Lodges I,* H.C. 1835 (377), XV, 303.

99. For the Belfast affray, see *Belfast Newsletter,* 23 June 1829; for Enniskillen, see *Dublin Evening Post,* 19 June 1829; for Lurgan, see *Dublin Evening Post,* 26 May 1829; for Rosslea, see *Dublin Evening Post,* 23 May 1829.

100. Police report, n.d., PRO, H.O. 100/231/103.

101. Sibbett, *Orangeism in Ireland,* vol. 2, 338–39.

102. *Dublin Evening Post,* 4 July 1829.

103. Sibbett, *Orangeism in Ireland,* vol. 2, 344.

104. *Dublin Evening Post,* 19 July 1829.

105. Appendix, *Rep. on Orange lodges III,* H.C. 1835 (476), XVI, 210–16, 227–37. The lawyer Randall Kernan testified that a drunken Orangemen had provoked the clash. Evidence of Randall Kernan, ibid., 84–85; 98–99. For press accounts of the riot and its aftermath, see *Dublin Evening Post,* 18 July 1829; *Enniskillen Chronicle,* 16 July 1829, 26 March 1830. For an Orange perspective, see Sibbett, *Orangeism in Ireland,* vol. 2, 344–48.

106. Orange tradition holds that Ribbonmen began the assault while the leaders of both parties attempted to work out a peaceful solution. See Sibbett, *Orangeism in Ireland,* vol. 2, 341–42.

107. *Belfast Newsletter,* 21 July 1829. Orange accounts place the number of Catholic casualties at forty (Sibbett, *Orangeism in Ireland,* vol. 2, 343). This figure, from one side of the communal divide, is assuredly inflated.

108. Quoted in Sibbett, *Orangeism in Ireland,* vol.2, 343.

109. Evidence of William Hancock, *Rep. on Orange Lodges III,* H.C. 1835 (476), XVI, 119; George Dawson to Sir George Hill, 23 July 1829, PRONI, Hill Papers, D.642/210; Sibbett, *Orangeism in Ireland,* vol. 2, 339–40.

110. See Senior, *Orangeism,* 241–42.

4. Ritual and Sectarian Violence

1. This narrative of the Maghery wreckings has been reconstructed from several sources, principally from the evidence given in the Appendix, *Rep. on Orange lodges III,* H.C. 1835 (476), XVI, 145–46, 172–77. For a press account of the conflict, see *Dublin Evening Post,* 27 Nov. 1830.

2. Black lodges were lodges that refused to abide by the official rules and regulations of the Orange Order. See Appendix, *Rep. on Orange Lodges I,* H.C. 1835 (377), XV, 22.

3. W.J. Hancock, a magistrate for Armagh and Down, compiled a list of the men attending the "black lodge." He listed thirty-six men, thirteen from Killyman parish and twenty-three from Derryinver. Of the Tyrone men, one was a bugle player in the local yeomanry corps and another was a soldier on furlough. Appendix, *Rep. on Orange Lodges III,* H.C. 1835 (476), XVI, 173.

4. Six men from the Killyman party were indicted for various acts of riot and assault despite the inactivity of Colonel Verner and other sympathetic local magistrates. All were found guilty. See *Belfast Newsletter,* 29 July 1831.

5. Buckland, *Ulster Unionism,* 37.

6. For example, see Garvin, "Defenders, Ribbonmen, and Others," 148.

7. Since Natalie Zemon Davis pioneered the examination of the relationship between festival and communal values, a quotation from her rightly famous

work seems appropriate here: "festive life can on the one hand perpetuate certain values of the community (even guarantee its survival), and on the other side criticize political order." See Davis, "Reasons of Misrule," 97.

8. Peter van der Veer, "Riots and Rituals," in Paul R. Brass, ed., *Riots and Pogroms,* 155.

9. Report of Sub-Inspector Waters, 12 July 1868, NAI, Official Papers, 1869/1.

10. Evidence of Earl of Gosford, *Rep. on Orange Lodges I,* H.C. 1835 (377), XV, 246.

11. See Kertzer, *Rituals, Politics, and Power,* 119.

12. Miller, *Queen's Rebels,* 68–69.

13. Stewart, *Narrow Ground,* 181.

14. *Belfast Newsletter,* 21 July 1829; *Dublin Evening Post,* 19 July 1829.

15. Dewar, Brown, and Long, *Orangeism,* 118.

16. Colonel Carew to Dublin Castle, 15 July 1869, Transcripts of the Official Papers, 1869–1872, PRONI, MIC.371/3. Incidentally, the trouble occurred less than a mile away from Dolly's Brae, site of the famous affray twenty years earlier.

17. William Butler to Dublin Castle, n.d., PRONI, MIC.371/3. While certainly understandable, the strategy reinforced strongly held Catholic suspicions that the police were allied with the marching Orangemen. It also fortified the Orange view that the police were on their side in their never-ending struggle against Catholic rebels. This feeling explains loyalist bitterness when police attempted to enforce laws impartially.

18. For a pioneering discussion of this notion, see Davis, "Rites of Violence," 161. Suzanne Desan provides an excellent critique in "Crowds, Community, and Ritual," 64–71.

19. *Belfast Newsletter,* 14 and 21 July 1829.

20. AM, Blacker MSS, 2/28.

21. Police Report, 1 July 1870, PRONI, MIC.371/3. Some of the bloodiest clashes in late nineteenth-century Belfast occurred between the police and Protestant mobs angry at the imposition of law in their territory. The worst of these clashes occurred in the midst of the infamous Belfast riots of 1886. For a description of these riots, see Conclusion.

22. *Dublin Evening Mail,* 4 Aug. 1864.

23. Appendix, *Report on Orange Lodges III,* H.C. 1835 (476), 179–82.

24. "The Anti-Boyne Water Act," in Orange Songbook, PRONI, D.2935/4/3.

25. Kertzer, *Ritual, Politics, and Power,* 67. Natalie Zemon Davis also stresses the idea that legitimacy could be reinforced by the group experience of procession. See Davis, "Rites of Violence," 168–69.

26. Lord Gosford to Lord Camden, 13 July 1796, PRONI, Gosford Papers, D.1606/1/188.

27. For an Orange history of the Scarva celebration, see M.W. Dewar, *Scarva Story.* The Apprentice Boys annually recreated a similar vision of Irish history

at their Derry celebrations, where an effigy of the "naive" Lundy is hanged and burnt.

28. Quoted in *Dublin Evening Post,* 19 July 1829.

29. Augusta Kiernan to Isabella and Sophia Hamilton, 25 Jan. 1832, PRONI, D.1728/18/21.

30. Prominent figures often paid a high price for their participation in such festivals. The three magistrates mentioned above lost their positions for their involvement in the Orange festivities that triggered the affray at Dolly's Brae. For the correspondence surrounding Lord Roden's dismissal, see the letters from Maziere Brady to Earl of Roden, Francis Beers, and William Beers, 6 Oct. 1849, PRO, H.O. 45/2603/88–93.

31. Zimmerman, *Songs of Irish Rebellion,* 300.

32. "To the Orangemen of Ireland," n.d., PRONI, MIC.506/2/24A.

33. Colley, *Britons,* 30–33.

34. *Loyal Orangeman's Song Book,* 5-6, 12-13. I would like to thank my friend Don MacRaild for this reference.

35. "Song without title," quoted in Zimmerman, *Songs of Irish Rebellion,* 302.

36. The exuberance of Orange music often attracted people to the festivities. In his memoirs, Lynn Doyle equated Orangeism with music: "Henceforth for me Orangeism connoted music. I longed to become an Orangeman; but it was as a musician, and no longer as a martyr in a great cause." See Lynn Doyle, *An Ulster Childhood.*

37. *Enniskillen Chronicle,* 28 August 1829.

38. Evidence of William Sharman Crawford, *Rep. on Orange Lodges I,* H.C. 1835 (377), XV, 305–9.

39. It is critical here to remember Emile Durkheim's notion that ritual can build solidarity without requiring uniformity of belief. For a good summary, see Kertzer, *Ritual, Politics, and Power,* 61–76.

40. Appendix, *Rep. on Orange Lodges I,* H.C. 1835 (377), XV, 2–34.

41. See *Laws and Ordinances.*

42. De Vere White, "Freemasons," 72–73.

43. This may have been particularly true of the evangelical circles of Ulster Protestantism. One influential Orange leader, Col. William Blacker, grew exasperated with what he termed the nonsensical millenarian ideas of certain Ulster preachers. See AM, Blacker MSS, 5/59.

44. Evidence of Rev. Holt Waring, *SOI evidence,* H.L. 1825 (181), IX, 334.

45. Donnelly, "Pastorini and Captain Rock," 107.

46. McFarland, *Protestants First.*

47. Appendix, *Rep. on Orange Lodges I,* H.C. 1835 (377), XV, 5.

48. Sibbett, *Orangeism in Ireland,* vol. 2, 192.

49. For example, see Foster, *Modern Ireland,* 293.

50. William Beers to ———, 17 March 1849, PRONI, Letter Relating to Ribbonism in County Down, D.682/146.

51. William Paxton to William Gregory, 18 March 1816, NAI, SOC, 1765/43.

52. Memorial to Viscount Ebington from Protestants of Creggan Parish, 26 March 1841, PRONI, Transcripts of Outrage Papers (County Armagh), T.3194/3.

53. Police Report, July 1869, NAI, Official Papers, 1869/1 (10368).

54. To cite one example of many, in 1797, United Irish sympathizers planted a bush decorated with several bunches of green ribbons in the center of Navan, County Meath. The bush represented the Tree of Liberty. Its life, however, in Navan was rather short-lived, as a "staunch" man quickly pulled it down and trampled it underfoot. George Lambert to Thomas Pelham, 9 May 1797, NAI, Rebellion Papers, 620/30/141. Nancy Curtin's work on the United Irishmen is particularly strong on ideology. See Curtin, *United Irishmen*.

55. *Enniskillen Chronicle*, 23 July 1829.

56. Faolain, *Blood on the Harp*, 220–21.

57. Daniel O'Connell certainly used this theme to great effect in his crusade for Catholic emancipation. See Donnelly, "Pastorini and Captain Rock."

58. *Belfast Newsletter*, 15 May 1829.

59. Ibid., 8 July 1828. In an effort to make the military threat seem more real, Protestant newspaper accounts often emphasized Ribbon regalia and uniforms. See *Enniskillen Chronicle*, 12 April 1832, and *Belfast Newsletter*, 8 April 1823, 24 July 1832.

60. Appendix, *Rep. on Orange Lodges III*, H.C. 1835 (476), XVI, 136–37.

61. *Enniskillen Chronicle*, 23 March 1826.

62. Ibid., 10 August 1826; *Dublin Evening Post*, 22 April 1829. Of course, such practices went both ways. In 1871 a similar event occurred in a Leitrim village, where a Catholic servant triggered a riot by pulling the hats off two small boys participating in an Orange procession.

63. For Ribbonism, see Carleton's "Wildgoose Lodge," in *Traits and Stories*, vol. 2, 349–62. For Orangeism, see his *Valentine McClutchy*.

64. Garvin, "Defenders, Ribbonmen, and Others," 145.

65. Carleton, *Autobiography*, 77–78.

66. Ibid., 78–79. For other Ribbon oaths, see PRONI, MIC. 448/2/186–87, 384–5. A copy of a Ribbon oath was also placed in evidence before the Select Committee on Orange lodges in 1835. See the evidence of Lt.-Col. William Blacker, *Rep. on Orange Lodges III*, H.C. 1835 (476), XV, 224–25.

67. Report of John O'Brien, 19 Nov. 1841, PRO, C.O. 904/8/393–96. This notion is reinforced by informers' statements lamenting the rise of corruption in the northern Ribbon society. See their statements in PRONI, MIC. 448/2/400–14, 444–46.

68. Davis, "Rites of Violence," 70–71.

69. For a good discussion of this theme, see Desan, "Crowds, Community, and Ritual," 64–71; and Sean Willentz, "Introduction," in Willentz, ed., *Rites of Power*, 1–5.

70. Garvin, "Defenders, Ribbonmen, and Others," 152–55.

5. Urbanization and Sectarian Rioting in Mid-Victorian Ulster

1. Thomas Larcom to Lord Naas, 7 June 1858, NLI, Larcom Papers, MS 7624/112.

2. *Telegraph,* 15 Aug. 1864.

3. Much of this was driven by major demographic shifts. For an astute analysis, see Hepburn, *A Past Apart,* 31–32.

4. The relative scarcity of historical writing on Belfast's industrial growth is one of the most problematic gaps in Irish historiography. The cotton industry is well served by Geary, "The Rise and Fall of the Belfast Cotton Industry," 30–35. The one excellent examination of the linen industry within Irish historical studies—Crawford, *Domestic Industry in Ireland*—is concerned with industry's rural origins. For lack of anything else, see Gill, *Rise of the Irish Linen Industry.*

5. Hepburn, "Catholics in the North of Ireland, 1850–1921," 86.

6. For a good example, see the editorials of the *Belfast Daily Mercury* concerning the demographic forces behind the Belfast riots of 1857. *Belfast Daily Mercury,* 25 Sept. 1857.

7. For the most detailed exposition of this argument, see Baker, "Orange and Green," 789–814. See also Boyd, *Holy War in Belfast;* Bardon, *Belfast,* 83; Fred Heatley, "Community Relations and the Religious Geography, 1800–86," in J.C. Beckett et al., *Belfast,* 135; and PRONI, *Problems of a Growing City,* x-xi. As so often, Frank Wright provides the happy exception to this reductionist rule. In particular, see Wright, *Two Lands on One Soil,* 241–83.

8. Baker, "Orange and Green," 89–93.

9. For a detailed history of Saint Patrick's Chapel, see Heatley, *Story of St. Patrick's.*

10. Baker, "Orange and Green," 789.

11. Young, *Tour in Ireland,* vol. 2, 48.

12. Witness Thomas Verner's comment to William Gregory about the sectarian tensions that surrounded an 1821 procession in Belfast: "I should observe that there was an angry appearance for a short time and a large gathering of mob." Thomas Verner to William Gregory, 13 July 1821, NAI, SOC, 2298/3.

13. Budge and O'Leary, *Belfast,* 27.

14. The best analysis by far being Wright, *Two Lands on One Soil,* 241–83.

15. Abrams, "Towns and Economic Growth," 10.

16. Moore, *Truth about Ulster,* 23–24.

17. The best history of Belfast undoubtedly is provided by Bardon in *Belfast.* For a helpful documentary guide to nineteenth-century Belfast, see PRONI, *Problems of a Growing City.*

18. S.C. and A.M. Hall, *Ireland,* vol. 3, 52–53.

19. *Repealer Repulsed,* 110–11.

20. Quoted in Bardon, *Belfast,* 89.

21. Malcolm, *Sanitary State of Belfast,* and O'Hanlon, *Walks among the Poor*

of Belfast. O'Hanlon's work is a compilation of letters published in the *Northern Whig.*

22. Malcolm, "Sanitary State of Belfast," in PRONI, *Problems of a Growing City,* 158.

23. O'Hanlon, *Walks among the Poor of Belfast,* 4.

24. Malcolm, "Sanitary State of Belfast," in PRONI, *Problems of a Growing City,* 9–10.

25. Froggatt, "Industrialization and Health in Belfast," 178.

26. The constricted nature of urban space in mid-Victorian Belfast is perhaps best illustrated by photographs taken from the 1870s onward. In his history of community relations in nineteenth-century Belfast, Fred Heatley includes an excellent photo of the demolition of Hercules Street in 1879. The picture truly captures the sense of just how narrow this major thoroughfare was. See Heatley, "Community Relations," 141.

27. For a model study, see Dyos, "Slums of Victorian London," 129–53.

28. The formation of segregated ethnic and occupational enclaves was, of course, not unique to Belfast. For example, a high percentage of Irish immigrants arriving in American cities created Irish neighborhoods. See Miller, *Emigrants and Exiles,* 315–28. These settlement patterns changed within a few generations, as Irish-Americans gradually became assimilated into American society (522). This dispersal did not occur in Belfast, where these same communal settlement zones largely survive to this day—a fact that attests to the power of the two conflicting visions described throughout this study.

29. Of the eighty-nine butchers listed in central Belfast in 1870, forty-nine lived on Hercules Street or Lane. See Patton, *Central Belfast,* 282.

30. This was especially true after the 1857 riots. Called before the commission of inquiry following the riots, John Hacket testified that prior to the riots his street in the heart of the Pound had been composed equally of Protestants and Catholics. Those few Protestants and Catholics living in the "wrong" west Belfast districts generally left these areas after 1857. See evidence of John Hacket, *Report of the Commissioners of Inquiry into the origin and character of the riots in Belfast in July and Sept. 1857* (hereafter cited as *Report on the Belfast Riots of 1857*), 134–38. The general outlines of west Belfast segregation can be seen in a map drawn up at Thomas Larcom's request following the 1864 riots (Map of Belfast, 1864, TCD, Larcom Papers, MS 7626).

31. O'Hanlon, *Walks among the Poor of Belfast,* 43.

32. Baker, "Orange and Green," 795.

33. Boal, Murray, and Poole, "Belfast," 77–131.

34. Ibid., 87–95.

35. Darby, *Conflicts in Northern Ireland,* 26.

36. By reducing contact between members of the two communities, urban segregation largely eliminates constant day-to-day conflict in favor of massive spo-

radic riots, thus allowing a facsimile of "normal" life to proceed. See Hepburn, "Catholics," 87. Recent literature on the survival of ethnic enclaves in urban centers has stressed the positive effects of ethnic segregation. For an interesting comparative overview, see Francis W. Carter, "Ethnic Residential Patterns," vol. 8, 375–90.

37. This was a substantial riot in which both sides wrecked several houses and a fifteen-year-old Catholic boy was killed by a stray bullet. Memorial of Hugh McQuirk and Police report, 14 July 1852, NAI, Outrage Papers (County Antrim), 1/129.

38. Information of William Watson and John Donnelly, 15 July 1852, NAI, Outrage Papers (County Antrim), 1/130. This document can also be found in PRONI., T.3280.

39. Lord Naas to Thomas Larcom, June 1858, NLI, Larcom Papers, MS 7624/ 111.

40. Summary of Forces Sent North for Twelfth of July, 1869, NAI, Official Papers, 1869/1 (10453).

41. This was not only an issue for proletarian Belfast Protestants. Witness the insecurity displayed when Bernard Hughes claimed that the strength and sinew of the city of Belfast was Catholic, not Protestant. Within a few months, Belfast Protestant leaders had published a pamphlet which rebutted Hughes's statement by listing the overwhelming economic, political, and social strength of Belfast Protestants. See *Statistics of Protestantism and Romanism in Belfast* (Belfast: Johnston and McClure, 1857).

42. Dewar et al., *Orangeism*, 118.

43. See Nowlan, *The Politics of Repeal.*

44. Riots between Repeal and anti-Repeal crowds accompanied the first two meetings of Gregg's Belfast Protestant Operatives Society. See Police reports, 4–5 April 1843, NAI, Outrage Papers (County Antrim), 1/6497 and 1/6553.

45. Police reports, n.d. [June 1843], NAI, Outrage Papers (County Tyrone), 28/14749 and 28/11277.

46. Police report, 13 July 1843, NAI, Outrage Papers (County Antrim), 1/13189.

47. *Northern Whig,* 29 July 1843. This issue gives an excellent retrospective narrative of the events of the weekend.

48. Ibid.

49. *Northern Whig,* 14 Sept. 1843; *Belfast Newsletter,* 15 Sept. 1843.

50. The critical turning point apparently came in July 1852, when the Sandy Row mob successfully reasserted its hegemony in west Belfast. See *Northern Whig,* 15 July 1852. See also Police report, 14 July 1852, NAI, Outrage Papers (County Antrim), 1/129.

51. Evidence of Harris Bindon, *Report on Belfast Riots of 1857,* 49; evidence of William Tracy, ibid., 32.

52. Evidence of Thomas Green, ibid., 69.

53. Evidence of John Hacket, ibid., 134.

54. *Downshire Protestant,* 17 July 1857. The text can be viewed in Appendix No. 1, *Report on Belfast Riots of 1857,* 248.

55. A process no doubt accelerated by John Hacket, an assistant editor of the *Ulsterman.* According to his own testimony, Hacket attended Dr. Drew's sermon at Christ Church but slipped out in the midst of his tirade. Evidence of John Hacket, *Report on Belfast Riots of 1857,* 134–35. See also Wright, *Two Lands on One Soil,* 250.

56. Evidence of Betty Ann Donohue, *Report on Belfast Riots of 1857,* 86–89; evidence of Bridget Kane, ibid., 143.

57. Evidence of Jonathan Jones, ibid., 100–107; evidence of William Watson, ibid., 126–27.

58. Bishop Cornelius Denvir to Earl of Carlisle, 19 July 1857, NLI, Larcom Papers, MS 7624/5.

59. Police behavior during the riots led to a full inquiry. See the *Report of the lord lieutenant by Messrs. Fitzmaurice and Goold, with the minutes of evidence taken by them at the inquiry into the conduct of the constabulary during the disturbances at Belfast in July and Sept. 1857.* Not surprisingly, the report found that while the constabulary did their duty admirably, the local force was more "a hindrance than a help"—findings that would be replicated in the aftermath of the 1864 riots.

60. Evidence of John Hacket, *Report on Belfast Riots of 1857,* 137; *Ulsterman,* 7 Aug. 1857. For additional information on the Catholic gun clubs, see the *Belfast Daily Mercury,* 18 Sept. 1857.

61. An Address from the Board of Management of the Belfast Parochial Mission, 9 Dec. 1856 (in Appendix No. 7, *Report on Belfast Riots of 1857,* 255–56).

62. Advertisements for McIlwaine's sermons are included in the *Report on Belfast Riots of 1857,* Appendix, No. 6, ibid., 254–55.

63. William Lyons, William Tracy, Thomas Verner et. al. to Rev. William McIlwaine, 26 July 1857, NLI, Larcom Papers, MS 7624/14.

64. Evidence of Captain William Verner, *Report on Belfast Riots of 1857,* 213–14.

65. Notice to Discontinue Open-Air Preaching, 2 Sept. 1857 (in Appendix No. 8, ibid., 256).

66. *Belfast Newsletter,* 5 Sept. 1857.

67. *Belfast Daily Mercury,* 8 Sept. 1857.

68. *Report on Belfast Riots of 1857,* 12–13.

69. Evidence of the Rev. Hugh Hanna, ibid., 167.

70. *Northern Whig,* 27 Aug. 1857.

71. Appendix No. 5, *Report on Belfast Riots of 1857,* 253–54. The placard is also quoted in Boyd, *Holy War,* 40.

72. At least one key figure in the open-air preaching debate, the Rev. William McIlwaine, believed that press reports that Drew was going to preach on 6 September were the ultimate cause of the riots that day. Evidence of Rev. William McIlwaine, *Report on Belfast Riots of 1857,* 75.

73. Evidence of Samuel Dunlop, ibid., 196.

74. Evidence of Thomas Lindsay, ibid., 46; evidence of Robert Thompson, ibid., 216–19; *Report on the Belfast Riots of 1857,* 13–14.

75. On 1 September the authorities had 15 officers and 344 members of the cavalry and infantry to complement an already substantial police force. By 18 September there were 434 members of the Irish Constabulary in Belfast. Constabulary and Military Force in Belfast, 1857, NLI, Larcom Papers, MS 7624/75.

76. *Belfast Daily Mercury,* 18 Sept. 1857. This evidence is reinforced by the testimony of Bridget Kane, a Catholic woman living on Tea Lane, off Sandy Row. Unwilling to live under threat, Kane moved from her residence on 9 September. Evidence of Bridget Kane, *Report on Belfast Riots of 1857,* 143–44.

77. In a letter to Thomas Larcom, William Tracy wrote that he had heard only one shot that evening: "I hope the farewell shot of the season." William Tracy to Thomas Larcom, 18 Sept. 1857, NLI, Larcom Papers, MS 7624/35.

78. This theory was shared by the interesting trinity of the *Dublin Evening Post,* the *Freeman's Journal,* and the *Times.* See the *Dublin Evening Post,* 8 Sept. 1857; *Freeman's Journal,* 28 Sept. 1857; *Times,* 9 Sept. 1857.

79. *Daily Warder,* 12 Sept. 1857.

80. *Belfast Daily Mercury,* 25 Sept. 1857.

81. *Nation,* 19 Sept. 1857.

82. Evidence of Harris Bindon, *Report on Belfast Riots of 1857,* 49.

83. See the evidence of James McIntyre, a head constable stationed in Ballymacarrett. Evidence of James McIntyre, *Report relating to the conduct of the constabulary,* 9.

84. For a solid overview of Derry's modern history, see Lacy, *Siege City.*

85. On 11 March 1868 a body of Derry loyalists assembled at Corporation Hall to draw up a petition to send to the British government. The petition centered on the injustice of banning loyalist processions, which were said to be "customary commemoration of the great victories of constitutional liberty." Declaration of the Protestants of Derry Meeting at Corporation Hall, 11 March 1868, to Benjamin Disraeli, 1st Lord of Treasury, NLI, Mayo Papers, MS 11,202/10.

86. *Londonderry Standard,* 14 April 1869.

87. For a celebratory account, see the *Orange and Protestant Banner,* 1 Jan. 1861. For a more critical perspective, see Acheson Lyle to Edward Cardwell, 19 Dec. 1860, TCD, Larcom Papers, MS 1710/42.

88. *Londonderry Standard,* 10 February 1869. For a detailed account, see Walker, *Ulster Politics,* 62–63.

89. Ibid., 1 May 1869.

90. The Catholic crowd collected on Bishop Street, while the Apprentice Boys were based in the Diamond. See *Londonderry Standard,* 2 June 1869.

91. At a later trial police defendants stressed the outrageous provocations that they had received from both sides. The prosecutor, the ubiquitous Ulster iconoclast John Rea, replied: "Yes, the police were practising at the Fenians, but I object

to them shooting Fenians or Apprentice Boys." For the various inquiries into the aftermath of the clash, see *Londonderry Standard*, 22, 26, 29 May and 2, 5, 12, June 1869.

6. The Campaign to Repeal the Party Processions Act, 1860–1872

1. Precis of all reported breaches of the Party Processions Act, 1867, NLI, Mayo Papers, MS 11,202/7. There is some question about attendance figures—Johnston claimed an audience of forty thousand. See Diaries of William Johnston, 12 July 1867, PRONI, D.880/2/19. In his biography of Johnston, Aiken McClelland suggests that fifty thousand attended the rally that day. See McClelland, *William Johnston of Ballykilbeg*, 36.

2. By 1866 Johnston was master of his local Orange lodge, a district master in Belfast, and a prominent member of both the County Down Orange Lodge and the Grand Lodge of Ireland.

3. See McClelland, *William Johnston*, 26–31.

4. *Belfast Newsletter*, 13 July 1867.

5. Most notably, Aiken McClelland, *William Johnston*, 59–73.

6. For the best treatment within contemporary Irish historical writing, see Wright, *Two Lands on One Soil*, 319–25. See also Patterson, *Class Conflict*, 1–11.

7. This aristocratic attitude often was maintained even in the most contentious political climates. For example, see the Earl of Roden's repeated warnings not to march at the very height of the Repeal campaign in the mid-1840s. Placard to the Protestants of Antrim, June 1843, NAI, Outrage Papers (County Antrim), 1/13715; Proclamation from Lord Roden, 3 July 1845, PRONI, Roden Papers, MIC.74.

8. For example, in 1852 Johnston wrote in his diary, "Not taking much interest in the Twelfth." Johnston Diaries, 12 July 1852, PRONI, D.880/2/5.

9. For a detailed account of the Dolly's Brae clash, see above. For the riot's impact on British establishment thinking about Orange processions, see Arthur McEvoy to Sir George Gray, 2 July 1851, PRO, H.O. 45/3472M/26–8.

10. The administration of the Party Processions Act often led to contention between law enforcement officials with different attitudes toward the processional tradition. One colorful example occurred in Antrim in 1871, when Andrew Montgomery, a resident magistrate in Ballymena, wanted to send additional troops to Mill Quarter near Toome Bridge. This angered the local justice of the peace, Thomas Hamilton Jones, who, in a vitriolic letter to the under-secretary, called Montgomery a "muff." See T.H. Jones to T.H. Burke, 8 July 1871, PRONI, MIC.371/2.

11. Summary of convictions of N.E. and N.W. circuits for violations of the Party Processions Act, 1850–1867, n.d., NLI, Mayo Papers, MS 11202/2. It should be noted that the figures are incomplete for 1853 and 1867, when numbers were unavailable for County Down. As we shall see below, the absence of statistics from County Down is an especially important omission. At least 134 people were charged

with violating the Party Processions Act in County Down in 1867. See Cases to be prosecuted for violations of the Party Processions Act at spring assizes, 1868, NLI, Mayo Papers, MS 11202/5.

12. H. Dalling to G.H. Wray, 13 July 1869, PRONI, MIC.371/1.

13. For two examples, see Memorial of Catholic clergy, merchants, and other inhabitants of Dungannon and neighborhood, n.d., PRONI, MIC.371/3[12048], and Petition of undersigned merchants, woolen drapers, and landed proprietors of Stewartstown, n.d., NAI, Official Papers, 1869/1 (9377).

14. As with so many sectarian riots, the Derrymacash affray of 1860 had its roots in events of the recent past. A riot had occurred in front of the Catholic church at Derrymacash on 12 July 1846. Subsequent loyalist processions in the Montiaghs areas of northeast Armagh avoided this contentious spot until 1860, when Orangemen marched again in front of the church. Local Catholics, angered by this affront to communal memory and territory, threw stones at the processionists. The riot escalated when a Protestant group returned to the site with firearms; two Catholics were killed in the ensuing struggle. The clash led to the proclamation of County Armagh and a renewal of legislation against party processions in 1860. For the Derrymacash riots of 1860 and the ensuing trials, see William Moore Miller to Thomas Larcom, 14 July 1860, TCD, Larcom Papers, 1710/40; Stewart Blacker to Thomas Larcom, 21 July 1860, TCD, Larcom Papers, 1710/40; and *Daily Express,* 11 March 1861. For an insightful examination of the relationship between the Derrymacash riots and the increased levels of sectarian contention of the 1860s, see Thomas Larcom to ————, n.d., TCD, Larcom Papers, 1710/40.

15. Quoted in McClelland, *William Johnston,* 24.

16. Alexander Fox to H.I. Brownrigg, 12 Dec. 1860, TCD, Larcom Papers, 1710/42.

17. See *Orange and Protestant Banner,* 1 Jan. 1861. Not everyone was enamored of the success of the day. One Derry correspondent wrote of his disappointment regarding the lax enforcement of legislation against party processions: "As all went off without a riot, they probably think that the day passed off satisfactorily. I must say that I am of a very different opinion; as you looked to the proceeding on that occasion as likely to form a precedent for the future in carrying out the provisions of the Emblems Act, you will consider them unfortunate." Acheson Lyle to Edward Cardwell, 19 Dec. 1860, TCD, Larcom Papers, 1710/42.

18. Most Orange commentators referred to the 1861 funeral procession for Terence Bellew MacManus and a more recent march in support of a Catholic university for Ireland.

19. Standard government policy was to allow processions that would not give offense to a substantial section of the local populace. Thus nationalist marches were allowed in the largely Catholic south, while both loyalist and nationalist processions were proscribed in the divided north. This distinction, however logical, understandably made little headway with Ulster loyalists.

20. *Dublin Evening Mail,* 4 Aug. 1864.

21. A lengthy account of the day can be found in the *Nation*, 13 Aug. 1864. For a modern examination, see Brendan Mac Giolla Choille, "Dublin Trades in Procession, 1864," *Saothar*, vol. 1, 1, 18–30.

22. *Nation*, 13 Aug. 1864.

23. Thomas Larcom to Sir George Grey, n.d., NLI, Larcom Papers, MS 7626/59.

24. For press accounts of the initial stages of the 1864 riots, see the *Northern Whig*, 9–12 Aug. 1864, and *Ulster Observer*, 13 Aug. 1864.

25. In detailing the primary causes of the Belfast riots for the government, Thomas Larcom went so far as to single out the *Dublin Evening Mail's* alarmist reports on the Dublin nationalist festival as particularly damaging. Thomas Larcom to Earl of Carlisle, 29 Aug. 1864, NLI, Larcom Papers, MS 7626/65.

26. Larcom provides a fine synopsis of the origin and course of the riots in several letters. In particular, see Thomas Larcom to Earl of Carlisle, 29 Aug. 1864, NLI, Larcom Papers, MS 7626/65.

27. The final force consisted of almost one thousand police constables, 150 members of the town police, six troops of the 4th Hussars, infantry from the 84th Regiment, and half of an artillery battery.

28. *Belfast Newsletter*, 14 March 1864.

29. Ibid., 2 Aug. 1864.

30. Ibid, 8 Aug. 1864.

31. Ibid.

32. Captain J.C. O'Donnell to Thomas Larcom, 5 July 1865, PRONI, MIC.371/3 (6413). In a similar vein Lord Dufferin pointed to "Lisburn, Banbridge, and perhaps Downpatrick as possible centers of disturbance." Lord Dufferin to Thomas Larcom, 6 July 1865, PRONI, MIC.371/3 (6413).

33. *Dublin Evening Mail*, 24 Oct. 1865.

34. *Correspondence between the lord lieutenant and William Johnston, esq. relative to a proposed meeting of Orangemen at Ballykilbeg on 12th July 1866*, H.C. 1866 (461), LX, 707. Much of this correspondence can also be found in the Official Papers at the National Archives, Dublin, NAI, Official Papers, 1866/49.

35. Precis of all reported breaches of Party Processions Act, 1867, NLI, Mayo Papers, MS 11,202/7.

36. William Johnston to Thomas Larcom, 17 Aug. 1867, TCD, Larcom Papers, 1710/45.

37. Diaries of William Johnston, 10 and 12 Feb. 1868, PRONI, D.880/2/20.

38. Ibid., 27 March 1868.

39. Johnston was released early due to potential health complications.

40. Drawn to the case by Johnston's notoriety, the Protestant press began to support calls for increased loyalist activism. Responding to information obtained from Bangor courthouse provided by a member of the Bangor L.O.L. No. 969, the *Dublin Evening Mail* called for Protestants to attend a massive anti-P.P.A. rally at Lisburn on 1 July 1868. *Dublin Evening Mail*, 22 June 1868.

41. Johnston's leadership of the forces of populist Orangeism was not unprec-

edented. In 1845 James Watson of Brookhill, County Antrim, lost his position as magistrate for his advocacy and participation in Orange processions. See *Memorial of James Watson, Esq.,* 40–43, 52–54.

42. Thomas MacKnight, *Ulster as it is,* vol. 1, 150–51.

43. *Northern Whig,* 13 Sept. 1867.

44. *Belfast Morning News,* 6 March 1868. This movement was confined to Belfast. On 11 March, hard-line Protestant activists met at Derry's Corporation Hall to draw up a lengthy petition against the Party Processions Act. Declaration of the Protestants of Derry, meeting at Corporation Hall, 11 March 1868, to Benjamin Disraeli, First Lord of Treasury, NLI, Mayo Papers, MS 11202/10.

45. Ulster Liberals supported Johnston as an anti-Conservative establishment candidate.

46. Walker, *Ulster Politics,* 59–82. For another excellent analysis of the 1868 election and its background, see Wright, *Two Lands on One Soil,* 284–332.

47. Witness a letter from a gentleman from the Portglenone area: "As regards the 12th, I am of the opinion that party spirit never was stronger than at the present day. Our radical House of Commons will never let this unfortunate country be at rest." J.W. Courtenay to ———, 9 July 1868, NAI, Official Papers, 1868/2 (8555).

48. For the land question, see Vaughn, *Landlords and Tenants in Mid-Victorian Ireland.*

49. For example, an estimated two thousand Orangemen met at Viscount Massarene's park near Antrim on 1 July 1869. Once there, Massarene gave the lodges permission to march in procession in full regalia. See Police report, 1 July 1869, PRONI, MIC. 371/1 (19592); Report of Andrew J. Montgomery, 3 July 1869, NAI, Official Papers, 1869/1 (9567). A similar event occurred in Fermanagh in 1868, when the Earl of Erne chaired the first meeting of the Fermanagh Protestant Defence Association in Enniskillen. See Police report, 22 July 1868, NAI, Official Papers, 1868/2 (9698).

50. Placard published by Henry Mervyn D'Arcy Irvine, 5 July 1869, NAI, Official Papers, 1869/1 (9386).

51. William Butler to T.H. Burke, n.d., PRONI, MIC.371/3 (14299). Predictably, the Rathfriland area proved to be particularly active in opposing the government's conciliatory legislation. On 1 July 1869 about three thousand men and women met near Rathfriland to petition against the church-disestablishment bill. See Police report, 1 July 1869, NAI, Official Papers, 1869/1 (8728).

52. William Butler to T.H. Burke, 1 and 8 July 1870, PRONI, MIC.371/1 (13206).

53. Among other places, Johnston spoke at massive Orange rallies at Derry, Omagh, and Killyman in 1869. For Derry, see *Londonderry Standard,* 14 Aug. 1869. For Omagh, see Police report, 19 Aug. 1869, PRONI, MIC.371/1 (12712). For Killyman, see Police report, 13 July 1869, NAI, Official Papers, 1869/1 (10203).

54. Rev. John O'Brien, P.P., to Lord Dufferin, 15 June 1869, PRONI, Blackwood Papers, D.1071 H/D2/6/233.

55. For the Banbridge riots of 1868, see *Downpatrick Recorder*, 13 July 1868; Report of J.M. Magee, n.d., NAI, Official Papers, 1868/2 (8738).

56. *Northern Whig*, 7 Aug. 1868. See also Rev. John O'Brien to Lord Mayo, 3 July 1868, NAI, Official Papers, 1868/2 (8738).

57. Police report, 12 July 1872, PRONI, MIC.371/3 (14143).

58. Abstract of reports of illegal processions, July 1868, NLI, Mayo Papers, MS 11,202/2; Police report, 13 July 1868, NAI, Official Papers, 1868/2 (9181).

59. For the Desertmartin riot of 1868, see Rev. James O'Laughlin to Earl Spencer, 5 July 1869, PRONI, MIC.371/1 (10481). At the ensuing trials eight Protestants and five Catholics were sentenced to two months' imprisonment with hard labor. See the *Londonderry Standard*, 10 March 1869. For Monaghan, see Police report, 17 July 1868, NAI, Official Papers, 1868/2 (9423); Informations following the riots in Monaghan town, 13 July 1868, NAI, Official Papers, 1868/2 (10182); Inquest in the death of Thomas Hughes of Crumlin, 14 July 1868, NAI, Official Papers, 1868/2 (9439).

60. Police report, 16 Aug. 1868, NAI, Official Papers, 1868/2 (11037).

61. For a detailed examination of the Derry riot of 1869, see chapter 5.

62. Summary of forces sent north for 12 July 1869, NAI, Official Papers, 1869/1 (10453).

63. *Londonderry Standard*, 14 July 1869; Police reports [County Down], 12 July 1869 PRONI, MIC. 371.1 (10101, 10172, 10219, 10224, 10255, 10312, 10314, 10368); Police report [County Fermanagh], 12 July 1869, NAI, Official Papers, 1869/1 (10290); Police reports [County Londonderry], 14 July 1869, NAI, Official Papers, 1869/1 (10402, 10407, 10473).

64. For the reflections of an overworked magistrate in County Down, see J. Eglinton to ———, n.d., NAI, Official Papers, 1869/1 (9723).

65. *Portadown News and County Armagh Advertiser*, 3 July 1869; *Londonderry Standard*, 7 July 1869.

66. *Portadown News*, 3 July 1869.

67. *Londonderry Standard*, 7 July 1869.

68. *Portadown News*, 17 July 1869.

69. *Portadown News*, 24, 31, July, 7 Aug. 1869; *Londonderry Standard*, 4 Aug. 1869.

70. *Londonderry Standard*, 4 Aug. 1869. Thirty-seven Catholics and ten Protestants were found guilty of riotous conduct for their participation in the riot in front of the convent. Thirty-three of the loyalist party involved in wrecking houses in Falloon's Row were sentenced for riot and assembly and bound over to appear at the Armagh assizes.

71. *Hansard's Parliamentary Debates*, 3rd Ser., 200 (30 March 1870): 938–39.

72. Several Catholic MPs from the south of Ireland supported Johnston's efforts to achieve repeal. These men justified repeal on the notion that the bill was ineffectual and merely reinforced sectarian divisions that otherwise might dissipate.

73. *Hansard*, 3rd Ser., 203, (12 July 1870): col. 165.

74. T.H. Burke to Hugh McTiernan, 11 July 1871, NAI, Official Papers, 1871/1.

75. Derry was proclaimed in the aftermath of the 1869 riot. To circumvent the authorities, Orangemen moved their Twelfth procession outside of the city. This led to a great deal of sectarian contention when Orange marchers attempted to walk through a Catholic district at Muff Glen, eight miles from Derry. In many ways this location acted as a substitute venue for the city's partisan rivalries, as both Derry Catholics and Protestants came determined to force the issue. Fortunately, magistrates, police, and the military arrived in force and prevented a serious party riot. Muff Glen had been the site of near-affrays in the previous two years, making it a particularly contentious flashpoint for the two parties. See *Freeman's Journal*, 14 July 1869; Report of J.C. O'Donnell, 13 July 1869, NAI, Official Papers, 1869/1 (10234); and Report of William Fitzmaurice, n.d., NAI, Official Papers, 1869/2 (9176).

76. *Hansard*, 3rd Ser., 210 (22 March 1872): 535.

77. Ibid., 210 (22 March 1872): 547.

78. Police report, 12 July 1872, NAI, Official Papers, 1872/2 (10163).

79. Police report, 5 July 1872, NAI, Official Papers, 1872/2 (9663).

Conclusion: Sectarian Violence and the Formation of Modern Ulster Politics

1. Walker, *Ulster Politics*, 255–67.

2. Ibid., 258–59. For a further examination of the relationship between the land question and Ulster liberalism, see Wright, *Two Lands on One Soil*, 432–75. Also see Walker, "The Land Question and Elections in Ulster, 1868–86," *Irish Peasants*, 155–91.

3. Major sectarian riots occurred in Belfast, Derry, and Portadown, prompting the typical series of government inquiries into the clashes. The inquiry into the Derry riots of 1883 provides particularly good reading for individuals interested in the links between political developments and sectarian riots in the north. See *Report of the Committee appointed to inquire into certain disturbances which took place in the city of Londonderry on 1 November 1883; together with the evidence taken before the commission*. Command C 3954, 38.

4. The revived Order was headed by Maj. Edward Saunderson, a Cavan landowner. For Saunderson's career, see Alvin Jackson, *Colonel Edward Saunderson*.

5. Not wholly so, however. In the general election of 1874, Home Rule advocates won two seats in Cavan and contested another in Monaghan.

6. For the Monaghan election, see Magee, "The Monaghan election of 1883," 147–66; Walker, *Ulster Politics*, 165–67; Wright, *Two Lands on One Soil*, 487–88.

7. MacKnight, *Ulster*, vol. 2, 44.

8. Statement re: Orangeism, n.d. [c. 1873], PRONI, Montgomery Papers, D.627/223B/1–4.

9. For a good overview, see Walker, *Ulster Politics,* 176–225.

10. For a good example of this theme, see the north Armagh campaign. Patrick Buckland, ed., *Irish Unionism,* 110–20.

11. Hugh de Feltenberg Montgomery was one of the first prominent Liberals to take such a position, arguing for a liberal-conservative alliance from mid-1885. See *Northern Whig,* 22 Aug. 1885.

12. MacKnight, *Ulster,* vol. 2, 100–102.

13. Ibid., vol. 2, 142–43.

14. *Northern Whig,* 1 May 1886.

15. For an excellent overview of the fusion of Ulster liberalism into an Ulster Unionism dominated by Conservative and Orange principles, see Walker, *Ulster Politics,* 234–54.

16. In his excellent work on nineteenth-century Ulster politics, Frank Wright convincingly argued that the extended electorate and contentious political climate presented a serious challenge to the traditional leaders of political Protestantism, who were forced to forge alliances with the demagogues of plebeian loyalism. See *Two Lands on One Soil,* 476–509.

17. Quoted in Walker, *Ulster Politics,* 179.

18. *Report of the Belfast Riots Commissioners [hereafter Report of the Belfast Riots of 1886]* (Dublin: Alexander Thom and Co., 1887), 8–9; MacKnight, *Ulster,* vol. 2, 149.

19. In 1886 Harland and Woolf employed 3,000 workers, 2,800 of whom were Protestant.

20. Seven to nine others were taken to hospital. *Report of the Belfast Riots of 1886,* 9.

21. Ibid., 11–13.

22. Many observers blamed the "Bower-street massacre" on the largely Catholic police, whose very presence in Protestant districts of Belfast was viewed as an unacceptable provocation by local loyalists. This feeling was apparently amplified by the nationalist press, which, according to MacKnight, claimed that the government was sending policemen from the south and west of Ireland to shoot down the loyal Protestants of Belfast (MacKnight, *Ulster,* vol. 2, 150).

23. *Report of the Belfast Riots of 1886,* 31–32.

24. Ibid., 34.

25. Ibid., 40–42.

26. Miller, *Queen's Rebels,* 4.

Bibliography

Manuscript Sources

Armagh County Museum, Armagh

Blacker Manuscripts (seven volumes).
Paterson Collection.

National Archives of Ireland, Dublin

Official Papers, Sectarian Conflict, 1832–1872.
Outrage Papers, 1837–1849.
Rebellion Papers, 620/1–65.
State of the Country Papers, 1383, 1390, 1403, 1537, 1544, 1560, 1565, 1682, 1711, 1765, 1831, 1955, 2084, 2086, 2187, 2188, 2298, 2358, 2360, 2520, 2622, 2623, 2723, 2882, 2885, 2886.

National Library of Ireland, Dublin

Brunswick Papers, MS 5017
Esmonde Papers, MS 5931
Larcom Papers, MS 7624–26
Mayo Papers, MS 11202

Public Record Office, London

Colonial Office Papers: C.O. 904/7–9, Ribbonism, 1798–1842.
Home Office Papers: H.O. 45, Orangeism and Ribbonism, 1841–1849.
Home Office Papers: H.O. 100, Party Conflict in Ulster, 1829–1840.

Public Record Office of Northern Ireland, Belfast

Abercorn Papers, T.2541
Anglesey Papers, D.619
Annesley Papers, D.1854
Armour Correspondence, D.1792
Beresford Papers, T.2772
Caledon Papers, D.2433
Calendar of Pelham Papers, T.755
Clogher Diocesan Papers, Dio.R.C.1
Diary of John Macky, T.925
Documents Relating to the Portadown Area, D.871
Downshire Papers, D.671
Dublin Castle Information on Ribbonism, MIC.448/1–3.
Dufferin and Ava Papers, D.1071
Erne Papers, D.1939
Fermanagh County Orange Lodge, Minute Book, D.1402/1
Foster Papers, T.2519
Foster/Massarene Papers, D.562
Gosford Papers, D.1606
Hill Papers, D.642
Johnston of Ballykilbeg Papers, D.880
Johnston of Kilmore Papers, D.1728
Letter Relating to Ribbonism in County Down, D.682
Material on Belfast Riots, MIC.327
McCance Papers, D.272
McCartney Papers, D.572
Mondooey Orange Lodge, Minute Book, MIC.157/1
Montgomery Papers, D.627
Orange Order Papers, D.2947
Orange Petition, D.1079/1
Orange Songbook, D.2935
Orange Songs, MIC.506
Papers of Mrs. Lowry, Bangor, Down, D.1494
Papers Donated by Crosslie, T.1689
Perceval-Maxwell Papers, T.1023
Poems Relating to the Orange Order, D.870
Roden Papers, MIC.74 and 147
Royal Black Preceptory, Enniskillen, Minute Book, D.1360/2A
Sharman Crawford Papers, D.856
Stewart of Killymoon Papers, D.3167

Transcripts of the Blacker Manuscripts, T.2595/1–6
Transcripts of the Official Papers, 1869–72, MIC.371/1–3
Wallace Documents, D.556
Waringstown Orange Lodge, Minute Book, MIC.202

Trinity College, Dublin

Larcom Papers, MS 1710

Newspapers and Periodicals

Belfast Daily Mercury
Belfast Morning News
Belfast Newsletter
Daily Express
Downpatrick Recorder
Downshire Protestant
Dublin University Magazine
Dublin Evening Mail
Dublin Evening Packet
Dublin Evening Post
Enniskillen Chronicle
Freeman's Journal
Irish Times
Londonderry Standard
Morning Chronicle
Nation
Newry Commercial Telegraph
Northern Star
Northern Whig
Orange and Protestant Banner
Portadown News and County Armagh Advertiser
Quarterly Review
Spectator
Star of Brunswick
Telegraph
Times
Ulster Observer
Ulsterman

Printed Material

Abrams, Phillip. "Towns and Economic Growth: Some Theories and Problems." In

Towns in Societies: Essays in Economic History and Historical Sociology, edited by Phillip Abrams and E.A. Wrigley. Cambridge: Cambridge Univ. Press, 1978.

Adams, J.R.R. *The Printed Word and the Common Man: Popular Culture in Ulster, 1700–1900.* Belfast: Institute of Irish Studies, 1987.

Akenson, Donald H. *Between Two Revolutions: Islandmagee, Co. Antrim, 1798–1920.* Hamden, Conn.: Archon Books, 1979.

———. *The Orangeman: The Life and Times of Ogle Gowan.* Toronto: James Lorimer and Company, 1986.

———. *God's Peoples: Covenant and Land in South Africa, Israel, and Ulster.* Ithaca and London: Cornell Univ. Press, 1992.

Baker, Sybil E. "Orange and Green: Belfast, 1832–1912." In *The Victorian City: Images and Realities,* edited by H.J. Dyos and Michael Wolff, vol. 2., 787–815. London: Routledge and Kegan Paul, 1973.

Bardon, Jonathan. *Belfast: An Illustrated History.* Belfast: Blackstaff Press, 1982.

———. *A History of Ulster.* Belfast: Blackstaff Press, 1992.

Barnard, T.C. "The Uses of 23 October 1641 and Irish Protestant Celebrations." *English Historical Review* 106, no. 421 (Oct. 1991): 889–919.

Barrington, Sir Jonah. *Personal Sketches of His Own Times.* London: Henry Colborn, 1827.

Bartlett, Thomas. "An End to Moral Economy: The Irish Militia Disturbances of 1793." *Past and Present* 99 (May 1983): 41–64.

———. "Selected Documents XXXVIII: Defenders and Defenderism in 1795." *Irish Historical Studies* 24, no. 95 (May 1985): 373–94.

———. *The Fall and Rise of the Irish Nation: The Catholic Question, 1690–1830.* Oxford: Clarendon Press, 1992.

Battle of Magheramayo. Report of the Evidence Taken Before the Government Commissioner, Walter Berwick, Esq., Q.C. at a Court Held in Castlewellan from 30 July to 4 August and by Adjournment on Tuesday, 18 September 1849. Newry: James Henderson, 1849.

Beames, Michael R. "The Ribbon Societies: Lower-Class Nationalism in Pre-Famine Ireland." *Past and Present* 97 (Nov. 1982): 128–43.

———. *Peasants and Power: The Whiteboy Movements and Their Control in Pre-Famine Ireland.* Brighton: Harvester Press, Ltd., 1983.

Blackstock, Allan. "The Social and Political Implications of the Raising of the Yeomanry in Ulster, 1796–8." In *The United Irishmen,* edited by David Dickson, Daire Keogh, and Kevin Whelan. Dublin: Lilliput Press, 1993.

Boal, Frederick W., Russell C. Murray, and Michael A. Poole. "Belfast: The Urban Encapsulation of a National Conflict." In *Urban Ethnic Conflict: A Comparative Perspective,* edited by Susan C. Clarke and Jeffrey L. Obler. Comparative Urban Studies Monograph No. 3. Chapel Hill, N.C.: Institute for Research in Social Science, 1976.

Bohstedt, John. "The Moral Economy and the Discipline of Historical Context." *Journal of Social History* (winter 1992): 265–84.

Bouton, Cynthia A. *The Flour War: Gender, Class, and Community in Late Ancien Regime French Society.* Philadelphia: Pennsylvania Univ. Press, 1993.

Bowen, Desmond. *The Protestant Crusade in Ireland, 1800–70: A Study of Protestant-Catholic Relations between the Act of Union and Disestablishment.* Dublin: Gill and Macmillan, 1978.

———. *History and the Shaping of Irish Protestantism.* New York: Peter Lang, 1995.

Boyd, Andrew. *Holy War in Belfast.* Tralee: Anvil Books, 1969.

Bradshaw, Brendan. "Nationalism and Historical Scholarship in Modern Ireland." *Irish Historical Studies* 26, no. 104 (Nov. 1989): 329–51.

Brady, Ciaran, Mary O'Dowd, and Brian Walker, eds., *Ulster: An Illustrated History.* London: B.T. Batsford, 1989.

Brass, Paul., ed. *Riots and Pogroms.* New York: New York Univ. Press, 1996.

A Brief Remonstrance to Mr. Justice Fletcher, Occasioned by His Charge to the Grand Jury of County Armagh, 12 March 1818. Ballynahone, Co. Westmeath: Thady Maguire, 1818.

Broeker, Galen. *Rural Disorder and Police Reform in Ireland, 1812–36.* London: Routledge and Kegan Paul, 1970.

Brown, Rev. John. *Social Peace Promoted by the Gospel: A Sermon.* Derry: Robert and James Hamilton, 1864.

Brown, Terence. *The Whole Protestant Community: The Making of a Historical Myth.* Derry: Field Day Pamphlets, 1985.

———. "Identities in Ireland: The Historical Perspective." In *Styles of Belonging: The Cultural Identities of Ulster,* edited by Jean Lundy and Aodan MacPoilin, 33–45. Belfast: Lagan Press, 1992.

Bryan, Dominic. "Interpreting the Twelfth." *History Ireland* 2, no.2 (summer 1994): 37–41.

Buckland, Patrick. *Irish Unionism: Ulster Unionism and the Origins of Northern Ireland, 1886–1922.* Dublin: Gill and Macmillan, 1973.

———, ed., *Irish Unionism: A Documentary History, 1885–1923.* Belfast: Her Majesty's Stationery Office, 1973.

Budge, Ian, and Cornelius O'Leary. *Belfast: Approach to Crisis.* London: Macmillan Press, 1973.

Byrne, John. *An Impartial Account of the Late Disturbances in the County of Armagh Since the Year 1784, Down to the Year 1791.* Dublin, 1791.

Canavan, Tony. *Frontier Town: An Illustrated History of Newry.* Belfast: Blackstaff Press, 1989.

Carleton, William. *Traits and Stories of the Irish Peasantry.* 2 vols. Gerrards Cross, Buckinghamshire: Colin Smythe, 1990.

———. *Valentine McClutchy, the Irish Agent.* London: H. Lea, 1846.

———. *Autobiography.* London: MacKibbon and Kee, 1968.

Carter, Francis W. "Ethnic Residential Patterns in the Cities." In *Ethnic Identity in Urban Europe: Comparative Studies on Governments and Non-Dominant Eth-*

nic Groups in Europe, 1850–1940, vol. 8, edited by Max Engman, 375–90. New York: New York Univ. Press, 1992.

Caulfield, James, First Earl of Charlemont. *The Manuscripts and Correspondence of James, First Earl of Charlemont.* 2 vols. London: Comprising Historical Manuscripts Commission, 12th Report, Appendix, Pt. X, and 13th Report, Appendix, Pt. VIII.

The Charge of Judge Fletcher to the Grand Jury of the County of Wexford at the Summer Assizes on Friday, 5 August 1814. Dublin: Thomas Reilly, 1814.

Civis [pseud.]. *Observations of the Impunity Enjoyed by Orangemen in the North of Ireland, with the Connivance of the Crown Prosecutors, as illustrated by the Late Newtownlimavady Riots, in Two Letters by "Civis."* Dublin: Nugent, 1855.

Clark, Samuel. *Social Origins of the Irish Land War.* Princeton: Princeton Univ. Press, 1979.

Clark, Samuel and James S. Donnelly Jr. "The Unreaped Harvest." In *Irish Peasants: Violence and Political Unrest, 1780–1914,* edited by Clark and Donnelly, 102–37. Madison: Univ. of Wisconsin Press, 1983.

Cleary, Rev. H.W. *The Orange Society.* London: Catholic Truth Society, 1899.

Comerford, R.V. *Fenians in Context: Irish Politics and Society, 1848–82.* Dublin: Wolfhound Press, 1985.

Connolly, Sean. "Catholicism in Ulster, 1800–50." In *Plantation to Partition: Essays in Ulster History in Honour of J.L. McCracken,* edited by Peter Roebuck. Belfast: Blackstaff Press, 1981.

———. *Priests and People in Pre-Famine Ireland, 1780–1845.* Dublin: Gill and Macmillan, 1982.

———. *Religion, Law, and Power: The Making of Protestant Ireland.* Oxford: Clarendon Press, 1992.

Copy of the proceedings of an investigation held in Armagh of the transaction which took place at Keady between the magistrates, the police, and the Orangemen on the 5th of November last. H.C. 1835 (362), XLV.

County Fermanagh Grand Orange Lodge. *Recall: A Little of the History of Orangeism and Protestantism in Fermanagh.* Omagh: Graham and Sons, 1990.

Correspondence between the lord lieutenant and William Johnston, esq., relative to a proposed meeting of Orangemen at Ballykilbeg on 12 July 1866. H.C. 1866 (461), LX.

Corrigan, S.L. *A New and Improved History of the Rebellion in Ireland in the Year 1798.* Belfast: James Wilson, 1844.

Counsel, E.P.S. *Our Orange Opponents.* Dublin: M.H. Gill and Son, 1886.

Crawford, William H. *Domestic Industry in Ireland: The Experience of the Linen Industry.* Dublin: Gill and Macmillan, 1972.

Cullen, Louis M. *The Emergence of Modern Ireland.* New York: Holmes and Meier, 1981.

———. "The 1798 Rebellion in Wexford: United Irishman Organisation, Membership, Leadership." In *Wexford: History and Society: Interdisciplinary Essays on the History of an Irish County,* edited by Kevin Whelan, 248–95. Dublin: Geography Publications, 1987.

————. "The Political Structures of the Defenders." In *Ireland and the French Revolution,* edited by Hugh Gough and David Dickson, 117–38. Dublin: Irish Academic Press, 1990.

————. "Late Eighteenth-Century Politicisation in Ireland: Problems in Its Study and Its French Links." In *Culture et Pratiques Politiques en France et en Irlande XVIe-XVIIIe Siecle: Actes du Colloque de Marseille, 28 Septembre-2 Octobre 1988.* Paris: Centre de Recherches Historiques, 1990.

Cullen, Mary. "Breadwinners and Providers: Women in the Household Economy of Labouring Families, 1835–6." In *Women Surviving: Studies in Irish Women's History in the 19th and 20th Centuries,* edited by Maria Luddy and Cliona Murphy, 85–116. Swords: Poolbeg Press, 1989.

Curtin, Nancy. "The United Irish Organisation in Ulster, 1795–8." In *United Irishmen,* edited by David Dickson et al., 209–21. Dublin: Lilliput Press, 1993.

————. *The United Irishmen: Popular Politics in Ulster and Dublin, 1791–8.* Oxford: Clarendon Press, 1994.

Darby, John. *Conflict in Northern Ireland.* Dublin: Gill and Macmillan, 1976.

Davis, Natalie Zemon. "The Rites of Violence." *Society and Culture in Early Modern France.* Stanford: Stanford Univ. Press, 1975.

————. "The Reasons of Misrule." *Society and Culture in Early Modern France.* Stanford: Stanford Univ. Press, 1975.

Davitt, Michael. *The Fall in Feudalism in Ireland or the Story of the Land League Revolution.* London and New York: Harper and Brothers, 1904.

De Paor, Liam. *Divided Ulster.* London: Penguin Books, 1975.

De Vere White, Terence. "The Freemasons." In *Secret Societies in Ireland,* edited by T.D. Williams, 46–57. Dublin and New York: Gill and Macmillan, 1973.

Desan, Suzanne. "Crowds, Community, and Ritual in the Work of E.P. Thompson and Natalie Davis." In *The New Cultural History,* edited by Lynn Hunt, 47–71. Berkeley: Univ. of California Press, 1989.

————. *Reclaiming the Sacred: Lay Religion and Popular Politics in Revolutionary France.* Ithaca: Cornell Univ. Press, 1990.

Dewar, M.W. *The Scarva Story.* Portadown: Portadown News, 1956.

Dewar, M.W., John Brown, and S.E. Long. *Orangeism: A New Historical Appreciation.* Belfast: Grand Orange Lodge of Ireland, 1967.

Dickson, Charles. *Revolt in the North: Antrim and Down in 1798.* Dublin: Clonmore and Reynolds, Ltd., 1960.

Dickson, David, Daire Keogh, and Kevin Whelan, eds. *The United Irishmen.* Dublin: Lilliput Press, 1993.

Donaldson, John. *A Historical and Statistical Account of the Barony of Upper Fews.* Dundalk: Dundalgan Press, 1923.

Donnelly, James S., Jr. *The Land and the People of Nineteenth-Century Cork: The*

Rural Economy and the Land Question. London and Boston: Routledge and Kegan Paul, 1975.

———. "The Rightboy Movement, 1785–8." *Studia Hibernica* 17–18 (1977–1978): 120–202.

———. "The Whiteboy Movement of 1761–5." *Irish Historical Studies* 21, no. 81 (March 1978): 20–54.

———. "Pastorini and Captain Rock: Millenarianism and Sectarianism in the Rockite Movement of 1821–4." In *Irish Peasants: Violence and Political Unrest, 1780–1914,* edited by Samuel Clark and James S. Donnelly Jr., 102–37. Madison: Univ. of Wisconsin Press, 1983.

———. "Republicanism and Reaction in the 1790s." *Irish Economic and Social History* 11 (1984): 94–100.

Doyle, Lynn. *An Ulster Childhood.* Belfast: Blackstaff Press, 1985.

Drew, Rev. Thomas. *Protestant Anniversaries.* Dublin: Curry and Co.,1858.

Duffy, Charles Gavan. *My Life in Two Hemispheres.* 2 vols. Shannon: Irish Univ. Press, 1969.

Dyos, H.J. "The Slums of Victorian London." In *Exploring the Urban Past: Essays in Urban History,* edited by David Cannadine and David Reeder, 129–53. Cambridge: Cambridge Univ. Press, 1982.

Edwards, Owen Dudley. *The Sins of Our Fathers: Roots of Conflict in Northern Ireland.* Dublin: Gill and Macmillan, 1970.

Elliott, Marianne. *Partners in Revolution: The United Irishmen and France.* New Haven and London: Yale Univ. Press, 1982.

———. *Watchmen in Sion: The Protestant Idea of Liberty.* Derry: Field Day Pamphlets, 1985.

———. "The Defenders in Ulster." In *The United Irishmen,* edited by David Dickson et al., 222–33. Dublin: Lilliput Press, 1993.

Faolain, Turlough. *Blood on the Harp.* Troy, N.Y.: Whitson Publishing Company, 1983.

Farrell, Sean. "Recapturing the Flag: The Campaign to Repeal the Party Processions Act, 1860–1872." *Eire-Ireland* 32, nos. 2 and 3 (summer/fall 1997): 52–78.

Fitzpatrick, David. "Women, Gender, and the Writing of Irish History." *Irish Historical Studies* 27, no. 107 (May 1991): 267–73.

Fitzpatrick, W.J., ed. *Correspondence of the Liberator.* 2 vols. London: J. Murray, 1888.

Foster, R.F. *Modern Ireland, 1600–1972.* London: Penguin Books, 1990.

Freitag, Sandria. *Collective Action and Communalism: Public Arenas and the Emergence of Communalism in North India.* Berkeley: Univ. of California Press, 1989.

Frogatt, Peter. "Industrialisation and Health in Belfast." In *The Town in Ireland,* edited by David Harkness and Mary O'Dowd, 155–86. Belfast: Appletree Press, 1979.

A Full and Authentic Report of the Proceedings of the First Annual Meeting of the

Brunswick Constitutional Club of Ireland, Held in the Rotunda on Tuesday, November 4, 1828. Dublin, 1828.

A Full, Faithful, and Impartial Report of the Trials of Messrs. H. and M. Hambridge, W. Graham, George Graham, J. Forbes, and W. Brownlow for an Alleged Conspiracy to Assassinate His Excellency the Marquis Wellesley, Lord Lieutenant of Ireland. Dublin: J. Charles, 1823.

Garvin, Tom. *The Evolution of Irish Nationalist Politics.* New York: Holmes and Meier, 1981.

————. "Defenders, Ribbonmen, and Others: Underground Networks in Prefamine Ireland." *Past and Present* 96 (November 1982): 133–55.

Geary, Frank. "The Rise and Fall of the Belfast Cotton Industry: Some Problems." *Irish Economic and Social History* 7 (1981): 30–35.

Geertz, Clifford. *The Interpretation of Cultures.* New York: Basic Books, 1977.

————. *Local Knowledge: Further Essays in Interpretive Anthropology.* New York: Basic Books, 1985.

Gendzel, Glen. "Political Culture: Genealogy of a Concept." *Journal of Interdisciplinary History* 28, no. 2 (autumn 1997): 225–50.

Gibbon, Peter. *The Origins of Ulster Unionism: The Formation of Popular Protestant Politics and Ideology.* Manchester: Manchester Univ. Press, 1975.

Gibson, Rev. F. Rupert. *Orangeism: Its Religious Origins, Its Scriptural Basis, Its Protestant Principles.* Belfast: Christian Irishman Office, 1940.

Gill, Conrad. *The Rise of the Irish Linen Industry.* Oxford: Oxford Univ. Press, 1925.

Gillespie, Raymond. "The End of an Era: Ulster and the Outbreak of the 1641 Rising." In *Natives and Newcomers: The Making of Irish Colonial Society,* edited by J. Brady and R. Gillespie, 191–214. Dublin: Irish Academic Press, 1986.

Grand Orange Lodge of Ireland. *The Formation of the Orange Order, 1795–8: The Edited Papers of Colonel William Blacker and Colonel Robert H. Wallace.* Belfast: Grand Orange Lodge of Ireland, 1994.

Grant, Lieut.-Col. G. Fox. *The Orange Society: Its Origins and Objects.* Dublin: George Herbert, 1884.

Gray, Tony. *The Orange Order.* London: Bodley Head, 1972.

The Great Protestant Demonstration at Hillsborough, October 30, 1867: Authentic Report. Belfast: William and George Baird, 1867.

Grieg, William. *General Report on the Gosford Estates in County Armagh, 1821.* Belfast: Her Majesty's Stationery Office, 1976.

Hall, S.C. and A.M. Hall. *Ireland: Its Scenery, Character, Etc.* 3 vols. London: Hall, Virtue, 1841–1843.

Hansard Parliamentary Debates, second series (1820–1830).

Hansard Parliamentary Debates, third series, vol. 191–213 (1868–1872).

Hart, James Verner. *Memoir of Orangeism.* Belfast: Adair's Steam Printing Works, 1875.

Heatley, Fred. *The Story of St. Patrick's, Belfast, 1815–1977.* Belfast: Bethlehem Abbey Press, 1977.

———. "Community Relations and the Religious Geography, 1800–86." In *Belfast: The Making of a City,* edited by J.C. Beckett et al., 129–42. Belfast: Appletree Press, 1983.

Hempton, David. *Evangelical Protestantism in Ulster Society, 1740–1890.* London: Routledge, 1990.

Hepburn, A.C. *A Past Apart: Studies in the History of Catholic Belfast, 1850–1950.* Belfast: Ulster Historical Foundation, 1996.

———. "Catholics in the North of Ireland: The Urbanization of a Minority." In *Minorities in History,* edited by A.C. Hepburn, 84–101. London: Edward Arnold, 1977.

Heslinga, M.W. *The Irish Border as a Cultural Divide.* Assert, Netherlands: Royal Van Gorcur, Ltd., 1962.

Hobsbawm, Eric. *Primitive Rebels: Studies in Archaic Forms of Social Movement in the 19th and 20th Centuries.* Manchester: Manchester Univ. Press, 1959.

Hogan, Patrick. "The Migration of Ulster Catholics to Connaught." *Seanchas Ardmhacha* 9, no. 2 (1979): 286–301.

Hoppen, K. Theodore. *Elections, Politics, and Society in Ireland, 1832–1885.* Oxford: Clarendon Press, 1984.

Hufton, Olwen. *The Prospect Before Her: A History of Women in Western Europe, 1500–1800.* New York: Alfred A. Knopf, 1996.

Jacob, Margaret. *Living the Enlightenment: Freemasonry and Politics in Eighteenth-Century Europe.* New York: Oxford Univ. Press, 1991.

Jackson, Alvin. *The Ulster Party: Irish Unionists in the House of Commons, 1884–1911.* Oxford: Clarendon Press, 1989.

———. *Colonel Edward Saunderson.* Oxford: Clarendon Press, 1995.

Jarman, Neil. *Material Conflicts: Parades and Visual Displays in Northern Ireland.* Berg: Oxford and New York, 1997.

Kelly, James. "Selected Documents XLIII: A Secret Return of the Volunteers of Ireland in 1784." *Irish Historical Studies* 26, no. 103 (May 1989): 268–92.

———. *That Damn'd Thing Called Honour: Dueling in Ireland, 1570–1860.* Cork: Cork Univ. Press, 1995.

Kennedy, Liam, and Phillip Ollerenshaw, eds. *An Economic History of Ulster.* Manchester: Manchester Univ. Press, 1985.

Kertzer, David. *Ritual, Politics, and Power.* New Haven: Yale Univ. Press, 1988.

Kisley, W.H. *Party Emblems in Ireland: A Letter to the Right Hon. Sir Robert Peel, Bart., M.P.* Belfast: Belfast Newsletter, 1865.

Knox, Alexander. *A History of the County of Down.* Dublin: Hodges, Foster, and Co., 1875.

Lacy, Brian. *Siege City: The Story of Derry and Londonderry.* Belfast: Blackstaff Press, 1990.

Laws and Ordinances of the Loyal Orange Institution of Ireland. Dublin: Edward Bull, 1849.

Lecky, William H. *A History of Ireland in the Eighteenth Century.* 5 vols. London:

Longmans, Green, and Co., 1892.

Lee, Joseph. "The Ribbonmen." In *Secret Societies in Ireland,* edited by T.D. Williams, 26–35. Dublin and New York: Gill and Macmillan, 1973.

———. *The Modernisation of Irish Society, 1848–1918.* Dublin: Gill and Macmillan, 1973.

———. *Ireland, 1912–85: Politics and Society.* Cambridge: Cambridge Univ. Press, 1989.

Letters from Ireland, 1886, by a Special Correspondent of the Times. London: W.H. Allen and Co., 1887.

Lewis, George Cornewall. *On Local Disturbances in Ireland and on the Irish Church Question.* London: B. Fellowes, 1836.

Lilburn, Richard. *Orangeism: Its Origin, Constitution, and Objects.* Armagh: Guardian Steam Printing Office, 1866.

Livingstone, Peadar. *The Monaghan Story.* Enniskillen: Clogher Historical Society, 1980.

Logan, John. "Oughteragh in 1826: A Case Study of Rural Sectarianism." *Breifne* 5, no.17 (1976): 74–120.

Londonderry Workingmen's Protestant Defence Association. Report of the Inaugural Meeting held on Friday, 17 April 1868. Derry: Londonderry Sentinel Office, 1868.

The Loyal Orangemen's Song Book. North Shields: J.K. Pollock, n.d. (1817?).

Luddy, Maria, and Cliona Murphy. "Cherchez la Femme: The Elusive Woman in Irish History." In *Women Surviving,* edited by Maria Luddy and Cliona Murphy, 1–14. Swords: Poolbeg Press, 1989.

Lyons, F.S.L. *Ireland since the Famine.* London: Weidenfeld and Nicolson, 1971.

Mac Giolla Choille, Brendan. "Dublin Trades in Procession, 1864." *Saothar* 1, no.1 (1974): 18–30.

MacDonagh, Oliver. *The Hereditary Bondsman: Daniel O'Connell, 1779–1829.* London: Weidenfeld and Nicolson, 1988.

MacKnight, Thomas. *Ulster as It Is.* 2 vols. London: MacMillan and Co., 1896.

MacNeven, William J. *Pieces of Irish History.* New York: W.J. MacNeven, 1807.

Malcolm, Andrew G. *The Sanitary State of Belfast, with Suggestions for its Improvement.* Belfast: Henry Grier, 1852.

Malcolmson, A.P.W. *John Foster: The Politics of the Anglo-Irish Ascendancy.* Oxford: Oxford Univ. Press, 1978.

Marshall, John J. *History of the Parish of Tynan.* Dungannon: Tyrone Printing Co., 1932.

Marx, Karl, and Frederick Engels. *Ireland and the Irish Question.* Moscow: Progress Publishers, 1971.

McClelland, Aiken. "The Battle of Garvagh." *Ulster Folklife* 19 (1973): 41–55.

———. *The Formation of the Orange Order.* Newcastle, Co. Down: Mourne Observer Ltd., 197-.

———. *William Johnston of Ballykilbeg.* Lurgan: Ulster Society, 1990.

McCollum, Rev. Randal. *Sketches of the Highlands of Cavan, and of Shirley Castle in Farney, Taken during the Irish Famine*. Belfast: J.Reed, 1856.

McEvoy, Rev. B. "The Peep O'Day Boys and Defenders in the County Armagh." *Seanchas Ardmhacda* (1987): 60–127.

McFarland, Elaine. *Protestants First: Orangeism in Nineteenth-Century Scotland*. Edinburgh: Edinburgh Univ. Press, 1990.

McMahon, Kevin, and Thomas McKeown. "Agrarian Disturbances around Crossmaglen, 1835–55: Part 1." *Seanchas Ardmhacda* 4, no.2 (1979): 302–32.

McNeill, Mary. *The Life and Times of Mary Ann McCracken, 1779–1866*. Belfast: Allen Figgis and Company, Ltd., 1960.

Memorial of James Watson, Esq., Brookhill, with Notices of His Contemporaries. Belfast: Newsletter Office, 1851.

Miller, David. *Queen's Rebels: Ulster Loyalism in Historical Perspective*. Dublin: Gill and Macmillan, 1978.

———. "Presbyterianism and 'Modernisation' in Ulster." *Past and Present* 80 (Aug. 1978): 66–90.

———. "The Armagh Troubles." In *Irish Peasants: Violence and Political Unrest, 1780–1914*, edited by Samuel Clark and James S. Donnelly Jr., 155–91. Madison: Univ. of Wisconsin Press, 1983.

———. *Peep O'Day Boys and Defenders: Selected Documents on the County Armagh Disturbances, 1784–96*. Belfast: Public Record Office of Northern Ireland, 1990.

Miller, Kerby. *Emigrants and Exiles: Ireland and the Irish Exodus to North America*. New York and Oxford: Oxford Univ. Press, 1985.

Minutes of the evidence taken before the select committee appointed to inquire into the disturbances in Ireland, in the last session of Parliament, 13 May-18 June 1824. H.C. 1825 (20), VII.

Minutes of the evidence taken before the select committee of the House of Lords appointed to examine into the nature and extent of the disturbances which have prevailed in those districts of Ireland which are now subject to the provisions of the insurrection act, and to report to the House, 18 May-23 June 1824. H.C. 1825 (200), VII.

Minutes of evidence and appendix. H.C. 1887 (C.4925–I), XVIII.

Moody, T.W., and J.C. Beckett, eds. *Ulster Since 1800: A Social Survey*. London: British Broadcasting Company, 1957.

Moore, Frankfort, *The Truth about Ulster*. London: Eveleigh Nash, 1913.

Murray, A.C. "Agrarian Violence and Nationalism in 19th-Century Ireland: The Myth of Ribbonism." *Irish Economic and Social History* 13 (1986): 56–73.

Nelson, Rev. Simon. *History of the Parish of Creggan in Counties Armagh and Louth*. Belfast: Public Record Office of Northern Ireland, 1931.

Niven, Richard. *Orangeism As It Was and Is*. Belfast: W. and G. Baird Ltd., 1899.

Nowlan, Kevin. *The Politics of Repeal: A Study in the Relations between Great Britain and Ireland*. London: Routledge and Kegan Paul, 1965.

O'Connell, Maurice, ed. *The Correspondence of Daniel O'Connell*. 8 vols. Dublin: Irish Manuscripts Commission, 1973.

O'Farrell, Patrick. *Ireland's English Question: Anglo-Irish Relations, 1534–1970.* New York: Schocken Books, 1971.

O'Ferrall, Fergus. *Catholic Emancipation: Daniel O'Connell and the Birth of Irish Democracy.* Dublin: Gill and Macmillan, 1985.

O'Grada, Cormac. *Ireland before and after the Famine: Explorations in Economic History, 1800–1925.* Manchester: Manchester Univ. Press, 1988.

O'Hanlon, Rev. W.M. *Walks among the Poor of Belfast.* Belfast: Henry Grier, 1853.

O'Malley, Padraig. *The Uncivil Wars: Ireland Today.* Boston: Houghton Mifflin Company, 1983.

O'Neill, Desmond. "Ulster Migration to Mayo, 1795–1796." In *Mayo: Aspects of Its Heritage,* edited by Bernard O'Hara, 84–87. Galway: The Archaeological, Historical and Folklore Society, 1982.

The Orange System Exposed, in a Letter to the Marquis Wellesley. Dublin: Richard Milliken, 1823.

O'Tuathaigh, Gearoid. *Ireland before the Famine, 1798–1848.* Dublin: Gill and Macmillan, 1972.

Palmer, Stanley H. *Police and Protest in England and Ireland, 1780–1850.* Cambridge: Cambridge Univ. Press, 1988.

Paterson, T.G.F. *Harvest Home: The Last Sheaf.* Dundalk: Dundalgan Press, 1975.

Patterson, Henry. *Class Conflict and Sectarianism: The Protestant Working Class and the Belfast Labour Movement, 1868–1920.* Belfast: Blackstaff Press, 1980.

Patton, Marcus. *Central Belfast: A Historical Gazetteer.* Belfast: Ulster Architectural Heritage Society, 1993.

Perceval-Maxwell, M. "The Ulster Rising of 1641 and the Depositions." *Irish Historical Studies* 21, no.82 (Sept. 1978): 144–67.

Phoenix, Eamon. *Northern Nationalism: Nationalist Politics, Partition, and the Catholic Minority in Northern Ireland, 1890–1940.* Belfast: Ulster Historical Foundation, 1994.

Porter, Frank T. *Gleanings and Reminiscences.* Dublin: Hodges, Foster, and Co., 1875.

Public Record Office of Northern Ireland. *Problems of a Growing City: Belfast, 1780–1870.* Belfast: Public Record Office of Northern Ireland, 1973.

The Repealer Repulsed: A Correct Narrative of the Repeal Invasion of Ulster. Dr. Cooke's Challenge. Also an Authentic Report of the Great Conservative Demonstrations in Belfast on the 21st and 23rd of January 1841. Belfast: William McComb, 1841.

Report by the commissioners of inquiry, 1886, respecting the origins and circumstances of the riots in Belfast in June, July, August and September, 1886. H.C. 1887 (C.4925), XVIII.

Report from the select committee of the House of Lords appointed to inquire into the state of Ireland. H.L. 1825 (181), IX.

Report from the select committee on the state of Ireland, ordered to be printed 30 June 1825, with four reports of minutes of evidence. H.C. 1825 (129), VIII.

Report from the select committee to inquire into the nature, character, extent and tendency of Orange lodges, associations, or societies in Ireland, with minutes of evi-

dence and appendix. H.C. 1835 (377), XV. (See also *Second report from the select committee to inquire...* and *Third report from the select committee to inquire...*)

Report of October 1879 made by the Lurgan riots commissioners. H.C. 1880 (130), LX.

Report of the commission appointed to inquire into certain disturbances which took place in the city of Londonderry on 1 November 1883, together with the evidence taken before the commission. H.C. 1884 (C.3954), XXXVIII.

Report of the commissioners of inquiry, 1864, respecting the magisterial and police jurisdiction, arrangements, and establishment of the borough of Belfast. H.C. 1865 (C.3466), XXVIII.

Report of the commissioners of inquiry, 1869, into the riots and disturbances in the city of Londonderry, with minutes of evidence and appendix. H.C. 1870 (C.5), XXXII.

Reports of the commissioners of inquiry into the charges made by Alexander Bell against the Dungannon magistracy, also on the charges against the magistrates contained in a memorial addressed to his excellency the lord lieutenant by certain Roman Catholic inhabitants of Dungannon, with a copy of the letter from the lord chancellor to the under secretary to the lord lieutenant, together with the minutes of evidence and appendix. H.C. 1872 (C.482), XX.

Report of the Commissioners of Inquiry into the origin and character of the riots in Belfast in July and September, 1857. H.C. 1857–8 (C.2309), XXVI.

Report of the Special Committee of the Grand Lodge of Ireland, Appointed Nov. 1849. Dublin: Edward Bull, 1849.

Report of the Trial Held at the Court-house, Green Street, on the 23rd, 24th, 25th, and 29th Days of June, 1840, of Richard Jones, Who Was Charged with Being a Member of an Illegal Society, the Members Whereof Did Communicate with and Were Known to Each Other by Secret Signs and Passwords. Dublin: Hodges and Smith, 1840.

Report of the Trial of Edward Browne and Others for Administering, and of Lawrence Woods for Taking, an Unlawful Oath. Dublin: J. Exshaw, 1822.

Report of the Trial of Michael Keenan for Administering an Unlawful Oath. Dublin: J. Exshaw, 1822.

Report of the trial of Richard Jones, who was charged with being a member of an illegal society. H.L. 1840 (241), XIV.

Report to the lord lieutenant by Messrs. Fitzmaurice and Goold, with the minutes of evidence taken by them at the inquiry into the conduct of the constabulary during the disturbances at Belfast in July and September 1857. H.C. 1857–8 (333), XLVII.

Rudé, George. *The Crowd in History: A Study of Popular Disturbances in France and England, 1730–1848.* New York: John Wiley and Sons, 1964.

Rules and Regulations for the Government of the Orange Institution. Manchester: C. Wheeler and Son, 1814.

Sagitarius [pseud.]. *Orangeism versus Ribbonism: A Statement on Behalf of the Orange Institution.* Dublin: Roe and Brierly, 1852.

Scott, James C. *The Moral Economy of the Peasant: Rebellion and Subsistence in South-east Asia.* New Haven: Yale Univ. Press, 1976.

—. *Weapons of the Weak: Everyday Forms of Peasant Resistance.* New Haven and London: Yale Univ. Press, 1985.

—. *Domination and the Arts of Resistance: Hidden Transcripts.* New Haven and London: Yale Univ. Press, 1990.

Second report from the select committee to inquire into the nature, character, extent and tendency of Orange lodges, associations, or societies in Ireland, with minutes of evidence and appendix. H.C. 1835 (475), XVI. (See also *Report from the select committee to inquire...* and *Third report from the select committee to inquire...*)

Senior, Hereward. *Orangeism in Britain and Ireland, 1795–1836.* London: Routledge and Kegan Paul, 1966.

Sibbett, R.M. *Orangeism in Ireland and Throughout the Empire.* 2 vols. Belfast: Henderson and Co., 1914.

Smyth, Jim. *The Men of No Property.* New York: St. Martin's Press, 1992.

Statistics of Protestantism and Romanism in Belfast. Belfast: Johnston and McClure, 1857.

Steele, E.D. *Irish Land and British Politics: Tenant-Right and Nationality, 1865–70.* Cambridge: Cambridge Univ. Press, 1974.

Stewart, A.T.Q. *The Ulster Crisis.* London: Faber and Faber, 1967.

—. *The Narrow Ground: The Roots of Conflict in Ulster.* London: Faber and Faber, 1977.

—. *A Deeper Silence: The Hidden Origins of the United Irish Movement.* London: Faber and Faber, 1993.

Strauss, Erich. *Irish Nationalism and British Democracy.* London: Methuen, 1951.

Sullivan, A.M. *New Ireland.* 2 vols. London: Sampson Low, Marston, Searle, and Rivington, 1877.

Teeling, Charles. *Observations on the History and Consequences of the Battle of the Diamond.* Belfast: Hodgson, 1838.

Third report from the select committee to inquire into the nature, character, extent and tendency of Orange lodges, associations, or societies in Ireland, with minutes of evidence and appendix. H.C. 1835 (476), XVI. (See also *Report from the select committee to inquire...* and *Second report from the select committee to inquire...*)

Thompson, E.P. *The Making of the English Working Class.* New York: Vintage Books, 1963.

—. "The Moral Economy of the English Crowd in the Eighteenth Century." *Past and Present* 50 (February 1971): 76–136.

—. *Customs in Common: Studies in Traditional Popular Culture.* New York: New Press, 1991.

Tohall, Patrick. "The Diamond Fight of 1795 and the Resultant Expulsions." *Seanchas Ardmhacha* 3, no. 1 (1958): 17–51.

Townshend, Charles. *Consensus in Ireland: Approaches and Recessions.* Oxford: Clarendon Press, 1988.

Trench, William S. *Realities of Irish Life*. London: Longmans, Green, and Co., 1869.

Trial of the Belfast Orangemen. Belfast: Joseph Smyth, 1813.

The Unknown Power behind the Irish Nationalist Party, by the Editor of "Grievances from Ireland." London: Swan Sonnenschein and Co., Ltd., 1907.

Vaughn, William E. *Landlords and Tenants in Mid-Victorian Ireland*. Oxford: Clarendon Press, 1994.

Verner, Col. William. *A Short History of the Battle of the Diamond*. Armagh: Ulster Gazette, n.d. (c. 1836).

Walker, Brian M., ed., *Parliamentary Election Results in Ireland, 1801–1922*. Dublin: Royal Irish Academy, 1978.

———. *Ulster Politics: The Formative Years, 1868–86*. Belfast: Ulster Historical Foundation and Institute of Irish Studies, 1989.

———. *Dancing to History's Tune: History, Myth and Politics in Ireland*. Belfast: The Institute of Irish Studies, 1996.

———. "1641, 1689, 1690, and All That: The Unionist Sense of History." *Irish Review* 12 (summer 1992): 56–64.

Ward, Margaret. *The Missing Sex: Putting Women into Irish History*. Dublin: Attic Press, 1991.

———. *Unmanageable Revolutionaries: Women and Irish Nationalism*. London: Pluto Press, 1983.

Wellington, Duke of, ed., *Despatches, Correspondence, and Memoranda of Field Marshal Arthur, Duke of Wellington, K.G.* 8 vols. London: J. Murray, 1867–1880.

Whelan, Kevin. "The Religious Factor in the 1798 Rebellion in County Wexford." In *Rural Ireland: Modernisation and Change, 1600–1900*, edited by P. Ferguson, P. O'Flanagan, and K. Whelan, 62–85. Cork: Cork Univ. Press, 1987.

———. "The Role of the Catholic Priest in the 1798 Rebellion in County Wexford." In *Wexford: History and Society: Interdisciplinary Essays on the History of an Irish County*, edited by Kevin Whelan, 296–315. Dublin: Geography Publications, 1987.

———. "Politicisation in County Wexford and the Origins of the 1798 Rebellion." In *Ireland and the French Revolution*, edited by Hugh Gough and David Dickson, 156–78. Dublin: Irish Academic Press, 1990.

Whyte, John. *Interpreting Northern Ireland*. Oxford: Clarendon Press, 1991.

Willentz, Sean. "Introduction." In *Rites of Power*, edited by Sean Willentz, 1–5. Philadelphia: Univ. of Pennsylvania Press, 1985.

Wright, Frank. *Two Lands on One Soil: Ulster Politics Before Home Rule*. New York: St. Martin's Press, 1996.

———. "Protestant Ideology and Politics in Ulster." *European Journal of Sociology* 14 (1973): 213–80.

Young, Arthur. *Tour of Ireland, 1776–79*. Edited by Arthur Hutton. 2 vols. London: George Bell and Sons, 1892.

Zimmermann, George-Denis. *Songs of the Irish Rebellion*. Dublin: Allen Figgis, 1967.

Index